WAORANI

The Contexts of Violence and War

WAORANI
The Contexts of Violence and War

Clayton Robarchek

Wichita State University

and

Carole Robarchek

Wichita State University

HARCOURT BRACE COLLEGE PUBLISHERS

Fort Worth   Philadelphia   San Diego   New York   Orlando   Austin   San Antonio
Toronto   Montreal   London   Sydney   Tokyo

Publisher	Earl McPeek
Acquisitions Editor	Brenda Weeks
Product Manager	Julie McBurney
Project Editor	Angela Williams Urquhart
Art Director	Lora Knox
Production Manager	Anne Dunigan Harris
Electronic Publishing Coordinator	Deborah Lindberg

ISBN: 0-15-503797-8

Library of Congress Catalogue Number: 97-76877

Address for Orders
Harcourt Brace & Company, 6277 Sea Harbor Drive, Orlando, FL 32887
1-800-782-4479

Address for Editorial Correspondence
Harcourt Brace College Publishers, 301 Commerce Street, Suite 3700, Fort Worth, TX 76102

Web site address:
http://www.hbcollege.com

Printed in the United States of America

7 8 9 0 1 2 3 4 5 6 039 10 9 8 7 6 5 4 3 2 1

Harcourt Brace College Publishers

Foreword

ABOUT THE SERIES

These case studies in cultural anthropology are designed for students in beginning and intermediate courses in the social sciences, to bring them insights into the richness and complexity of human life as it is lived in different ways, in different places. The authors are men and women who have lived in the societies they write about and who are professionally trained as observers and interpreters of human behavior. Also, the authors are teachers; in their writing, the needs of the student reader remain foremost. It is our belief that when an understanding of ways of life very different from one's own is gained, abstractions and generalizations about the human condition become meaningful.

The scope and character of the series has changed constantly since we published the first case studies in 1960, in keeping with our intention to represent anthropology as it is. We are concerned with the ways in which human groups and communities are coping with the massive changes wrought in their physical and sociopolitical environments in recent decades. We are also concerned with the ways in which established cultures have solved life's problems. And we want to include representation of the various modes of communication and emphasis that are being formed and reformed as anthropology itself changes.

We think of this series as an instructional series, intended for use in the classroom. We, the editors, have always used case studies in our teaching, whether for beginning students or advanced graduate students. We start with case studies, whether from our own series or from elsewhere, and weave our way into theory, and then turn again to cases. For us, they are the grounding of our discipline.

ABOUT THE AUTHORS

Clayton Robarchek was born in McCook, Nebraska, in 1939. His father was a meat-cutter, and his mother a bookkeeper. After completing high school in Grand Island, Nebraska, he spent more than a decade in a variety of jobs. In the mid-1960s he enrolled in a night class, an introduction to anthropology, at the University of Nebraska, and was hooked. He completed his BA in anthropology at the University of Nebraska in 1970, and his PhD at the University of California at Riverside in 1977. He has taught in the California State University system at Los Angeles, Bakersfield, and Chico; at the University of California, Riverside; and at Wichita State University. He also served as a Senior Fulbright-Hays lecturer in Anthropology at Universiti Kebangsaan Malaysia.

Carole Robarchek was born in Kingman, Arizona, in 1943. Her father was an officer in the Air Force, her mother a homemaker. After high school, she worked as a model in Japan, and for the telephone company in California. She discovered anthropology at the University of California, Riverside, where she received her BA in

1971, entering the PhD program the same year. In 1974, on returning from her dissertation fieldwork in Malaysia, she was diagnosed with advanced cancer and given a 50% chance of surviving the year. During the years of surgery and intensive chemotherapy that followed, academic deadlines passed with her dissertation uncompleted. Later, however, as survival began to appear to be a real possibility, she resumed her ethnographic research. She has since conducted fieldwork in Malaysia and Ecuador, and has taught at the California State Universities at Los Angeles and Bakersfield and at Wichita State University.

The authors met and married while they were graduate students. They have collaborated on four field research projects. Two studies among the Malaysian Semai in 1973–1974 and 1979–1980 analyzed various aspects of the dynamics of peacefulness in this nonviolent society, and two studies among the Ecuadorian Waorani in 1987 and 1992–1993 examined the Waorani warfare complex and its transformation into a much more peaceful way of life. The results of their research have been published in numerous journal articles and edited volumes including, among others, *The Anthropology of War* (J. Haas, ed.), *Societies at Peace* (S. Howell and R. Willis, eds.), *The Anthropology of Peace and Nonviolence* (L. Sponsel and T. Gregor, eds.), *Aggression and Peacefulness in Humans and Other Primates* (J. Silverberg and J. Gray, eds.), *A Natural History of Peace* (T. Gregor, ed.), *Anthropological Contributions to Conflict Resolution* (A. Wolfe and H. Yang, eds.), and *Cultural Variation in Conflict Resolution* (D. Fry and K. Bjorkqvist, eds.). Clay is Associate Professor of Anthropology at Wichita State University. Carole is a social research consultant in Wichita.

ABOUT THIS CASE STUDY

This case study is devoted to exploring and explicating the conditions surrounding the spectacular violence that, until recently, characterized the Ecuadorian Waorani. Prior to the beginning of peaceful contacts, more than 60% of Waorani deaths were homicides, making this the most violent society on earth. They saw all outsiders as mortal enemies, and they left many who ventured into their territory dead, bristling with 9-foot chonta palm wood spears. But their hostility was not limited to outsiders; they also killed each other, often their own relatives. Even today, in the remote fastness of the Oriente where Ecuador and Peru meet, there are still a few Waorani bands that continue to kill all interlopers.

The authors, Clayton and Carole Robarchek, did much of their early fieldwork in settlements on the Waorani Protectorate, in communities where most people had foresworn killing. Later they left the reserve, travelling to visit remote and more recently "pacified" bands. Although most Waorani are no longer at war, the memory of the recent bloodshed remains fresh and, with careful fieldwork and genealogical study, the authors were able to document many raids from the perspectives of both the killers and the surviving victims.

In search of an explanation for why the Waorani killed so prolifically, the fieldworkers studied the material, historical, social, cultural, and psychological contexts of Waorani life. They found no single "cause" for the violence, however. Rather, they identified a complex set of conditions, all of which channeled Waorani behavior further and further in directions where homicidal violence was seen, within their culturally defined reality, to be an appropriate and effective alternative.

Other anthropological studies of warfare have concentrated on Amazonia and the highlands of New Guinea, both areas steeped in war and only recently occupied. Although much is known about the people and places where warfare was endemic, the underlying causes of that warfare are by no means clear. The Robarcheks enlarge the scope of their enquiry to address the question of the roots of warfare in these other human groups as well. After careful consideration, they reject sociobiological and ecological explanations and turn to psychological, cultural, and historical circumstances for answers. While they clear away some of the debris of the debate, they come to no final conclusion. Perhaps there is none; the capacity to kill seems latent in all human groups, and a variety of circumstances seems to be able to call it forth.

This case study is rich in both questions and explorations of possible answers. It is a thoroughly honest study that does not claim more than it can produce, worth studying in depth, both because it is about a uniquely interesting culture and important problems that are universal to the human condition.

George and Louise Spindler
Series Editors
Calistoga, California

Acknowledgments

Our initial fieldwork in 1987 and the subsequent data analysis were supported by research grants from the Harry Frank Guggenheim Foundation. Support for the 1993 fieldwork was provided by the Harry Frank Guggenheim Foundation and the United States Institute of Peace. We gratefully acknowledge their support, without which this project would not have been possible.

Our thanks also to the Instituto Nacionál de Patrimonio Cultural del Ecuador for serving as sponsor for both projects, and to Wichita State University for granting a leave of absence in 1987 and a sabbatical leave in 1993 to allow us to undertake the fieldwork.

Over the course of our two projects the cooperation, kindness, and assistance of a great many people have been invaluable. We are especially thankful to Sra. Josefina Torres de Peñaherrera, who offered us the hospitality of her home in Quito, assisted us in obtaining visas and research permits, and shared with us many recollections of her youth on the Napo River. In Wichita, Martha Peñaherrera also assisted us in obtaining visas and has graciously loaned us rare books on the Oriente.

Among our many Waorani friends and neighbors, we are especially indebted to Dyuui and to Oba, whose recent death we mourn deeply. Our thanks also to Nyïiwa and Wängïngkämö for their friendship and patience in helping us to understand, and to Gaba for helping us learn the language. We thank Oömä, Ana, Kïnta, Paba, and Tïwë of Tïwënö; Koba, Tëmënta, Gaya, Ongkayï, and Dabo of Kiwarö; Kïmö and Dawä of Tzapino; and Tamata and Yeti of Nyönënö for spending many hours talking with us and furthering our understanding of Waorani language, history, and culture. We also thank the many other Waorani who extended the hospitality of their hearths to us on various occasions.

Many people involved in missionary activities assisted us. Glen Turner, director of the Summer Institute of Linguistics (SIL) in Quito, provided a great deal of vital information about the Oriente, and gave us access to the SIL communication network. Frank Kallinger helped us in numerous ways, including finding hard-to-get supplies and getting them to us during our first month in Tïwënö. Miriam Gebb allowed us to rest and recuperate in her home and gave us the pleasure of her company on many occasions.

We also acknowledge the many kindnesses of Rachael Saint, and we mourn her passing. Despite our philosophical differences, she was unfailingly friendly, helpful, and nurturant.

We are grateful to the pilots of the Missionary Aviation Fellowship, without whose assistance, consideration, good judgment, and good humor this project would have been vastly more difficult and uncomfortable. Only those who have spent months in the jungle or in some similarly isolated setting can appreciate what a packet of mail tossed from a low-flying airplane can mean. In their names we thank especially Jan Zwart and Gene Jordan, directors of MAF in Ecuador in 1987 and 1993, respectively.

We owe a special debt of gratitude to Rosie Jung and Catherine Peeke for spending many hours answering our questions and assisting us with the Waorani language. We also thank them for allowing us to use their vacant house in Tɨwënö for part of our fieldwork in 1993. Dr. Peeke has continued to keep us up-to-date on current developments among the Waorani.

We thank Jim Yost for spending a day answering our questions, and Randy Smith of the Rainforest Information Center for sharing with us his observations and insights gained from working on the demarcation of Waorani territorial boundaries, his census, and his investigation of tourism. Our thanks to Father Miguel Angel Cabodevilla of the Capuchin Mission in Coca for sharing his observations with us.

We are especially grateful for the hospitality and friendship of Dan and Michael Buzzo in whose canoe and good company we made the long journey down the Napo from Coca to Nuevo Rocafuerte and up the Yasuní.

We are also indebted to Doug Robarchek who visited us in Tɨwënö in 1987, bringing much-needed equipment from the United States, and from whose detailed editorial suggestions this book has benefitted greatly. We thank George and Louise Spindler for their many helpful comments and suggestions on the organization of the manuscript. Needless to say, we bear responsibility for whatever shortcomings remain.

Parts of the theoretical discussion in chapter 8 were previously published in *American Anthropologist 91* (4), 903–920 (1989) under the title, "Primitive Warfare and the Ratomorphic Image of Mankind."

C. R.

C. O. R.

Dedication

This book is dedicated to our parents, Sharlaine and Clarence Robarchek
and Jeanne and Philip Obley, who taught us that everything is possible.

Contents

Introduction   1
    Orthography   5
    Pronunciation Guide   5

Part 1: Studying War

1 Preparations   9
    Getting to the Field   13

2 The Waorani War Complex   19
    External War   20
    Internal War   24
    The Decline of War   26
    A Tenuous Peace   27

3 The Fieldwork   31
    Getting Started   31
    Language   33
    Church   34
    The Community   36
    The Daily Routine   38
    Structured Data Collection   41
    The Company   45
    Participant Observation   46
    Soccer   55
    Homosexuality   56
    Domestic Relations   57
    The Killings of Father Alejandro and Sister Inez   58
    Fieldwork, 1993   60
    Soccer Tournaments   61
    The ONHAE Congreso   64
    Tourism   68

Part 2: The Contexts of War

4 The Material Context: Environment and Technology   73
    The Physical Environment   73
    The Waorani Ecological Adaptation   74

5 The Historical Context   85
    The Fifteenth–Nineteenth Centuries   85
    The Twentieth Century   91

6 The Social/Cultural Context 97
The Human World: Kowudɨ and Waorani 97
Kinship and Marriage 99
Residence 101
Politics: Authority and Social Control 102
Economic Relations 103
Men, Women, and Sexuality 104
The Nonmaterial World: Magic, Sorcery, and Christianity 106

7 The Individual/Psychological Context 117
Culture, Self, and Emotion 117
The Cultural Construction of Self 118
The Cultural Constitution of Emotion: Rage 120
Egalitarianism 123
Homicidal Rage and Waorani Ethnopsychology 123

8 Waorani Warfare in Context 127
The Anthropology of Violence and War 127
Waorani Warfare in Context 137
Explaining Waorani War 146

Part 3: Contexts Revised

9 The Renunciation of Violence 151
Information and the Decline of War 151
The First Peaceful Contacts 151
Information and Culture Change 158
Constructing a Culture of Peace 159
World View, Emotion, and Culture Change 162

10 Action in a New World: Ethnogenesis and the Return of Violence 165
Oil 165
Colonists 166
Ethno-Politics, Eco-Politics, and the "Noble Savage" 167
Ethnogenesis 168
The Resurgence of Violence 170
Conclusion 173

Epilogue (Clay) 175

Afterword 177

Glossary 183

References Cited 185

Index 189

Introduction

The Waorani resisted outside contact and pacification longer and more successfully than any other indigenous group in Amazonian Ecuador. They were engaged in warfare with all surrounding groups and in lethal vendettas among themselves well into the last half of the twentieth century. During the past century, more than 60% of Waorani deaths have been the result of homicide, making this the most violent society known to anthropology (Yost, 1981). Even today, a few small bands remain hidden in the vast expanse of rainforested ridges and swamps that span the disputed frontier between Ecuador and Peru, still at war with each other and with all outsiders.

While the fieldwork on which this book is based is recent, the study itself grew out of our research interest (going back more than 20 years) in the natures and sources of violence and nonviolence in human societies. We began our ethnographic exploration of the subject during 1973–1974 when we first went to live with the Semai of the highland Malay Peninsula, a people described in an earlier monograph in this series as "a nonviolent people of Malaysia" (Dentan, 1968). We returned to the Semai for a second study in 1979–1980. The objective of those projects was to understand how, in a world where violence and war seem to be inescapable, these people had managed to organize their lives so that violence was not seen as an option in human relations.

Shortly after returning from our last Malaysian fieldwork, we became aware of the existence of the Waorani, a people about whom almost nothing appeared in the anthropological literature but who were reported to be extremely violent. What was particularly intriguing to us was that in most other respects, including their environmental settings, subsistence practices, technology, political organization, and systems of descent, the two societies seemed almost identical.

We spent the next several years planning and preparing for a field research project that would allow us to compare the psychological and sociocultural underpinnings of these two societies' radically divergent orientations to violence. This presented an opportunity for us to test some of the hypotheses about the psychological and sociocultural dynamics of violence and nonviolence that we had drawn from our earlier studies among the Semai. In the process, we also hoped to cast some light on current theoretical explanations of human violence and war.

We spent 1987 in Ecuador, living in and visiting communities in the Waorani Protectorate. In 1992–1993, we returned for an additional 5 months that we spent contacting and visiting groups living outside the Protectorate, groups that

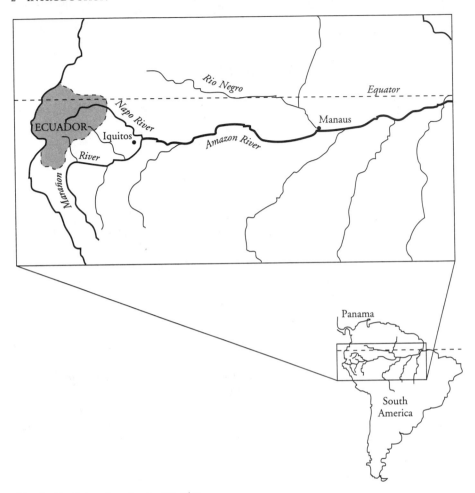

Map 1   South America, showing Ecuador

had experienced less intensive contact with missionaries and other representatives of the outside world.

We mention our Semai research here because, while this case study does not explicitly compare the two societies (that work is in progress; for preliminary reports, see Robarchek & Robarchek, 1992, 1996a), a comparative perspective nonetheless informs all of what follows. This is necessarily the case because our day-to-day observations of and reflections on Waorani life took place against the background of our earlier studies and were sharpened by conscious or unconscious consideration of how what we were seeing was similar to or different from what we had seen among the Semai.

Thus, for example, when we discuss the Waorani world view in chapters 6, 7, and 8, our conception of it and its social and behavioral implications are, at least in part, conditioned by how strongly it contrasts with that of the Semai. Similarly, in chapter 6, when we argue that the world of the supernatural is of little day-to-day practical concern to the Waorani, we are seeing them against the background of a people for whom virtually every act, no matter how mundane, has actual or potential ramifications in the world of nonmaterial beings and forces.

While the primary goal of our study was to describe and analyze Waorani violence and the psychological and sociocultural contexts within which it occurs, organized violence had, by 1987, already decreased dramatically. Although in comparison with other societies the homicide rate for Waorani society remains high, over the previous three decades there has been a more than 90% decline. The most recent raids staged by bands that we were able to contact ranged from as long ago as 30 years prior to our 1987 study to as recently as a few months after our 1993 fieldwork.

To assess continuity and change in behavior and in basic beliefs, values, and assumptions, we drew on the accounts of the early contact period from missionaries and others, and we lived with and interviewed as wide a range of Waorani as possible, from young people who have lived on the Waorani Protectorate and been exposed to the influence of missionaries all their lives, to those who have never lived on the Protectorate; from multiple killers to those who have never taken part in a raid. What we found was, in part, a continuum of change over time and space, ranging from the earliest contacted and most Christianized individuals and groups living on the Protectorate, to a few groups who have never been peacefully contacted and who remain at war with all outsiders and other Waorani.

We should make it clear at this point that while our objective was to try to understand the homicidal violence of Waorani society, we did not, we are glad to say, witness or experience it directly. Although there were a few occasions when we felt threatened, in nearly 18 months of living in various Waorani settlements, we did not actually witness a single violent act. This is a little like saying that although we have lived in Kansas for a decade, we have never seen a tornado (which is also true). Nonetheless, we have seen (and, if we were meteorologists, we could have studied and analyzed) the atmospheric conditions that generate the tornados that give Kansas its well-deserved reputation for violent weather. Similarly, in the Ecuadorian Amazon, we were able to see and study the sociocultural and psychological conditions that underlie the violence for which the Waorani are justifiably known.

All of this is by way of introducing the central theoretical premise around which this book is organized: People's behavior is not the determined result of ecological or biological or socioeconomic forces acting on them but, rather, is motivated by what they want to achieve in their world as they perceive and understand it. Within their experienced reality, people make choices based on the information available to them—information about themselves, about the world around them, and about possible goals and objectives in that world.

From this perspective, both individual and social behavior are governed by systems of information and control, or *schemata* (singular: *schema*). These constitute both maps of the world and plans for action in it. Most relevant to our purposes here are the schemata operating on the individual and social levels, the structures and processes sometimes designated by the terms *personality* and *culture,* respectively.

These are the systems of information (the maps/plans) that generate the assumptions, values, meanings, options, possibilities, and constraints that individuals and societies use in defining, making sense of and acting in their worlds (Laszlo, 1969).

Like all people, Waorani inhabit a reality that is, to them, all-encompassing and seamless. For purposes of description and analysis, however, that seamless reality can be conceptualized as a hierarchy of contexts—material, historical, social/cultural, and individual/psychological—that offer opportunities for action and constrain its possibilities. In the chapters that follow, we will show that understanding the ways that these contexts are culturally constructed and interpreted by Waorani goes a long way toward explaining the behavioral choices that they make, choices that ultimately constitute both their traditional orientation to violence and the changes that are now occurring.

The most encompassing of these contexts is the social/cultural context, because it defines and gives meaning to all the others. The conceptualization of culture employed in the approach that we have been developing here, however, differs rather markedly from some current approaches. In our view, culture is neither a construct nor an abstraction: It is an open system of information encoded in the minds of the individual members of the society. While our *characterization* of Waorani culture, drawn from inferences based on our observations, is most certainly an abstraction, the culture itself is quite real. It is a systematically interrelated body of knowledge and information by means of which people, as individuals and as groups, make sense of and decide how to deal with the other contexts that inform their realities.

Violence and warfare, like other behaviors, occur when they are perceived and selected from a field of possible alternatives as viable means of achieving specific goals within such culturally constructed realities. Understanding and explaining Waorani behavior, including warfare, requires that we attend to people's motives and goals, to what *they* want to achieve. We must consider cultural and individual assumptions, beliefs and values, the social order in which they are embedded and the purposes and intentions that they inform. These elements constitute the behavioral environments within which people make their choices and chart their courses of action.

What that means is that Waorani violence must be explained, at least in part, in terms of the sociocultural processes of Waorani society and the psychological processes of Waorani individuals. Such an approach requires that we take people—and their aspirations, motives, and goals—seriously. People are not considered passive machines pushed into action by ecological, biological, or even sociocultural determinants but active decision-makers picking their ways through fields of options and constraints in pursuit of individually and culturally defined goals in a culturally constituted reality that they are continually constructing and reconstructing.

There is a potential problem with presentation of the kinds of data necessary to such an approach. The necessity of putting the events of the present into a historical context and of dealing with both continuity and change, with the present and the past simultaneously, means we will sometimes be referring to the present, sometimes to the past, and sometimes to the continuity between them. In general, our use of the past tense indicates some state of affairs that existed in the past but that no longer obtains. Use of the present tense, unless we specifically indicate otherwise with terms like "now," "recently," or "today," refers to conditions that held true both in the past and in the present. Our use of the pronoun "we" throughout this work reflects the fact that this, like all of our previous ethnographic research, has been a thoroughly collaborative endeavor.

ORTHOGRAPHY

Some writers have attempted to use the Spanish alphabet and Spanish spelling conventions to represent the Waorani language. Unfortunately, Spanish has neither /w/ nor /k/, and both consonants are prominent in Waorani—for example, "Waorani" becomes "Huaorani." Many other words, however, become nearly unrecognizable: këwëiri (cannibals) becomes quehueiri, kɨwɨngkodɨ (manioc garden) becomes quihuinquodi, and so on.

The Spanish alphabet is not capable of adequately representing the 10 distinct vowel sounds in Waorani (vowel length is also phonemic). This can lead to the confusion of quite different morphemes, for example, awɨnɨ (leader) with awënɨ (in a tree) (Rival, 1992, 1993).

Others have used a phonemic system of transcription. This, however, is very confusing for speakers of European languages, because in Waorani, vowel nasalization is phonemic but consonant nasalization is not: for example, nänögëngä (husband) becomes dädögëgä. (For a system of phonemic transcription of Waorani, see Peeke, 1973.)

In this book, we are using a modified phonetic transcription that is intended to more accurately represent the sounds of spoken *Wao tɨdɨdo* (person speech) to speakers of European languages.

PRONUNCIATION GUIDE

VOWELS (TWO DOTS INDICATE A NASALIZED VOWEL.)			
/a/	as in "father"	/i/	as in "beet"
/ä/	as in "mom"	/ï/	as in "mean"
/e/	as in "bad"; includes the allophone "bed"	/o/	as in "hope"; includes the allophone "put"
/ë/	as in "man"; includes the allophone "men"	/ö/	as in "home"; includes the allophone "Nurenburg"
/ɨ/	as in "pit"	/u/	(allophone of /o/) as in "hoop"
/ɨ/	as in "mint"	/ü/	(allophone of /ö/) as in "moon"

Repetition indicates a long vowel, as in "üüntɨ" (shooting).

CONSONANTS

/b/, /g/, /k/, /m/, /n/, /p/, and **/t/** as in English	**/ny/** as in ca<u>ny</u>on; also occurs in initial position
/d/ in initial position, as English /d/	**/w/** as English **/w/**
/r/ (allophone of /d/) between vowels, as Spanish "flap" /r/	**/y/** in initial position, as **/y/**, **/dy/**; between vowels, as **/dy/** or **/gy/**
/ng/ as in "si<u>ng</u>er, thi<u>ng</u>"	

NAMES

With the exception of those listed in the acknowledgments, the names of all living Waorani have been replaced by psuedonyms. We will be happy to provide a key to these names upon request from legitimate researchers.

PART 1

STUDYING WAR

1 / Preparations

East of the massive volcanic wall of the Ecuadorian Andes lies the Oriente—the East. Here, in a vast expanse of steep ridges, deep valleys, and impassible swamps, all mantled in dense equatorial rainforest, rise the headwaters of the Amazon River. The contrast with the dry, cool Mediterranean climate and sparse vegetation of the highlands could hardly be more stark, and to the people of the mountains, from the time of the Incas through the colonial era and into the modern age, the Oriente has represented the Heart of Darkness. This is the realm of savagery in all its possible forms, from the raw animal ferocity of jaguars and anacondas, to the *tigres mojanos*—men who assume the form of jaguars and stalk the forest trails— to the savage *Aucas,* naked cannibals who kill with spears and sorcery and devour the flesh of their victims. This myth-image of the rainforest and its inhabitants has in one way or another infused the perceptions and the actions of all who have come here, whether seeking adventure, rubber, gold, oil, or souls.

In this century, the label "Auca," with all it connotes, has come increasingly to refer to one ethnic group, the last "wild Indians" in Ecuador, a people who call themselves *Waorani:* "people." Although they possessed no firearms and in the last years of their isolation numbered fewer than 700, their fearsome reputation and viciously barbed 9-foot palmwood spears allowed them to maintain control over a vast territory, some 8,000 square miles of densely forested valleys, ridges, and swamps lying between the Napo and Curaray rivers. With only those spears, they kept the modern world at bay until well into the second half of the twentieth century.

Their reputation for ferocity was, in fact, well-founded. The course of their history of contact with people they call *kowudï* (foreigners) has been characterized by unremitting violence perpetrated both by and against them. They also fought each other; blood feuds and vendettas arising from past killings, from quarrels over marriage arrangements, and from accusations of sorcery were a way of life among the widely dispersed extended family bands.

As "Aucas" (a pejorative label), the Waorani are very famous in the Oriente and, indeed, throughout Ecuador (there is even a soccer team in the highlands named "Aucas"). They first came to the attention of the world beyond Ecuador in 1956, when five young American missionaries, seeking to make contact with them, ferried themselves by small plane onto a sandbar in the Curaray River, where a band of Waorani promptly speared them all to death. The story was carried worldwide by newspapers, magazines, and radio. *Life* magazine sent a reporter and photographer to the Oriente to cover the story, and gruesome photos testified to the "savagery" of the Aucas.

Paradoxically, events triggered by the killing of the missionaries led, within a few years, to the abandonment of large-scale violence, both within Waorani society and between them and the world outside their forest stronghold. At the time, however, for the members of the band involved—people who would later be our neighbors and friends—it was merely another encounter with the incomprehensible *kowudɨ*, another violent episode in a world where most people could expect to die at the point of a spear.

Until very recently, the Oriente was one of the least known regions in the world. The large geological map of South America that hangs in the hall of the Geology Department at Wichita State shows Waorani territory as only a blank space. When we undertook our first study, many of the topographic maps we purchased from the military map office in Quito were, except for blue lines indicating the courses of major rivers, also completely blank.

In January of 1987, after several years of planning and preparation, we arrived in Ecuador, supported by a research grant from the Harry Frank Guggenheim Foundation. The foundation has, for a number of years, devoted its resources to the support of projects that have a potential for casting new light on the problems of violence and war. We had proposed an ethnographic research project to gather data on the Waorani, but our ultimate objective was a comparison of the Waorani and the Malaysian Semai.

At that time, very little was known ethnographically about the Waorani. James Yost, a missionary anthropologist, had written several articles and had, together with a botanist from the Harvard Botanical Museum, published a survey of the Waorani uses of native plants (Davis & Yost, 1983). Catherine Peeke, a missionary linguist associated with Wycliffe Bible Translators and the Summer Institute of Linguistics (organizations devoted to translating the Bible into native languages) had published a structural analysis of the grammar of Auca (as the Waorani language is still officially known) (Peeke, 1973).

There were also several books written by missionaries and by those sympathetic to their efforts, describing the period of initial contacts and the almost miraculous conversion of an entire tribe of bloodthirsty savages into devout and pacifistic Christians (e.g., Wallis, 1960, 1973). Although these books were useful in reconstructing recent historical events, the pictures they painted of both pre- and post-contact Waorani life sometimes bore only the slightest resemblance to reality. With these materials, we had prepared ourselves, as best we could, to undertake a study of what had until recently been the most violent society on earth.

Our intention was to establish ourselves in a settlement on the Waorani Protectorate, recruit a bilingual informant, and set about learning the language. Since American Protestant missionaries had been in contact with some bands for a number of years, we hoped to find an informant who was bilingual in English but, if not, we were prepared to work in Spanish until we could function in the native language. As it turned out, neither of those options existed; there was no one in the hamlet where we settled who spoke English or more than the most rudimentary Spanish.

The Waorani Protectorate, lying between the Challua and Nushiño rivers and encompassing the headwaters of the Curaray River, is accessible only on foot, by canoe, or by small, single-engined airplanes. These latter are operated by missionary pilots affiliated with an organization called the "Mission Aviation Fellowship" (MAF).

Known locally as *"Alas de Socorro"* ("Wings of Mercy"), their mission is to provide emergency medical transportation out of the jungle. They land in clearings made in the forest by Waorani and other Indians, and transport victims of illness, injury, and snakebites to the small missionary-operated hospital in the Andean foothills near the town of Shell-Mera. They also ferry missionaries, schoolteachers, medical teams, and local government officials in and out of the jungle and carry small amounts of forest products and other cargo. On the Waorani Protectorate, they provide access to a half-dozen remote settlements otherwise accessible only on foot or by canoe.

Thus, after reporting in with the Instituto Nacional De Patrimonio Cultural (National Institute of Cultural Heritage), the government agency through which our research was authorized, one of our first priorities was to make contact with the Summer Institute of Linguistics (SIL), the missionary organization that has been involved with the Waorani since the initial contacts were made in the late 1950s.

We had first tried to contact the SIL when we began planning the project, in the hope of developing a working relationship with them and perhaps tapping into their communications network. When we wrote and phoned their headquarters in Texas, however, we were clearly brushed-off when we said we were contemplating work in Ecuador. Nevertheless, we decided to try again in Quito.

We located the SIL offices in Quito, and had a polite meeting with the director during which we explained the nature of our project and its objectives. We also discussed our earlier fieldwork among the Semai and gave him copies of some of our previous publications. He was friendly, but reserved, and he was clearly unwilling to offer us any assistance or even to provide much information about the Waorani. At the conclusion of the meeting we agreed to return in a few days, after he had had a chance to read our articles. It was apparent that there were things afoot that we did not understand.

At our next meeting he was much more forthcoming and as we talked some of the reasons for his earlier wariness, and for the cool response we received from the SIL in the United States, became apparent.

In the 1970s and early 1980s, Marxist ideology had become very influential in anthropology, and particularly in Latin American anthropology. Missionaries in general and the SIL in particular had been condemned by Marxists and accused in several books of being agents who were laying the groundwork for the capitalist exploitation of traditional peoples. The missionary anthropologist who had been working with the SIL had, he told us, been vilified for his collaboration with missionaries when he presented a paper at a scientific conference in the United States. The missionaries were obviously and understandably apprehensive that we, too, were seeking to enlist their assistance in order to attack them and their work.

Once it became clear that missionary-bashing for its own sake was not part of our agenda, however, he willingly provided us with a great deal of useful information on the current situation in the Oriente. He also introduced us to others in his organization and to the director of the Missionary Aviation Fellowship, who invited us to dinner at his home where we worked out our immediate plans for finding a field site. Over the next year, and during our second study five years later, we developed a friendly working relationship with many of the people involved in these organizations.

At this point, perhaps we should make clear our position with regard to missionaries and their activities. It is fair to say that, at the beginning of our careers, we shared the generalized antipathy toward missionaries that is common among anthropologists and among academics generally. We still have the same fundamental philosophical disagreement with the primary goal of missionization: that of convincing people that their traditional beliefs are false and that another's are true. (It is also the case, however, that we see little difference in this regard between Christian missionaries whose objective is to replace the belief in "demons" with the word of Christ and his disciples, and the Marxist missionaries of recent decades whose goal was to destroy the "false consciousness" of traditional cultures and to inculcate the revealed truth of *their* prophet and his disciples.)

The undeniably negative consequences that missionization often had in the past notwithstanding (and this was certainly the case in the Oriente—see chapter 5), it is clear to us, after having lived and worked in traditional societies on both sides of the world, that now, at the end of the twentieth century, it is not the ideological and social changes introduced by missionaries that are destroying traditional societies like those of the Semai and Waorani.

Any negative psychological, social, and cultural effects of missionary activity are today utterly insignificant compared to the catastrophic impact of the worldwide industrial megaculture—in both its capitalist and socialist variants—with its insatiable hunger for resources: land, water, food, timber, oil, minerals, and labor. It is "development": mining, oil extraction, lumbering, ranching, plantation agriculture, dam construction, and environmental degradation through deforestation, soil erosion, and toxic wastes that is obliterating the cultures and societies, and often the very lives, of native peoples the world over.

"Development" forces or entices them from their lands and ways of life, robs them of their economic self-sufficiency and destroys the social and cultural coherence of their traditional lives. If all of the world's missionaries were to disappear tomorrow, it would have no salutary effect whatsoever on that process.

In a world such as this, the missionaries we have met provide native peoples with some basic medical care, a little education, and an occasional voice on their behalf in the capital cities' corridors of power, often at the cost of considerable discomfort and even danger to themselves. By way of example, although it often seems that every individual and group in Ecuador with an axe to grind among indigenous people has tried to claim credit for the designation of the Curaray headwaters as a Waorani Protectorate, it was, in fact, the Protestant missionaries who were primarily responsible for its creation.

We spent two weeks in Quito, meeting with government officials, making contact with missionary groups, and buying supplies. As luck would have it, the day after we arrived in Ecuador, the president was taken hostage by the military. We understood imperfectly the intricate political issues in dispute, but the practical effect for us was that there were demonstrations, counterdemonstrations, and police activity everywhere in the streets of Quito. It seemed that whenever we set out to track down rubber boots or plastic buckets or shotgun shells, we would walk around a corner and into a street demonstration. We managed to get teargassed three times that first week. Nonetheless, government offices and businesses remained open and we were able to complete our preparations on schedule.

GETTING TO THE FIELD

Our first problems were the tactical ones that confront every anthropologist: finding a suitable community, getting settled in it, and learning the language. By means of the MAF shortwave radio network, we had made arrangements to visit a settlement where Dr. Catherine Peeke and Rosie Jung, Bible translators affiliated with the SIL, resided periodically while working with local informants to translate the Bible into the Waorani language. They had been involved with the Waorani since the early contacts, and our intention was to meet with them and discuss possible research sites.

We had learned from the director of the Missionary Aviation Fellowship that the airstrip at Shell-Mera had been closed for resurfacing by the military authorities who also used it. In the meantime, MAF was operating out of a shed on a gravel strip at Tena, a small town some 60 miles to the north. Since we had no idea what supplies would be available in Tena, we decided to buy our disposable field gear—cooking utensils, storage containers, sleeping pads, basic tool kit, blankets, towels, and so on—in Quito.

We rented a Land Rover in Quito and hired a driver to return it to the city. Into it we packed the gear for a year in the field stuffed into two footlockers, a large fiberglass suitcase, and two duffel bags. There were also two foam sleeping pads; a mosquito net and two blankets; two pair of rubber boots; four small boxes of food; four large rectangular cans holding rice flour, noodles, and assorted bagged staples; a box of kitchenware; a portable computer; two solar electric panels; a lantern; a one-burner pressure stove; a 5-gallon plastic jug of kerosene; a single-shot 16-gauge shotgun and shells; assorted odds and ends; the driver; and ourselves.

There are two roads over the Andes from the highlands to the region of the upper Napo River. The best one heads south from Quito, down the central plateau between two rows of volcanos, then turns east dropping (sometimes quite literally) into the spectacular gorge of the Pastaza River.

The first third of the trip, to the town of Baños, is by a comfortable, paved two-lane highway. The last two-thirds follows a terrifying narrow, winding, unpaved track that clings precariously to the sheer wall of the canyon, with the wheels of vehicles sometimes only inches from a sheer drop of hundreds of feet. In places, waterfalls and streams pour across the road, and it is frequently closed for long periods when landslides or earthquakes drop whole stretches of roadway into the gorge. It had been closed by an immense landslide when we got ready to leave the city.

The other road climbs eastward out of Quito into the Andes. Once over the high passes, it drops southeast to Baeza, then south to Archidona and Tena. This would be our route to the Oriente, the path used since the mid-sixteenth century (and probably before) by all travelers to the Upper Napo River region. Historical accounts of this route in the eighteenth and nineteenth centuries, when it was only a foot trail,

A bulldozer works to clear the narrow, unpaved road that connects the highland cities to the frontier towns at the headwaters of the Amazon. The road is frequently closed by massive landslides such as this.

emphasized the deep mud and the difficulty of hiring guides and bearers for the journey.

We left the paved streets of Quito behind and began to climb out of the basin in which the city lies. The road was surfaced with crushed rock, but it soon narrowed to a single lane. For several hours we wound our way upward until we emerged onto a high, cold, windswept plateau, a vast area of grasslands at nearly 13,000 feet, with no animals in sight nor any sign of human habitation.

Climbing again, we came to the top of a pass that presented a breathtaking view of Antesana, an immense black volcano with glaciers on its flanks and clouds around the summit.

Then we began the descent. In places, the road was just a rutted dirt track; most of this leg of the journey was made at 25 miles an hour or less. We waited anxiously for our first glimpse of the Amazon basin, imagining a cloud- and fog-shrouded sea of green stretching to the horizon; but such a view never appeared. Long before the road emerged onto the eastern flanks of the mountains, it had already plunged into the dense tropical forest of the *montaña,* the eastern slopes of the Andes.

Tena is a small provincial town and the capital of Napo Province. We ate lunch in a small, dingy concrete hotel built over an open-fronted café. We had one of the two meals commonly available in the cafés of the Oriente: fried potatoes, rice cooked with oil, half an avocado, some shredded lettuce and a piece of tough fried beef. (The other meal is exactly the same, except it features chicken instead of beef.)

After lunch we drove the Land Rover to the gravel airstrip, where we met some of the MAF pilots. They told us there was no secure building at the strip (in fact, there were no buildings at all) and that we would have to keep our supplies and equipment in the hotel until we could fly out. We made arrangements to meet them at the hotel café that evening for dinner and to discuss our travel plans.

Back at the hotel we carried our supplies up a narrow concrete stairway to our room. It had two single beds, a toilet, and a bare shower pipe sticking out of the wall. The water flowed away via a drain in the bedroom floor.

The room was tidy and neatly swept, although it smelled of the mold and mildew that blotched the concrete walls; the windows were missing several panes of glass. Compared with many of the places where we have stayed, it was actually quite comfortable; at least it had running water (cold), and walls that went all the way to the ceiling.

That evening we had dinner at the hotel with the pilots and listened to them talk about their day of flying patients to and from various sites in the jungle, of delivering goods, of the weather, and of the condition of the various air strips. We queried them about the various Waorani settlements.

We were looking for a community with a large enough population to have a reasonable distribution of people of various ages, but where the subsistence cycle and the routine of daily life were not distorted by the requirements of a school. We also wanted it to be remote enough to be inacccessible to tourists. (We had heard that, at one or two of the more accessible settlements, guides had begun bringing "adventure tourists" in by boat and trail to see "the savages.") We had contacted Dr. Peeke and Ms. Jung in Tɨwënö by radio, and they were expecting us to arrive the following day to discuss possible research sites.

The next morning found us standing on the airstrip in our knee-high rubber boots and carrying our emergency travel pack. We had long since learned from painful experience that, when traveling in the jungle, it is prudent always to expect to be stranded, whether by bad weather, swollen rivers, sickness, or any of a dozen other typical misfortunes. So, in a nylon duffel bag, we carried a small dome tent, a tiny backpack stove and fuel, two old army mess kits, rice, canned fish, eggs, oatmeal, powdered milk, a change of clothes each, flashlight, knife, lighter, medical kit, toiletries, some antibiotics, two vials of snakebite antivenin, and a hypodermic syringe.

When weather and the condition of the grass-covered jungle airstrips permitted flights, first priority went to medical emergencies; second to other missionaries; third to government officials, teachers, and so on. We would fly on a space-available basis, with our fare calculated on the basis of cargo weight and distance flown.

The settlement that was our destination lay, we soon learned, at the bottom of a narrow, steep-sided valley. It has the shortest landing strip on the reserve, truncated by a bend of the river at one end and by a swamp at the other, and is frequently un-usable because of mud.

Standing at the edge of the airstrip in Tena, we experienced for the first time what would soon become routine: the pilots listened to weather reports and requests by shortwave radio from settlements scattered over the Oriente, checked out the planes, and organized cargo and people waiting to fly out. They drew gas out of the wing tanks to check for dirt and for water (which condenses in the tanks as the fuel is consumed and replaced by moisture-saturated air). The flights came and went throughout the morning. Around 11:30 A.M. it was our turn to be strapped into one of the tiny single-engined planes.

Almost immediately we were over dense forest, with rivers curling in elaborate meanders below us. For the first few minutes we could see occasional clearings with houses and fields, but soon we were over primary rainforest. From a thousand feet up, it was a seemingly endless expanse; only the tops of trees were visible, reaching for sunlight 150 feet or more from the forest floor and stretching, like an endless expanse of broccoli, to the horizon.

Here and there were splashes of color, a tree covered in red or yellow flowers, brilliant against the profusion of shades of green. Occasionally there were red slashes in the intense green where, under the presure of torrential rain and perhaps triggered by an earthquake deep beneath one of the Andean volcanoes, the satu-rated soil on a steep ridge had given way, collapsing into the valley below in an avalanche of red mud, trees, and boulders.

The terrain was deeply dissected, with steep ridges, deep valleys, and rocky outcrops. We quickly noticed that there was no place to land in an emergency; but even if one survived a forced landing, the topography was so rugged that walking out would be very difficult.

After about 20 minutes we saw a rectangular clearing and a scattering of palm-thatched houses in a narrow valley between two steep ridges. At one end of the clearing was a swamp, at the other a bend of the river that swung across from one side of the narrow valley to the other.

Circling twice, the pilot dropped between the ridges and, flying just above the water, approached the airstrip from directly downriver. From that angle, the clear-ing looked about 10 yards long. The landing, however, was smooth and uneventful and, as we came to a stop, the plane was immediately surrounded by people.

Several had the large holes in their earlobes that once held the balsa wood earplugs that had immediately identified them as "wild Aucas." One man displayed a wide, gap-toothed grin. He was Omëni̵, we soon learned, the elder of the primary kindred in the settlement and one of the men who had speared the five North Americans.

The two missionaries were also there, and they escorted us to their house—made of split bamboo and raised on posts like the others—where we had a lunch of packaged soup, crackers, and canned Vienna sausages. The villagers stood or sat along the walls inside the house or peered in through the windows, laughing and talking.

One ancient woman was wearing a faded red dress made of some synthetic fab-ric, her dark, crinkled skin clearly visible through the transparent material. Other women wore similar dresses in bright colors. As we had observed before in

The airstrip in Tïwënö is kept clear of trees and undergrowth by men and women wielding machetes. The house clusters reflect the clustering of kin relations within the community.

Malaysia, somehow clothes that are unsalable anywhere else in the world—T-shirts with misspelled words, clothes made from garishly ugly materials or with the pieces sewn together crooked—filter down and finally find a market in the trading shops of these places at the ends of the earth.

Some of the young women wore what looked like bright red lipstick, not only on their lips but also painted in large round dots, one on each cheekbone. Men wore shorts or bathing trunks; some had T-shirts. Most were barefoot, although a few wore rubber boots. There did not appear to be one full set of teeth among them.

We discussed with the two women the pros and cons of various communities as possible research sites. Based on our previous experience in learning Semai, we anticipated spending about three months acquiring the rudiments of the language, and then using the settlement as a home base from which we could extend our research to other communities. Once they understood that we were experienced field researchers and that we did not expect them to act as interpreters for us, they suggested Tɨwënö as a possibility. The population was about right—around 70—and there was no school. There was also an old abandoned bamboo and thatch building that had been used as a schoolhouse during the late contact period that we might be able to live in. They told us they would be leaving in a little more than a month, which would allow us to take advantage of their linguistic expertise as we were getting started.

Later, standing outside at the edge of the airstrip, we asked Dr. Peeke to explain our objectives to the community and to request permission from the elders for us to live there. She spoke to Omënɨ, and his response was to look in our direction and take a sharp intake of breath, a gasp, as if he had been startled. We quickly looked to the forest behind us for the source of his alarm and Dr. Peeke smiled and said, "He's not telling you there is something behind you, he is telling you, emphatically, 'Yes!'"

2 / The Waorani War Complex

In this notably violent part of the world—the western Amazon basin—the Waorani were among the people most feared. They were at war with all their neighbors, but their enforced isolation had left them with no access to the firearms that the surrounding groups possessed. Still, their fearsome reputation and their 9-foot palmwood spears kept the outside world at bay. They also raided each other. Blood feuds and vendettas arising from previous killings, from conflicts over marriages, and from accusations of sorcery persisted over generations and were a way of life and a constant threat.

Over at least the past several generations, more than 60% of Waorani deaths have been homicides. While nearly 20% of those deaths were the result of warfare with outsiders, more than 40% grew out of internal vendettas (cf. Yost, 1981; Robarchek & Robarchek, 1989, 1992).

Before we undertake to analyze and attempt to explain this warfare complex, however, we must first try to put the violence into perspective. First, we must admit that most published descriptions of Waorani society and culture, ours no less than others', are distorted by an overemphasis on violence. The bulk of this material has been written by missionaries and those who sympathize with their efforts to Christianize and "civilize" the Waorani and, as a result, it focuses on the contrast between pre- and post-contact life. When the pre-contact period is discussed, the violence is emphasized to the exclusion of almost everything else.

Our own descriptions suffer from a bias similar in content, if not in motivation. Since no description can truly present the vision of reality perceived by its creator, much less that of its subjects, all observations and descriptions must be selective; ours are certainly no exception.

It is the violence of Waorani society that gives it significance in terms of the theoretical issues that interest us. Much of our time in the field has, therefore, been devoted to exploring, documenting, and attempting to understand the complex of historical circumstances, the patterns of social relations, and the beliefs, attitudes, and values that motivate raids and vendettas. Not surprisingly, our published reports reflect this emphasis, focusing on violence while neglecting much of the rest of Waorani culture and social life.

This book, similarly, persists in that emphasis. At some point, however, we must attempt to put the violence (which is quite real) into perspective, and, if only briefly, to restore some balance to the presentation of Waorani life.

It would be well to remember that, even in the pre-contact period when violence was a constant threat, it was seldom a constant reality. For any given group, years might pass between raids. While it is difficult to ascertain or even estimate the frequency of raids in the past, it is clear that at least the internal violence was, to some extent, cyclical. There were periods of greater and lesser intensity in the raiding, and the late pre-contact period appears to have been a period of higher intensity for at least some bands.

But our data suggest that, even then, a typical residence cluster of around 40 people was likely to take or lose a life on an average of no more than once every year or two. Since raids seldom claimed only a single victim, the actual frequency of attacks was certainly much lower than that. The following autobiographical account from one of our neighbors is typical:

> In my early childhood, my mother abandoned me and fled. Right here (Tɨwënö) we lived; then we moved further downriver, living and drinking manioc we lived. Further downriver, making more gardens, we lived on that side of the Dayönö under only lean-to shelters. Then Möipa speared Wɨwä. He speared and even further we fled, further into the forest, further downriver! We reached the Villano, going cross-country then going down trail. All of our manioc plantings we abandoned; we fled into the unplanted forest.
>
> For four chonta fruit seasons [years] we lived like that before we dared to come back upstream to get some manioc stalks [to plant]. For all that long time we did not drink manioc. We did not drink plantains. We made drink from the wild *pɨtümö* palm fruit and ate meat from hunting. There was very little wild chonta fruit. We lived on the ridges of the Villano River, far downstream from here.
>
> Living like that for so long, I became a young man. By the time we returned to this area, I was already grown. Then Downriver people came up. Wawë speared my stepfather, Wamönyɨ. After that there was only Paä, Gïngata and Kipa. We came upstream as far as Möi's place and lived in houses again, but we speared and they retaliated. Finally Imä was speared. We moved and moved, upstream and downstream. Finally we lived about three years near Damöïntarö.

It is clear from accounts such as this that, while raiding was certainly a constant concern, it was not a constant reality. Even during this period when the raiding was comparatively intense, years passed between raids.

Although the cultural and psychological significance of violence is great, and while the death toll was spectacularly high and remains high in relative terms today, everyday life was, and is, devoted primarily to the economic and social activities common to all such societies everywhere: gardening, hunting, fishing, house building, feasting, dancing, sex, arranging marriages, and all the other activities that evidence a stable, culturally structured social life.

EXTERNAL WAR

We have no way of determining how long this complex of warfare and violence has been in existence. Prior to the beginning of this century there are no accounts of contacts with people who can be confidently identified as Waorani.

A map produced by Jesuit missionaries in 1707 shows the area between the Napo and Curaray rivers to be occupied by the "Abijiras," and variants of that label— "Awishiris," "Avishiris," "Auxiris," and, most commonly, "Aushiris"—were applied to the inhabitants of what is now Waorani territory until well into the twentieth century. Just who the Aushiris were, however, remains an open question. Lists of words collected in the early years of this century indicate that the label has been used to designate several different groups, at least one of which was probably Waorani.

By the 1920s, information collected by missionaries and others, including lists of words collected from captured Indians, makes it clear that at that time those called Aushiris were Waorani, and they occupied much or all of the territory that they still hold today. They were violently hostile to outsiders, and all observers agreed that to enter the realm of the Aushiris was to court sudden and violent death.

In 1925, Monsignor Cecco from the Josefina mission in Tena wrote "It is not possible to visit those pagan tribes who live on the right shores of the Napo . . . because they are very fierce and are enemies of the whites whom they assault frequently, robbing and assassinating them" (Spiller, 1974, p. 95; translated by the authors).

Mission records from 1907 to 1924 report 10 attacks on settlements near the Nushiño and Napo rivers, attacks attributed to "the infidel tribe of Aushiris" (Muratorio, 1991, p. 251). By the late 1920s, the term *Aushiri* had been largely replaced by the Quichua word *Auca*, and those to whom it referred were clearly Waorani.

In 1931, a geologist traveling down the Napo to Coca observed that

> The south bank of the river below the mouth of the Arajuno is given over entirely to an unsubdued and murderous tribe of Indians, called by the Spanish-speaking people 'Infieles' or pagans. This tribe still lives in the Stone Age, using weapons of wood and stone and going unclothed   their ambition seems to be to murder anyone who enters their domain. Owing partly to fear inspired by these Indians and partly to economic reasons, the upper Napo, which once had a number of more or less populous settlements with numerous haciendas, is now almost deserted (Holloway, 1932, p. 413).

In the 1920s and 1930s travelers on the Napo were routinely given advice such as the following from a local hacienda owner: ". . . never spend the night on the right bank of the Napo. That's where the Auca Indians live, and they kill peaceable Indians and whites alike, just as a matter of principle" (Blomberg, 1957, p. 13).

Through the 1950s, Waorani had few peaceful contacts with the outside world. So complete was their isolation, they had no regular access to iron tools or to the cheap shotguns that were ubiquitous among other Indian groups. Our informants described how they cleared their fields with stone axes and cut weeds with sharp-edged chonta palm wood "machetes."

Unlike the surrounding Indians, they did not even have dogs. Instead, a harpy eagle was often kept tethered in the clearing to scream a warning at the approach of strangers. Armed only with the barbed and feathered hardwood spears that are their trademark in Ecuador (and, to this day, the preferred weapons for killing people), they attacked any hunter or settler foolhardy enough to venture south of the Napo River.

Many people remember clearing the forest for gardens with stone tools. They found the stone axe blades left behind by earlier gardening peoples. The sharp chonta palm wood "machetes" were used to clear undergrowth and also sometimes used as war clubs.

The following recollection from Omënɨ gives an indication of the Waorani attitude toward outsiders:

> *Kowudɨ* came to that place where we were living and Paä, angry that they came into our territory, said, "You all go to the Ahuano River and spear the *kowudɨ!*" So we went and speared. Paä and Gïngata went with us.
>
> From the Ahuano we all went to the Todoborö (Napo) River to spear the *kowudɨ* who came into our territory. They came so often there was a trail from Ahuano to the Kɨrɨmïnënö (Tzapino) River. When we got to the Napo River, it was full and there was no sun, and we got cold there, so we went back home. After about a month, we went back but didn't see anyone. We kept going back and not finding anyone to spear and Gïngata was getting angry. One day, when the sun was shining, we went with Gïngata and speared two women who were cutting palm trunks down for flooring. It was our spears we left in those women that Nate Saint [one of the missionaries later killed by this band] found and, knowing we were somewhere near, started to look for us in his plane.
>
> Earlier, Möipa speared at Arajuno when the oil company came there. Anyone who came across the Curaray would get speared.

Occasionally, small Waorani raiding parties, often including both men and women, even crossed the Napo to raid the settlements of the lowland Quichua on the north bank. The increasing population of non-Indian colonists and the scattered haciendas were also at risk. Writing in 1931, Monsignor Cecco observed that

> . . . [U]p to a few years ago along the river there were 34 haciendas, located in a manner which was very easy for the traveler to encounter hospitality and assistance. Today the haciendas are diminished because the inhabitants descended to the Aguarico and there, the course of the Napo, from Vargas Torres to Providencia, for a stretch of 256 kilometers, is abandoned. This immense solitude is truly impressionable. The causes which have induced the masters of the old haciendas to relocate further downriver were the difficulties of selling their produce and the danger of the *Aucas*. These infest

the right banks of the Napo, in the zone which goes from Vargas Torres to Coca; and they don't hestitate to repeat, from time to time, their terrible incursions, assaulting and killing with their lances of chonta, whomever they encounter, Indians and Whites. (Spiller, 1974, pp. 135–136)

In 1937, exploration for oil began in the Oriente when Royal Dutch Shell was granted a concession. Laborers, usually Indians hired locally, were set to clearing trails and sites for camps and seismic tests. Waorani attacked them at every oppportunity. In 1942, the company reported that "Aushiri Indians who inhabit the region between the Rio Napo and the Rio Curaray east of Arajuno, and whom it has proved impossible to civilize, attacked our workers and killed three of them" (Blomberg, 1957, p. 16). The next year, three more workers were speared to death.

Even today, the personnel working at isolated drilling sites are vulnerable to threats and demands. Armed with spears or shotguns, Waorani often appear and demand food, pots and pans, and tools. A directive from one American oil company currently working in Waorani territory advises field staff that "if the demand is urgent, offer the Waorani some food."

In the 1960s, a priest based in the Quichua settlement of Curaray attempted to contact a band of Waorani living on the Cononaco:

Padre Nardi in 1964 crossed to the Cononaco and established a ranch to make contact with the savages. The soldiers came and built a house too. A few days after the soldiers arrived there was a bloody battle between them and the Aucas; a few members on both sides were lost. The final result was that the soldiers returned to their base on the Curaray and the Aucas pursued them causing new casualties not far from the general quarters. (Spiller, 1974, p. 262)

A Quichua who had worked for Shell in Waorani territory, but who had never actually seen the Aucas, offered the prevailing Quichua view of them: "They're worse than beasts. They kill girls and women at their feasts. When a baby girl is born, they are disappointed and embittered, and sometimes they murder her . . ." (Blomberg, 1957, p. 121).

If these excerpts reflect the perceptions of the Waorani by their neighbors, the Waorani view of them was no less sanguinary. From the Waorani perspective, all *kowudï* were enemies who had a taste for human flesh. Waorani folklore recalls their ancestors' encounters with these dangerous foreigners and chronicles their cannibalistic practices. One story describes how the *kowudï* bound their victims and then cut off strips of their flesh, which they roasted and ate (cf. Saint, 1964).

Besides raiding for territorial defense and for retaliation, Waorani raided to acquire the manufactured goods that their hostility to the outside world denied them. Raids against the *kowudï* were the only reliable source of metal tools, especially axes and machetes. One of our neighbors recalled his family fleeing to avoid retribution after they had raided an enemy band and speared several people in retaliation for an earlier raid that had killed some of their kinsmen. When they arrived at their new residence site, they discovered that no one had a machete to clear land for gardens.

Paä said, "how will we live without drink? I am angry, and I will take spears and kill *kowudï*." Paä, already angry over the deaths of his kinsmen, and always having lived by killing, went to the Villano river and speared some Quichua. He brought back three machetes.

Another of our neighbors described how a relative had, for several days, patiently watched from the cover of the densely forested river bank while a Quichua man fashioned a dugout canoe on a sandbar. When the canoe was finished and he had seen the entire process, he speared the Quichua and took the tools so he could make his own canoes.

Surrounding Indians and whites raided them as well, both in retaliation and for women and children who were taken to work, essentially as slaves, on the haciendas that persisted into the 1960s. A hacienda owner described one such raid:

> . . . [A] year ago some of my Indians and others from the Garces' and Peñaherreras' haciendas made a combined punitive expedition against the savages. They were twelve strong and all had firearms. The reason was—apart from their earlier misdeeds—that the Aucas had just killed three Yumbo [Quichua] children, a girl and two boys. The poor little things were found nailed to the beach with Auca spears. They had been home alone in a Yumbo hut on the Huachi Yacu—that's a small tributary of the Napo—when the bloodthirsty devils came. . . .
>
> Well, the Yumbo Indians managed to locate a large Auca house—it was really two houses joined together—near the Rio Tzapino. They crept right up without being seen and attacked. But nearly all of the Aucas got away, even if a lot of them were wounded. Two Auca women were killed—and one or two children as well, I've heard, but my Yumbos won't talk freely about that. The two women, who had only been wounded in the shooting, were killed with machetes—slaughtered! These so-called Christian Indians showed no mercy. They were too full of hate. (Blomberg, 1957, p. 31)

INTERNAL WAR

Although the internal feuding was, at least at times, intense, even less information is available regarding the historical depth of this pattern of internecine warfare. The patriarch of the primary kindred in our home settlement, an old man, probably in his eighties and one of the oldest living Waorani, recounted how, when he was a small child, his father was accused of sorcery and speared to death by other Waorani. If the sorcery/raiding complex was already well developed during his father's lifetime, it must have existed for at least a century, and perhaps much longer. In any case, it is clear from the deaths recorded in our genealogies that internecine raiding had been going on for at least the last five generations (cf. Yost, 1981).

Much of the raiding was among the major regional subgroups. In the early 1960s, when direct information about the Waorani first began to become available, there were a number of widely dispersed subgroups, each occupying a more or less discrete region within the larger territory.

Three major subdivisions were identified by the first missionaries as the "Upriver," "Downriver," and "Ridge" bands. The Upriver group was centered in the region between the Challua and Nushiño rivers (headwater tributaries of the Curaray), the region that later became the Auca Protectorate. The Downriver bands occupied the headwaters of the Tiputini and Tivacuno rivers. The Ridge bands held the headwaters of the Nashiño and Yasuní rivers to the southeast. There were additional smaller groups scattered along the Tiguino, Shiripuno, and Cononaco rivers and eastward to the Peruvian border (Map 2). There are at least two, and perhaps more, of these smaller bands that continue to resist all contacts, still at war with both *kowudï* and with other bands of Waorani.

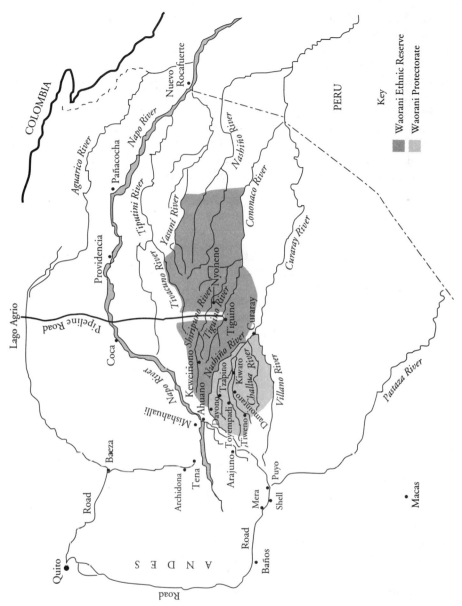

Map 2   *Waoraniland: rivers (Napo, Curary, Yasuni, Cononaco, Shiripuno. . .), towns (Coca, Tena, Puyo, Nuevo Rocafuerte), settlements, Via Auca*

Bonds of kinship and marriage link the members of each of these subgroups and, more distantly, link the various subgroups to each other. For Waorani, how-ever, such ties are as likely to be sources of conflict as of congeniality, sometimes a result of disputes that arise over marriage arrangements. The most common imme-diate motive for killings, however, is revenge.

In the past, raids were often undertaken to avenge previous spearings. Today, they are more likely to be in retaliation for deaths caused by sorcery, whose practice is inferred from the occurrence of serious illnesses, accidents, and snakebites.

The logic underlying this inference is straightforward. Waorani are, in general, remarkably healthy; food is abundant and varied and their diet is more than adequate to sustain good health. Their enforced isolation, low population density, and wide dispersal has insulated them from most of the diseases that have repeatedly devastated similar peoples. Still, hazards abound: scorpions and venomous spiders are common, and poisonous snakes are everywhere.

Every adult has been snakebitten—most several times—and around 4% of Waorani deaths are the result of snakebite (Larrick, Yost, & Kaplan, 1978). Although this may be the highest snakebite death rate in the world, even here only one in perhaps 50 or more snakebites actually results in a fatality.

Since serious illnesses are infrequent, and since most of those bitten by snakes and other venomous creatures survive, a death from any of these causes is an abnormal event. Such an event requires an explanation, and the explanation that is almost certain to be offered is sorcery by someone who has a grudge against the victim or his/her kin.

The appropriate response to such an event was, and occasionally still is, a retaliatory raid on the suspected sorcerer's household. Typically, the raiders strike at night, bursting into the house and spearing the suspected sorcerer and as many of his or her housemates—men, women, and children—as possible. Raiders have always tried to wipe out the primary victim's entire family so that there would be no one left to retaliate at some future time.

These killings, in turn, generated their own momentum. Long-term blood feuds developed and were sustained by the desire for revenge. In earlier times the killers and their families would abandon their houses and fields following a raid. In the hope of avoiding retaliation, they would flee into the forest and establish a new hamlet many miles away. Years might pass before a telltale footprint betrayed their location to hunters from another band and triggered another round of killing.

This internecine violence apparently went through cycles of greater and lesser intensity. Among the upriver band with whom we principally lived and worked, the late 1940s and 1950s had been a period of particularly intense raiding.

This was due in part to the actions of a notorious killer named Möipa, who apparently enjoyed killing for its own sake. He and his kinsmen raided *kowudï* and Waorani alike. Not only did his raids against other Waorani bands bring devastating retaliatory raids against his own group, he himself also killed many of his own kin. "He even," we were told, "speared his own grandfather who adopted and raised him."

Even in more "normal" periods, however, the spearing deaths that we recorded in our genealogies show that the rate of killing was, in cross-cultural comparative terms, astronomically high.

THE DECLINE OF WAR

The first sustained peaceful contacts betwen Waorani and the outside world began when two American missionary women—Elisabeth Elliot, the widow of one of the young men killed on the Curaray, and Rachael Saint, the sister of another—made contact with some young Waorani women who had fled the raiding to take refuge with Quichua Indians.

From them, they began learning to speak the Auca language and making plans to contact those who remained in the jungle. After a year, the Waorani women returned to their homeland to locate their kinsmen and to prepare them for the arrival of the missionaries. They soon came back for the two American women, and led them into the forest to meet the very people who had killed their husband and brother.

Although the missionaries' primary goals were to bring the word of God to the Aucas and, thereby, to bring an end to the violence, they had no coercive power at their disposal to accomplish these ends. There were no police or soldiers at hand; if the missionaries were to be successful, the Waorani had to be persuaded to forsake the vendettas and abandon their implacable hatred for and fear of *kowudɨ*. We will discuss the dynamics of that process in chapter 9; for the present, it is sufficient to note that they were spectacularly successful.

In a very short time, most bands of the three main subgroups had been contacted and persuaded to abandon their vendettas. Seeking to shed their identity as "savages," most soon abandoned the nudity and the large balsa wood earplugs that had made them instantly recognizable as Aucas. Within only a few years, the number of killings had declined by more than 90%.

A TENUOUS PEACE

Although there has been a remarkable change in behavior—from a situation where all men (and some women) were killers to one where very few of the most recent generation to grow to adulthood have killed—this has not become an inherently peaceful society. In comparative perspective, it remains fairly violent, with a homicide rate among contacted groups that we have conservatively estimated to be at least six times that of the United States as a whole.

Moreover, the process of "pacification" remains uncompleted. During our first field trip in 1987, the Tagëiri ("Tagë's group"), one of the bands still resisting all contact, speared to death two Catholic missionaries, a bishop and a nun, who had been ferried into their hamlet by an oil company helicopter. When the plane returned the following day, both the missionaries were lying dead in the clearing, pierced by at least 20 spears. The Tagëiri were gone; having once again disappeared into the forest.

Another incident occurred shortly after our most recent fieldwork in 1993, when a group of Waorani living on the fringe of the reserve made several forays into the territory of this same group (instigated, according to one account, by a writer seeking an adventure story for a European magazine).

They found the Tagëiri settlement with little difficulty, but the inhabitants had fled. The searchers made three attempts and each time, when they left, they made off with as many of the Tagëiri's belongings as they could carry. On their last foray, they were ambushed and one of their number suffered a mortal wound from a Tagëiri spear. His relatives have pledged to avenge him and to wipe out the Tagëiri.[1]

---

[1]Randy Smith, personal communication.

This man is immediately recognizable as a Wao by the large holes in his earlobes that once held balsa wood earspools. These were abandoned soon after contact as Waorani strove to shed their image as "savages."

As this incident makes clear, even among those groups that have abandoned large-scale warfare, the new peacefulness is often tenuous. The violence of the recent past is never far from consciousness, and almost any event triggers accounts of past attacks inflicted and suffered. A journey downriver by dugout canoe is punctuated, as the sites of old houses and gardens slip by, with recollections in graphic and gory detail of the deaths of kinsmen who lived and died there.

Collecting genealogies invariably elicits graphic accounts of the raids that took the lives of parents and grandparents, brothers and sisters, spouses and children. Even members of the younger generation who never experienced the wholesale violence of the past have grown to young adulthood listening to these stories and can recite them from memory.

The current peacefulness is fragile in part because it remains institutionally unsupported. Changes in economic and political arrangements from the pre-contact period are largely superficial and the fundamentals of social organization and social life are little changed. As in the past, there is still little basis for the creation of mutual interest groups or for generating interdependence and mutual obligations among individuals or kindreds. There are still no institutionalized mechanisms for resolving disputes or for controlling or limiting conflict.

The fragility of the current peacefulness is graphically evidenced by its occasional breakdown, usually precipitated by accusations of sorcery. There have been at least two raids against accused sorcerers in the past several years in which, in the traditional pattern, entire families—men, women and children—have been speared to death.

This, then, is the warfare complex that brought us to the Oriente: a pattern of homicidal violence with roots extending back a century or more that still occasionally finds expression in the behavior of the members of what was until recently the most violent society on earth.

3 / The Fieldwork

GETTING STARTED

Before we left Tɨwënö that first day, we were able, with the help of the two missionaries, to get the community's approval to use the abandoned schoolhouse and to contract for someone to repair the rotted thatch on one side of the roof and to clear the weeds and grass from around the building to reduce the danger from snakes.

We arrived back in Tɨwënö with our gear around noon the following day. Together with the pilot, we unloaded the plane, and the villagers helped us carry our bags and boxes to the schoolhouse. The two missionaries told us who had worked to repair and make ready the house for us, and let us know how much we owed to each one. They again fed us lunch while a crowd watched us take every bite.

These two women (they told us to call them "Rosie" and "Cathy") had been involved with the Waorani, in one way or another, for more than 20 years. Both had arrived within a few years of the first contact. Rosie Jung, trained as a midwife, had helped to treat the sicknesses that swept each new group during the time of the relocations to the Protectorate. Catherine Peeke, a linguist, had been directly involved in many of the initial contacts and had written her PhD dissertation on the Waorani language. They were nearing the ends of their careers and were striving to complete their translation of the New Testament into Waorani before their retirement. Their routine was to spend several months in Tɨwënö working with informants and then to return to the SIL complex in Quito for several months to work on their translations.

We asked them for suggestions regarding an informant to hire to work on language with us. They suggested Imäa, a boy about 17 years old whose father, Tönyë, had been one of the first Christian converts. In 1972, Tönyë had gone to contact the Ridge people to try to persuade them to give up their vendettas and move to the Protectorate. He had been there for about 3 months when they killed him with an axe. His son was among the crowd that was following us around, so Cathy asked him if he wanted to work with us. He just grinned and looked away; we decided to let the matter rest for the time being.

After lunch, we went back to the old schoolhouse and began to turn it into a home base for the next year. Omënɨ had replaced the rotted palm thatch, and the ground around the house was now completely bare. Someone had even washed the mud off the floor.

The house, a single room, was raised on pilings about 4 feet off the ground. Three of the split bamboo walls went halfway up, with the rest covered by old metal screenwire. There were only a few holes in the gables to be patched to keep out vampire bats. The floor was made of 3- to 4-inch-wide slats split from palm trunks.

It even had furniture—of a sort. There were two wooden benches and a large wooden frame, about 7 feet square and 2 feet tall, that originally had planks laid across it to serve as school desks. Round trunk sections of balsa trees served for the seats. We pushed this frame into one corner, covered it with split bamboo to make a platform, put our foam pads on top, and hung our mosquito net over it all. Underneath we pushed the suitcase and two footlockers that held our tape recorders, cameras, computer, and our clerical supplies and clothes.

Hanging on one wall was a sheet of Masonite that had been painted green to serve as a blackboard. There were two large barrels full of school supplies and a small wooden cupboard.

We filled the cupboard with canned goods, covered a board with a sheet of plastic and put it across the space between the cupboard and the barrels. That gave us a surface that could be washed, a place for our dishes and kerosene pressure stove.

Beneath that, we stored the 5-gallon plastic container of kerosene; beside it we stacked the large reusable tins that held our rice, beans, noodles, flour, sugar, and so on. Above it, we drove some nails into the wall posts and hung our pots and pans— and our kitchen was finished.

As Carole finished stowing away canned goods, Clay set up a wooden pole in front of the house and built a frame to hold the two small solar panels that would charge the battery for our laptop computer. All the while, people sat on the two benches which we had pushed against one wall, laughing and making unintelligible comments.

The ancient woman whom we had seen the day before sat just inside the door, chattering away at us, gesturing, pointing in different directions and counting on her fingers. She was barefoot and wore the same transparent red dress. She also had the elongated earlobes that had once immediately identified all Waorani. She stayed for more than two hours and never stopped talking, completely unaware, it seemed, that we could not understand a word she said.

In the months to come, we would listen to her rambling accounts on many occasions, and would come to know that she was compulsively recounting stories of the spearing raids that had killed most of her generation. It was a topic that obsessed her—especially when rumors or threats of spearings reached the settlement— because she was old and was widely believed to be a witch, and, because she expected that, one night the killers, perhaps her own grandsons, would come for her.

A few days later, we found out that she had named us. Clay was henceforth "Näntowë" and Carole was "Abare," the names of a couple in her parents' generation. This, we also later learned, conferred on us some of the obligations of relatives to her kindred. When they came to Tiwënö, we were obligated to give them fishhooks, line, safety pins, and anything else that we would let them extract from us, but it didn't seem to confer any discernable reciprocal rights. Moreover, since she was an outsider in this community, it meant that we had few fictive "kin" in the community where we had our primary residence.

LANGUAGE

Within a few days of our arrival, we had arranged for Imäa to come and work with us every morning on the language. Since he spoke only Waorani, we began with a short list of words from *El Idioma Huao*, a grammar of Waorani written in Spanish by Catherine Peeke, and with words that we extracted from grammatical examples in her dissertation, which had been published by the SIL. Slowly we began memorizing and learning to pronounce a basic vocabulary.

On the Masonite "greenboard" we wrote the complex paradigm of Waorani pronouns so it would be constantly in front of us. As we painfully worked out the meanings of new words, Carole used the laptop computer to construct and constantly revise a Waorani-English and English-Waorani dictionary.

The Waorani language may be unrelated to any other known language.[1] We found it appallingly difficult to learn, the most difficult of any language that we have attempted. This is a perception shared by the half-dozen or so missionaries who, over the past 20 years or so, have also managed to learn it.

In 1987, no Wao (the singular form of Waorani) in Tɨwënö was bilingual in either English or Spanish, and the few Spanish words spoken by some were difficult for us to recognize because of the differences in phonology between Waorani and Spanish. For example, the basic unit of currency in Ecuador is the *sucre*. In Waorani, it became *tukudi*, because Waorani has no *s* and always places a vowel between consonants.

"Words" are made by putting together long strings of mostly monosyllabic particles, the sounds of which change depending on the sounds that precede or follow them, and all of which must be in the proper sequence or the entire utterance becomes unintelligible.

Here is a simple sentence:

Kɨmöntadɨwodiiri Omënɨ ïngäntɨ tënönäni wëngakäïmba.

Kɨmöntadɨ [person's name]; -wodi- [dead person]; -iri [group/kind]; Omënɨ [person's name]; ïngäntɨ [object marker, indicating that Omënɨ is the object of some action]; tënö- [to spear]; -näni- [third-person plural: they]; wë- [to die]; -nga- [far past]; -kä- [third-person singular: he/she]; -ɨ- [inferential (the speaker didn't witness it)]; -mba [declaration]: "The dead Kɨmöntadɨ's group speared Omënɨ and he died (in the distant past)."

One day, after we had been working intensively on the language for several weeks, Carole, beginning to feel a bit more confident, leaned out the window and shouted to Mïngkayɨ, as he passed by, "Is your father biting yet?" The young man stopped in mid-stride, open-mouthed and puzzled, and then grinned as he realized

---

[1]Greenberg (1987) classifies Auca with the Andean languages; however, the data upon which he bases that conclusion are extremely sketchy.

what she had intended to ask: "Has your father arrived yet?" The difference was that she had forgotten to nasalize one vowel.

CHURCH

Every Sunday at about 7 A.M. people began to gather outside the church, a small, rectangular bamboo building with a rusty corrugated tin roof. It was raised, like the houses, about 4 feet off the ground and had a ladder leading up to the doorway. Inside, several rows of crude benches and blocks cut from the trunks of balsa trees were arranged along the left side of the single room. At one end was a recognizable pulpit, made of split bamboo.

The first Sunday, we climbed the ladder and sat on two balsa logs by the door. Gämï, Omënï's sister-in-law, stood behind the pulpit and seemed to be telling a story. We understood a word here and there, but no sentences, and we could not even tell what the story was about.

The old woman, whose name we now knew was Dyiko, was sitting on the floor near us. One of the pet marmosets that seemed to be in every house came in, screeching and running between the benches, poking its tiny hands in all the holes in the logs as it searched for large cockroaches that crunched noisily as it chewed them. It raced across people and up onto the pulpit; finally, it settled in Dyiko's lap.

Gämï's story seemed interminable but, finally, she began what was clearly a long prayer; most people covered their eyes with their hands and silently prayed along with her.

Next, Omënï stood to speak. He held a copy of Matthew, the only portion of the Bible translation that had been completed at that time. As he spoke, he moved his finger across the page as if he were reading from the text.

Later, Cathy and Rosie told us that he cannot read the Waorani text, and that he says much the same thing every Sunday. From memory, he recounts a Bible story and talks about how, in the old days, Waorani killed each other, but now they live together peacefully. He also says that soon he is going downriver to preach to the still uncontacted groups.

After he finished speaking, he led the group in a chanted song that we later learned he had composed himself, and then he said a short prayer.

Next, a man who was one of Cathy's informants and who had arrived the previous day from another settlement with his wife and two children, came to the front and read from Matthew. Then he led a song and said a long prayer. After him, Nängkä, Omënï's son, did much the same. During the last session, several women with fussy babies went outside and stood around the ladder; we wished we could join them. After what seemed an eternity, it ended, and we really had no idea what had gone on.

We attended these meetings every Sunday when we were in Tïwënö and we also attended in the settlements of Tönyëmpadï and Kiwarö. Slowly, we began to understand what was being said and done.

In Tïwënö, the service generally began with the recitation of one or more Bible stories by single individuals, either men or women. One at a time, people came to the front to speak, to lead a prayer or, in the case of some of the young men, to read

Women in their best dresses enter the church. Participation in the ritual of the church service is a public statement of their commitment to nonviolence and a "civilized" self-image.

haltingly from the book of Matthew. When Cathy and Rosie were in the settlement, they sat near the front and participated, but the entire service was under the direction and control of the Waorani themselves.

The Old Testament stories—the Creation, Noah and the Ark, Samson and Delilah, and David and Goliath were favorites—seemed to be told as literally true accounts of the past, and there was usually little attempt to extract morals or messages beyond the most obvious from them.

Meetings lasted from one to two hours, depending upon how many people wanted to speak and how long they spoke. All the while, women played with their babies and stripped fibers for making string. Naked children became restless and played on the floor; people talked softly among themselves. Sometimes people brought along marmosets and other pets. Some people attended irregularly, while others were always there.

Omënï was one of the latter, and he almost always began the meeting in Tïwënö. Standing in front of the gathering, he usually told a Bible story while pretending to read from his copy of Matthew. His favorites included the serpent in the Garden of Eden and The Flood. He emphasized that God punishes those who behave badly. He almost always spoke of "how badly the Waorani had lived" in the past before they believed in God. They lived, he said, by killing and then fleeing into the forest to escape retribution, living with no access to gardens and suffering from snakebites.

Snakebites were often explicitly characterized as a punishment that God inflicts on unbelievers and on those who allow themselves to become angry or otherwise behave badly. Omënï's son, Nängkä, on one occasion, observed that "At Tönyëmpadï many people are very angry and many dogs and snakes are biting them. We here are not angry."

Omëni's wife's sister, Gämi, also usually told a story or read a passage from Matthew (she could read, haltingly, the text in Waorani). She used the stories to make one or two points about how people should behave. She also reported any current rumors that people in other settlements were quarrelling, that someone was angry, that someone had threatened to spear, that someone was sick or had been snakebitten, and so on.

In her prayers, said aloud with eyes closed, she asked that people let go (*piyëni keti*) of their anger, that the sick become well, and that people behave well and live well together. Usually, others also would come to the front to tell a story or read a passage. Nängkä tried to teach people to sing some Quichua songs.

By the time of our second visit in 1993, a school had been established and many of the young people could read Spanish. Many of the songs were sung in Spanish and some in Quichua. Most people had learned these by rote, however, and did not actually understand the words.

The church meeting was one of the few occasions when virtually the entire settlement came together. This was the time to make announcements of general interest and to organize the rare community projects such as filling a muddy spot in the airstrip.

Regardless of what else went on, however, there was one constant refrain: because they heard/believed/understood/obeyed (*inyi-*) the word of God, they no longer allowed themselves to become angry and therefore they no longer speared. The commitment to this nonviolent way of life distinguished them from other Waorani who did not believe, and ensured a good and a peaceful life for them all.

THE COMMUNITY

From our house, we could see the two households directly across the clearing. One was occupied by Omëni and his wife, Ditë, and their four unmarried children, three daughters and one son. Another son, Nängkä, occupied the other with his wife and three children. Omëni's house was constructed in Quichua style, as were all the others in this settlement, and consisted of two structures. One was a sleeping house, raised on pilings and built tightly closed and with no windows (this to exclude vampire bats); it had split bamboo walls, a split palmwood floor and a palm-thatched roof. The other structure was the kitchen, built on the ground with split bamboo walls, a palm-thatched roof, and hammocks strung up around the hearth. Later that year, their teenage son built a second small sleeping house off the kitchen area.

In some houses, the kitchen areas were strongly built, almost palisaded, with stout planks of chonta wood and solid doors, a reminder of the days when houses were built to resist the assaults of raiders. Other kitchens were barely enclosed at all, with only low walls of split bamboo.

Stalks of plantains hung ripening in the kitchens; smoked monkeys and other meat and fish were stacked on bamboo shelves; tin dishes and aluminum pots were heaped about; the fibers used in making string were evident in every stage of preparation.

There were clay pots of curare dart poison hanging on the walls and blowpipes, quivers, spears, and shotguns leaned against the walls or were were stuck in the

An extended family house cluster. The residents are a husband and wife, their four unmarried children and a married son and his wife and children.

A man relaxes in his kitchen as pet birds and a dog scavenge for scraps of food. Aluminum pots hold cooked food; bananas and plantains hang ripening; and blowguns and spears are readily at hand.

rafters. The peelings of manioc, bananas, and chonta palm fruit littered the floors, and the mash made from manioc and chonta was stored, covered with leaves, in aluminum pots or in the large, shallow, hand-carved wooden bowls in which it is prepared.

The sleeping houses were variously furnished. Some people slept on the floor, some slept in hammocks, and some slept on raised platforms of split bamboo or chonta. Some households had blankets and mosquito nets.

Clothes were hanging on lines, stuffed into bags or woven baskets, and heaped on the floors. The debris of the modern world—scraps of paper and plastic, empty bottles and cans, and bits of plastic string and rope—littered most sleeping house floors. Chickens, dogs, and other pets wandered in and out freely.

All the houses had pets. These included marmosets, woolly monkeys, spider monkeys, parrots, macaws, agoutis (jackrabbit-sized rodents), and in one case a peccary (wild pig). One common method of feeding pet birds was to pick up a pile of clothes from the floor and shake out the roaches, which the birds pounced on hungrily.

Between our house and the river, on a high bank right at the edge of the water, was the household of Ompudë, Omënï and Dïtë's daughter, and her husband Mïngkaiyï. A short distance farther upriver were two more households occupied by a son and a daughter of Omënï and Dïtë and their spouses and children.

Across the river and up a short trail lived Dïtë's half-sister Gämï and her husband, Omënï's half-brother Wämönyï. Gämï and Wämönyï's newly married son and his young wife lived in the same house with them. Farther up the same trail, near the top of the ridge, lived another married daughter and her husband. Downstream on our side of the airstrip was the church and, a short distance farther on, Cathy and Rosie's house. Both structures were hidden from view from our house by trees.

At the downstream end of the airstrip and on the side opposite our house was another cluster of households occupied by Mïmä, abandoned wife of Gämï's father Gïngata; Mïmä's married son Baï and his wife and children; her married daughter Nyäwadë with her husband and children; and her dead son's widow Mïnta with her daughter and son Imäa, our language informant.

Still farther removed, spatially as well as genealogically, was the household of Ongkayï, half-sister of Gämï, and her husband Näntowë. A trail descended into the river from the downstream end of the airstrip; emerging on the other side, it traversed a swamp, then climbed a steep ridge to their house. Ongkayï's father is Gïngata, which makes her a sister to Gämï (but not to Dïtë), and to Baï and Nyäwadë. Her mother is Dyiko, the old woman in the red dress. Ongkayï's husband Näntowë is her classificatory cross cousin from one of the Downriver bands.

From their house, a trail led down the other side of the ridge to Dyiko's house, hardly more than a hut, located well away from that of her daughter and grandchildren. We always suspected that this was so that, if raiders came to spear Dyiko, who was widely believed to be a sorcerer, they might spare the rest of the family.

THE DAILY ROUTINE

Tïwënö ("Chonta Palm River") is at an altitude of around 1,300 feet. The nights are chilly and mornings are sometimes foggy or rainy. We slept under two blankets and often wore long-sleeved shirts in the mornings and on rainy days. Typically, however, days were mostly sunny and enervatingly hot and humid.

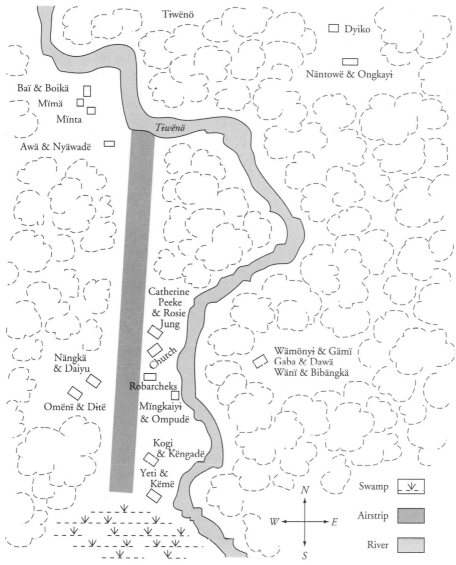

Map 3   Tɨwënö

We always woke up before dawn. It was impossible not to awaken when roost-ers started crowing and people began shouting from one house to another, chopping firewood, and coming down the trail beside our house to fetch water from the river.

We quickly established the routines that constituted our daily lives for much of the next year. We had long ago learned the importance of controlling the necessary chores of daily life: cooking, clothes washing, firewood gathering, and so on. If these tasks are not simplified and kept to a minimum, they will consume much of every day (as they do for the local people) and leave little time for the research and especially for any specialized data collection.

One part of that simplification was our reliance on a one-burner portable kerosene pressure stove for the majority of our cooking. That immediately freed us from much of the time-consuming task of cutting and hauling firewood.

Another simplification was a small pressure cooker. This made it possible to cook enough food at one time for two to four meals. The tightly closed pot kept insects out, and bringing the contents up to pressure every day eliminated the danger of food poisoning in the absence of refrigeration. Food was generally pretty tasteless after it had been recooked three or four times, but it was safe.

In large part, of course, our daily routines were tailored to those of our neighbors. In the initial months of the project, while they were hunting or gardening in the mornings, we worked with Imäa on language and on clarifying other data. After lunch we did household chores, including hauling and boiling drinking water and washing dishes and clothes. In the afternoon, we resumed our fieldwork, visiting houses as people returned from hunting and gardening. At night we cooked at least enough food for dinner and for lunch the next day. Sometimes, especially if we received a quantity of fresh meat, we could cook enough to last for two or even three days. We usually had visitors in the late afternoon and often late into the night.

We spent part of every day at the river, as did our neighbors. The Tïwënö River, at this point in its course, usually flows with perfectly clear water, about knee-deep in most places, over a rocky and sandy bottom. The river was not as big as we would have liked for fishing, but was delightful for bathing, for washing dishes and clothes, and for swimming in one of several deep pools. After heavy rains upstream, the river would become muddy and sometimes dangerously swift and deep, sweeping away huge trees that fell as the current undercut the riverbanks.

One morning, after torrential rains and high water, we found the fuselage of a small airplane deposited on a sandbar, an incident that tended to come to mind later when we were flying over the jungle.

The river was usually a pleasant place to chat and listen to news and gossip. Sometimes, when a tree trunk was left behind by high water, someone would cut off the bark with a machete and smooth a surface on which to wash clothes, or peel and chop manioc, or butcher a deer or a pecccary.

When we went to wash dishes, children inspected our plates to see what we had been eating, and pet ducks nibbled at stray crumbs. More than once while Carole was washing clothes, Gämï's almost full-grown pet peccary startled her by swimming across the river, snorting at her, and snapping its teeth together menacingly.

We were rarely alone at the river, or anywhere else. Since we were usually the only show in town, people were in our house almost constantly. Two or three young women with their babies in slings and two or three toddlers following behind would climb the ladder, seat themselves on the floor or on the benches against the wall, and spend the morning sitting, talking, and laughing, openly discussing us, our belongings, our behavior, our appearance, and who knows what else.

As the months wore on, of course, we became less and less the objects of these conversations, and more and more participants in them. This daily gossip was an important source of insight into people's concerns, beliefs, values, goals, and so on. All the while, each woman was constantly pulling lengths of fibers from a bundle, rolling them against her thigh with the flat of her palm, and twisting them into an endless coil of string that she carried with her.

String making is a constant task; whenever a woman has her hands free she is rolling string which she weaves into hammocks, dip nets, and carrying bags. These articles are in daily use, but they can also be carried out to the frontier towns and sold. This provides an important source of cash income.

STRUCTURED DATA COLLECTION

Genealogies

Because one of the first things that we needed to know was how people were related, we focused early on learning the kin terms and on how to ask questions like "What was your grandmother's name?" and "How many children did she have?" and "Is that person male or female?" That allowed us, while our linguistic competence was still rudimentary, to begin collecting useful data from the people who were constantly sitting in our house anyway.

Compiling genealogies was not as simple a task as it might seem. Waorani traditionally have only one name, which is taken from someone in their grandparents' generation. This means that names repeat every other generation and, in each generation, a number of people are likely to have the same name. As the Waorani acquire national identity cards and begin to register births and deaths, they are being drawn into the Western system of surnames. Some people now have, as surnames, words such as *ënömïngä* ("he who comes upriver"; that is, "a Downriver person"). This is obviously the result of a census taker asking someone what another person's name is, and getting, as a response "He's so-and-so, a Downriver person." Some of the younger generation have been given European rather than Waorani names by their parents; one young woman is "Mariana"; a young man is "Tantun" (Samson).

As we began to sort out genealogical relationships, it became clear that the leading roles taken in church by Omënï and Gämï are indicative of the fact that the two sibling sets they represent form the core of the settlement. This primary social fact is also represented in the spatial distribution of the households within the settlement. The households are clustered into three units, one at the upstream end of the settlement and two at the downstream end (see map 3).

In the upstream cluster are the households of Omënï and Wämönyï, half-brothers who are married to a pair of half-sisters: Dïtë and Gämï. These marriages express the Waorani ideal pattern of cross cousin marriage: one should marry one's father's sister's child or one's mother's brother's child. Omënï and Dïtë are cross first cousins and Wämönyï and Gämï are double cross first cousins (see figure 3.1).

Around each of their houses are clustered the houses of their children and *their* spouses. Two of Omënï and Dïtë's children and two of Wämönyï and Gämï's children are married to four siblings from another settlement who are their cross second cousins (see figure 3.1). This region where they all live (and that is now the Waorani Protectorate) was the traditional territory of the ancestors of all of them.

The two downstream groups derive, respectively, from marriages of Mïmä and Dyiko to Gïngata, who is mother's brother to both Omënï and Wämönyï. This makes the children of Mïmä and Dyiko half-siblings of Gämï, wife of Wämönyï. Even though Gïngata now lives in another settlement, he is the connection that links the upstream and downstream households.

A woman weaves a small carrying bag from string that she has produced and dyed.

People in the upstream households say that Gïngata was not properly related to Mïmä, who was originally from a Downriver band, or to Dyiko, who was originally from the Ridge group between the headwaters of the Yasuní and Nashiño rivers far to the east. In fact, they say that he did not properly marry these two women at all, but only "gave them his seed." The two women's children are married to spouses from the Downriver and Ridge groups, further indicating that they are *warani* "different people" from the Upriver group.

This genealogical division is reflected in other ways as well. In church, for example, the division between the upstream and downstream households was evident both in the ways that they assorted themselves and in their interactions. Omënï and Dïtë preferred to sit on the floor up near the pulpit to sitting on the uncomfortable backless benches. Young women from the upstream group sat together on the benches, giggling and snickering behind their hands and exchanging whispered comments about those from the downstream group.

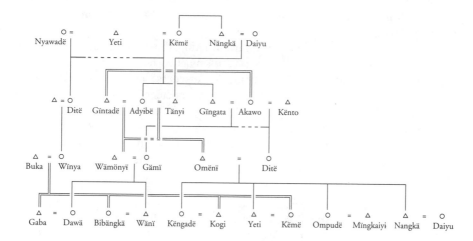

Figure 3.1 The upstream group

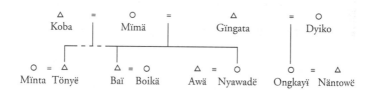

Figure 3.2 The downstream group

Ongkayɨ and her daughters sat with the upstream group on the benches. The two old women from the downriver group, Mïmä and Dyiko, never sat on the benches with the rest, always preferring to sit on the floor near the door. They were joined there by Mïmä's daughter and daughter-in-law when they attended church.

On the rare occasions when the two segments agreed to work together on a community project, the work was usually divided between them. When the entire community was mobilized to cut the grass on the airstrip with machetes, for example, the downstream people cut the downstream half and the upstream people cut the upstream half.

As we began collecting genealogical information, those conversations narrowly focused on genealogical relationships gave us practice both in speaking the language and in understanding it; but keeping the discourse in the realm of kinship, where we had begun to develop some linguistic competence, was impossible. Asking about a parent or grandparent typically brought forth a graphic account, often told at machine-gun speed and complete with gestures and explicit descriptions, of how that person died, of the location of the spear wounds, of who the killers were, where they were from, how they were related, and so on. The following, from Dïtë, is typical:

> Grandfather Kare's first wife was Ïnë and he had three children by her, Kënto (my father), Mïmä, and Wïnyamï. One day two *kowudï* came to the house when Ïnë and her two daughters were there alone. They shot Mïmä with a shotgun and she died. Wïnyamï was a young unmarried girl at that time, but she was very pregnant and did not try to run away and Ïnë stayed with her. Seizing these two, the men took them away cross-country to their dwelling place.
>
> Grandfather Kare then fathered two children with Dyiko [Ongkayï's mother], a boy, Nïmüngkä and a girl, Dabeta. After Kare and his son, Kënto, were speared by Möipa (the orphan he raised), his third wife, Omïnïa, wanting to escape the spearing, fled to the *kowudï* taking Dabeta and her own child by Kare. There, in the *kowudï's* house, Omïnïa married an Oruna [Quichua] and had another child, before dying in childbirth. Her child by Kare died of sickness they say. Dabeta grew up in the *kowudï's* house.
>
> After Dabeta grew up, she married an Oruna who beat her. When Nïmö [Rachael Saint] brought her back, Dyiko cried out, "It is my child!" When Dabeta came back, her head was bleeding from the beatings, we cleaned her wounds and she became well and married downriver Gïngata.
>
> Her brother, Nïmüngkä, on the other hand, grew up with us, but recently he died of sorcery. Oruna were coming into our land to hunt and Nïmüngkä tried to stop them. An Oruna sorcerer put powder in his food and his insides rotted and he died.

All this was, of course absolutely crucial to the problem that we had set out to investigate, which centered on untangling the roots of the warfare complex. Our problem was that people were giving us volumes of valuable ethnographic information, but we could understand only a fraction of it. We quickly realized that we had to have a tape recorder running whenever we discussed genealogies so that we would have a permanent record of these stories. Later on, we worked with the same person or with other informants to clarify, transcribe, and translate the accounts.

As we began trying to trace the network of vendettas through sequences of raids and retaliatory raids and counter-retaliatory raids, we always asked "Why did you (or they) spear?" "We/they were enraged" was the inevitable reply, and that seemed to be a sufficient explanation.

One night, as we sat going over the day's field notes by the light of a kerosene lantern, Clay was trying to trace one of those sequences: "Let's see," he said,

"Nëngkiwi killed Awänyïte and the dead Gaba and he threatened to kill Wämönyï; then Nïmüngkä and Omënï killed Nëngkiwi." At that point he stopped. "You know," he said, "it's still a little bizarre to realize that these are our friends and neighbors that we're talking about."

Economic and Social Relations Survey

As soon as our language capacity allowed, Carole began a month-long period of structured daily data collection. She interviewed everyone in the village every day, asking them what work they had done that day, with whom, what they had brought back to the settlement, what they did with what they brought back, whether or not they had received anything from anyone or had given anything to anyone, and if they had given or received any money, and why.

This replicated a data set that we had collected among the Semai. It was intended to provide data on the patterning of social relationships within Waorani society as well as to provide a basis for comparing the economic systems and the patterning of social relations in the two societies.

As this data collection progressed over the 30-day period, people first became accustomed to it, and then tired of it. Some people helped by rounding up their children and having them available when Carole arrived; some others bore the questions with only the thinnest veneer of civility. After the period of daily data collection was over, however, many people continued to drop by our house in the evenings to tell us what they had been doing that day.

THE COMPANY

During the period of the survey, several young men were absent. They had gone to work as laborers for "*La Compania*" (The Company), the more-or-less monolithic conception that most Waorani have of the various government entities and national and international companies involved in the exploration for and production of petroleum in the Oriente. By 1987, most of the younger men had spent some period of time working for The Company.

They work as laborers, cutting trails for seismic crews, clearing campsites and drilling sites, carrying supplies and equipment, and hunting game for the camps. Their wages go primarily for the purchase of clothes, flashlights, aluminum pots, axes, machetes, cheap single-shot shotguns, and so on.

This has not, with rare exceptions, led to abandonment of traditional subsistence activities; most men time their outside employment around the demands of clearing forest for their families' swidden gardens. Nonetheless, the resulting exposure to the world of the *kowudï* has been a major force in acculturation and culture change. They began to learn at least simple Spanish; they learned to work side by side with Quichua, Shuar, and Blancos (whites); they learned to play soccer and volleyball, and they acquired new material wants, such as battery-operated radios and cassette players. Some also learned to drink alcohol.

A boy hunts birds with a blowpipe. It is customary for him to give game to his grandmother, but he may choose to eat it himself.

PARTICIPANT OBSERVATION

As our language skills improved, we were able to enter more and more into the life of the community: we joined a work party hauling rocks from the riverbed to fill muddy spots in the airstrip; we attended many *ëëmë* drinking feasts; we accompanied people as they went fishing or worked in their swidden fields; we sat in kitchen-houses and chatted and asked questions, we joined in the late afternoon gatherings at the airstrip and we almost always had people in our house in the evenings.

One day, while Carole and Dïtë were working in one of Dïtë's manioc gardens, she told Carole that Awä (originally from the Ridge group) did not clear any fields, and that his wife's brother, Baï, had to do all the cutting for himself, for his mother, and for his dead brother's wife. He and his wife had to plant enough to feed themselves and to feed Awä and his wife and children.

"Awä also told lies," she said. (We had discovered that for ourselves during Carole's economic survey; he routinely lied about what he had given to others, claiming to have given gifts the "recipients" denied receiving.) "And he is lazy," she said. "He steals from other's gardens when his family has no manioc to drink." The only reason he lived in Tïwënö, she confided, was because he had married

Gĩngata's daughter, Nyäwadë, who was brain-damaged and whom no one else would marry. He had agreed to marry her because he had no proper cross cousins (or none who would marry him).

Nyäwadë could barely speak and was clearly retarded. She also had a scar above one eye and her face was slightly asymmetrical. Later on, her mother Mïmä told us what had happened to her. Mïmä had been on the verge of giving birth when her settlement was raided, and she fled headlong into the jungle. As she ran for her life, she went into labor, but she ignored the pain and continued to flee into the night. Finally, she said, in terror of being speared by pursuers who might have been just behind her, she had to squat and give birth.

Nyäwadë came out face-first onto a snag, a root projecting from the trail, and her face was smashed. Mïmä snatched up her injured infant daughter and continued her flight. Although she is elderly now, she still does almost all the garden work for this daughter and her ne'er-do-well husband.

Another member of the same downstream house cluster was Mïnta, a widow with two teenaged children, a girl, Eru, and Imäa, the young man who became our first language informant. People said that Imäa did not help his uncle Baï cut trees for the gardens his mother planted and that he did not hunt, as other young men his age did. The laziness of both households was the subject of merciless gossip by members of the upstream group who frequently made their derisive comments within earshot of the downstream people.

This exemplifies the classic anthropological method of participant observation. Through such ongoing involvement in the daily life of a community, the tone and texture of life in another society becomes, first familiar, and then, as the values and assumptions on which it rests begin to emerge into consciousness, comprehensible.

Food

Merging into the community's economic system provided further clues to these underlying premises. Our plan called for us to fly out every two months to buy supplies. This meant that we needed to bring in a two-month supply of food. Unfortunately, the selection of edibles that will keep for months and are available in Amazonian frontier towns is, at best, limited. Flour, rice, beans, and noodles provided our carbohydrates, although by the end of two months, they were crawling with bugs and had to be sorted by hand or, in the case of flour, sifted before use. The only canned meats available in the frontier towns were corned beef and something euphemistically called "luncheon meat" (both mostly congealed fat), mackerel, and tuna.

The prospect of a year of that diet was not attractive. We hoped that we would be able to integrate ourselves into the exchange system as we had done among the Semai and, thereby, get access to manioc, fruit, and fresh meat. Our plan was to give out gifts of perishable food when we came back from supply trips; to have fishhooks, line, matches, soap, and other desired imported goods available to give away on request; and, in return, to receive food as we needed it.

While we were preparing for this project, one report we read had described their economic system as one of "generalized reciprocity." This is a system whereby goods, especially food, are shared freely, with the expectation that each person's generosity will be reciprocated when he or she is in need. Since we had extensive experience with that type of exchange among the Semai, we immediately set about to establish our place in the Waorani system.

Accordingly, the second day after our arrival, accompanied by a gaggle of naked children, we visited each house, taking gifts of canned fish, flashlight batteries, soap, and other items. Although we couldn't understand a word that was spoken, it seemed that people didn't quite know what to make of our arrival or of our gifts. Still, we knew that, in a system of generalized reciprocity, gifts of food would be understood. Afterward, we set off for the river to bathe and fetch water, confident that we could expect fruit, manioc, and perhaps meat as we needed them.

That turned out to be excessively optimistic. Several days went by and no food arrived at our door. We saw women coming back from their fields, backbaskets laden with manioc and plantains; women and men with net bags of fish; and men returning from hunting with large and small birds of all sorts, and with larger animals—peccaries and monkeys, even deer. We had seen more game coming into the households nearby in a few days than we had seen in months among the Semai. It was apparent that game was plentiful, but still we received nothing.

After a few days, Dïtë, Omënï's wife and our neighbor across the clearing, brought us a few manioc and some plantains. Then she asked if we had any powdered milk. Dïtë, it turned out, was raising her infant grandson, one of a pair of twins born to her daughter-in-law.

Waorani see multiple births as unacceptably animal-like and believe that a woman cannot produce enough milk for more than one baby at a time. When twins are born, one will usually be "thrown away"—abandoned in the forest. In this case, probably as a consequence of the influence of Protestant missionaries who condemned infanticide, the infant boy had been taken by his paternal grandmother while the other twin, a daughter, was kept by her mother. When we arrived in the hamlet, the girl, who was being nursed by her mother, was fat and healthy. The boy, around three months old, was pale and thin and was obviously not thriving.

We inventoried our supplies and gave her some powdered milk, but made it clear that we needed manioc and plantains. This developed into a relationship of more or less balanced reciprocity; we began to provide her with dried milk for the baby, and she kept us supplied with manioc, plantains, bananas, and chonta palm fruit. The arrangement almost amounted to a contract. Occasionally other women would bring us a half-dozen manioc tubers or a bunch of bananas, almost always with an accompanying request for needles, thread, matches, pins, fishhooks, and so on (all of which we had brought to give away). But we still had no meat.

One evening a man was sitting in our house describing the day's hunting when he noticed the single-shot 16-gauge shotgun that we had purchased in Quito, leaning against the wall. He asked if we had any shotgun shells. Clay said, "I have shotgun shells; I don't have any meat," and gave him a shell. He took it and seemed pleased. Other men soon appeared as word quickly spread that we would give away shotgun shells; to each man, we made it clear that we had no meat. We were confident that, at last, some fresh meat would be forthcoming. It wasn't.

We began trying to take explicit notice of meat when we saw it. Among Semai and in many other societies, this is tantamount to a request. One day we were in a kitchen where some kind of animal was being boiled with manioc tubers in a large pot. "What kind of animal is it?" we asked. "*Iwä*" was the reply. "*Iwa*?" we said, not recognizing that the final vowel was nasalized and, therefore, not recognizing the word. "*Iwä*," they said, loudly and repeatedly.

Exasperated, the wife finally picked up a stick and began to stir around in the pot. Finally, the head of a howler monkey floated to the surface, its fur burned off, its lips drawn back and teeth bared in a death grimace. "Oh! *Iwä*," we said, finally recognizing the word from our word lists. She didn't offer us any of that, either.

Due to the weight limitations on the plane, we had allocated ourselves one can of tuna per day and, for some weeks, we lived on tuna noodle soup, tuna fried rice, tuna patties, and creamed tuna over noodles. Then one evening one of Dïtë's daughters brought us the breast of a pheasant shot by her father. We discussed what to do about it and, the next day, Carole took a shotgun shell to their house and called out to Dïtë who opened the door a crack (and carefully blocked Carole's view of the interior of the kitchen so she couldn't see what other game they had). Carole gave her the shell and told her that it was in exchange for the meat. Dïtë took the shell, told her two better ways of saying the same thing, and closed the door. The next day we received some pork from the upstream group, and we gave them another shell.

We had finally found the key and, after we made it absolutely clear that we would give shells only in return for meat, hunters finally began to appear at our door with a piece of wild pork, a howler monkey leg, perhaps a toucan or a parrot. From then on, we resorted to what would have been absolutely unthinkable among the Semai: the direct exchange of goods for food.

Generalized reciprocity, we found, applies only within the kindred—parents, their siblings, their married and unmarried children, and perhaps a grandparent— essentially those who would have constituted a traditional household. These family members are freely admitted to each others' houses and can expect to eat in each others' kitchens. Sharing of meat and other foods among them is the norm. Since we had been named by Dyiko, we bore names from the Ridge group and were marked as "different people" from the Upriver people among whom we lived. We later learned that our initial giving of food to non-kinsmen was so bizarre as to be utterly incomprehensible. When one of our neighbors was asked if the *kowudï* had come to her house, she responded, "Yes, and they must be coming back, because they left some of their food here."

Tïpë

The Waorani staple food is *tïpë*, a sort of porridge made from manioc. Women prepare it by boiling the tubers and mashing them into a pulp in a large wooden bowl or trough. Then they scoop up handfuls of the mash, stuff their mouths full, chew it for a few minutes, then spit it out and mix it back into the remainder. Their saliva starts a fermentation process, and the mash is then covered with leaves and set aside to ferment for a day or two. When it is ready, people scoop out handfuls of the pulp and mix it into gourd bowls of water to produce a nutritious drink which has something of the taste and consistency of buttermilk.

The Quichua and other surrounding groups allow the mash to ferment longer, until it becomes mildly alcoholic. Waorani, however, traditionally discard the mash

A woman prepares tïpë *from boiled and mashed manioc tubers. She chews some of the mash a mixes it into the remainder, which is then allowed to ferment for a day or two before being mixed with water for drinking.*

when it begins to turn alcoholic. As contact with outsiders has increased, some Waorani have begun to let their *tïpë* ferment longer, but usually only for feasts.

The process of producing and storing *tïpë* assures that it will contain virtually every illness-causing microorganism that exists in the community. We tried, as best we could, to avoid drinking it because we soon learned that we could not afford the sick time that was an almost certain result.

Avoiding it was usually not a problem because, as we had already discovered, offering food to unrelated visitors is in no sense obligatory—although it is sometimes done as an indication of a continuing relationship or with the intention of cultivating one. We have seen visitors from other settlements stand for hours in the sun waiting for someone to invite them into a house and offer them *tïpë*.

One morning, early in our first fieldwork, Clay went to visit one of the households at the downstream end of the settlement. As he entered Baï's house, his elderly mother immediately dipped a gourd bowl full of water, scooped up a handful of manioc mash, mixed it with the water, and brought it to him. Clay feared that to refuse might offend them, so he drank it down. The diarrhea that commenced early and urgently the next morning lasted for more than a month. (Sickness, we have long since learned, is one of the expected consequences of participant observation research.)

In order to reduce the likelihood of repeat occurrences, or worse, we tried to drink only *pëënëmë*, a drink made from boiled and mashed plantains. Since it is not pre-chewed or left to ferment, but is mashed in the water in which it is boiled, it is considerably safer. Even so, by the time we finished our first project, Clay had lost nearly 40 pounds to various illnesses, and Carole had contracted hepatitis B.

Repairing Shotguns

On our second day in Tɨwënö, a man brought a flashlight to the house. Somehow, he managed to communicate to us that it didn't work and that he wanted to know if we could fix it. Clay cleaned all the contacts with steel wool, tested the bulb, replaced the batteries with some not quite dead ones from our tape recorder, and it worked. A few days later, another man brought an old rusty shotgun with a broken hammer spring, which Clay replaced with a piece of a hacksaw blade. That began a service that we continued to provide throughout both periods of our fieldwork.

There are two types of shotguns locally available: muzzle-loaders and those that take shells. Both kinds are poorly made and their maintenance is even worse (the standard Waorani technique for cleaning a shotgun is to take it to the river and scrub it with water and sand). It is not surprising that the weapons are rusty, unreliable, and dangerous. There are several men who have lost an eye when shotguns blew up in their faces.

Many of these guns, with broken hammers or split barrels, were beyond redemption with the simple tools we had, but perhaps half or more were repairable. The first task was to take the gun apart and get the mud, sand and roaches out of the firing mechanism, and then to assess the problems. Broken leaf springs can be replaced with hacksaw blades snapped to the correct lengths; firing pins in various diameters and shapes can be filed from nails; small parts for the firing mechanisms can be filed from iron nails hammered flat on a rock and hardened in the hearth; and rust can be removed with oil and steel wool. The process was almost always carried on inside a circle of men who closely watched every step.

As word spread, people came from considerable distances. On one occasion two Záparos, members of a once-powerful group that has almost ceased to exist (see chapter 5), spent two days walking to Tɨwënö, each carrying a broken shotgun.

Repairing shotguns allowed us to make a substantive contribution to the communities where we lived, and it also served us well. Clay always took his tool kit whenever we visited a new settlement, and it generated instant rapport and good will. Nearly every Waorani household has at least one old, rusty, nonworking shotgun stuck up in the rafters somewhere.

Carole's Snakebite

In our seventh month in the field, Carole was bitten by something, probably a snake, although she never saw it. We had just returned to Tɨwënö from a visit to another settlement and she went down to the river to bathe and wash clothes. When she got back to the house, she stowed our travel gear under the bed platform. Shortly thereafter, Clay noticed her rubbing the crook of her elbow, where an examination revealed two small punctures.

Within fifteen minutes she said she felt dizzy and weak, and she crawled under the mosquito net to lie down. Within a few more minutes she was feverish and beginning to be delirious. Her temperature climbed through that night and the next day. Clay gave her aspirin every few hours to try to bring the fever down. If it kept rising, the only thing to do would be to carry her down to the river to try to bring it down down by immersing her in the cool water.

Her temperature finally stabilized at 104 degrees. Neighbors came to see her and to examine her arm, which had swollen to more than twice its normal size. She was delirious for several days and bedridden for the better part of a week, during which time she could only swallow water and *pëënëmë* (banana drink). After that, she recovered quickly. The consensus of medical people whom we consulted later was that it was most likely a snakebite.

Drinking Feasts (ëëmë)

Periodically, individual households host *ëëmë*, drinking feasts. These are occasions when other kindreds are invited for several days and nights of dancing, feasting, and sex with cross cousins.

The first one that we attended was hosted by Bibängkä, the young wife of Wämönyɨ and Gämï's son, Wänï. She was newly married and obviously reveling in the opportunities presented by a settlement full of classificatory cross cousins. She flirted extravagantly during the soccer games and, we were told, had been disappearing into the forest with Imäa. To make matters worse, they were classificatory siblings, not cross cousins. Her young husband was also fairly obviously less than pleased with the whole situation and, for a time, he left and went to work for The Company.

In addition, Gämï complained that Bibängkä was not living up to her responsibilities; she did not work hard enough in her gardens nor would she prepare *tɨpë* for her husband. These complaints had apparently reached her father in Tzapino, and he ordered her to give an *ëëmë*, a banana-drinking feast, to publicly demonstrate her commitment to her adult responsibilities.

Bibänkä began harvesting the huge stalks of plantains and carrying them home to ripen for the feast. As she came through the settlement with burdens of 100 pounds and more suspended from a tump line across the top of her head, others, mostly men, teased her and hooted. Her husband Wänï helped her to harvest the fruit of the tall, thorny, chonta palms. Gathering food for the feast took more than a week; no one but her husband helped her carry anything.

The day before the feast, her father-in-law Wämönyɨ started out before dawn, running barefoot to invite people in another settlement to the feast. An hour or so from Tɨwënö, he stepped on a fer-de-lance and it bit him on the ankle. He started back, but kept losing consciousness and falling. One of the falls broke his nose.

Nängkä, his brother's son, who was also going to spread the word of the *ëëmë*, found him, but assumed he could make his way back alone, so he left him and went on. Mïngkayɨ, heading out along the same trail to inform another group, found him and helped him back. By the time they got back to the settlement, he was semiconscious and barely able to walk. It was a Sunday and the MAF shortwave radio network was not in service, so there was no possibility of calling in a plane.

We went to his house to see how he was. He was lying on a sleeping platform covered by a ragged blanket. Gämï, his wife, had been trained by the missionaries to administer antivenin, and she had just injected him with a second vial, about an hour after the first. The fang marks on his ankle were only about ⅜ inch apart, so it must have been a very small snake. His foot was severely swollen and the swelling had progressed about ⅔ of the way up his calf. He said his head hurt; he was also spitting blood.

A few feet away in the kitchen, preparations for the *ëëmë* continued. There were several hundred pounds of ripe plantains hanging on the walls; beneath them were five large pots of plantain and chonta mash. Dyiko was pounding chonta fruit in a large wooden trough. Bibängkä was tending a pot of boiling chonta fruit and talking with Imäa's sister, who was cutting up cooked chonta. Periodically, Dyiko stuffed her mouth full of chonta, chewed it for a few minutes, then spat it out and and mixed it into the rest. When she was not chewing, she chanted a song about preparing for a feast.

Wämönyɨ's snakebite precipitated stories of others' experiences with snakes and other related information. Gämï told of having been bitten on the top of her head as she and a group were walking through the forest to a feast several years before. Someone said that Omënɨ's son Tuka had been bitten two days earlier but that it had just bled and did not swell.

Someone else said that, after a person has been bitten, the victim will die if his father or brothers use a blowpipe; if they eat meat or drink plantains the limb will turn black and be full of pus. Gämï said the *duuräni* (ancestors) used the leaves of a certain plant to make a drink that the victim drank in large quantities; they also took a certain kind of fish and rubbed it on the affected part. When they returned the fish alive to the water, it took the poison away with it into the stream.

About mid-afternoon the next day we heard shouting and hooting (a falsetto "huuuuuuu") coming from the forest to the north. Tɨwënö people hooted and shouted in response. Shortly thereafter, about 15 men carrying spears and shotguns and four women with children came in on the trail. People always sing out with high-pitched hoots as they approach another settlement (and sometimes when approaching their own). This announces their arrival and makes it clear that they are not sneaking in for an attack. Across the river at Gämï's house we could hear old Dyiko leading a chant, so we went across the river to wait for the visitors there.

They stopped for a few minutes at Mïngkayɨ's house at the edge of the river, but soon we could hear them hooting as they came up the trail toward the house where we were waiting. They had replaced their weapons with palm fronds, making clear their peaceful intentions. They came in, single file, through the door at one end of the kitchen and shuffled, each man with his hands on the shoulders of the man in front of him, in a line that snaked through the kitchen and out through a door on the far side.

Still in a line, they looped around and danced back in, hooting all the way. Then they clustered around the pots of banana drink at one end of the kitchen, reached out their hands, and sang a song demanding bowls of drink (*bɨkɨ*). Bibängkä passed out bowls of banana drink to the outstretched hands as fast as she could; the men gulped it down and immediately thrust the bowls back at her to be refilled and passed back to the men crowding from behind.

After this rather spectacular entrance, the men settled down along the walls of the kitchen-house, talking, laughing, hooting when someone made a good joke, and drinking. The women went down to the river to bathe, and some of the men went down to the airstrip to play soccer.

A few feet away, Wämönyɨ's condition remained about the same. The bleeding had slowed, although he still had a nosebleed, and the swelling, now extending to just

Hooting loudly, visitors arrive for a feast. They are carrying palm fronds instead of spears to show their peaceful intentions.

above his knee, seemed to have stopped increasing. He still had a severe headache. During the feast, Gämï never left Wämönyï's side. Their daughter and her husband came out to the kitchen for a while, but did not join in the dancing and singing.

In the late afternoon, the visitors and people from Tïwënö reconvened in the kitchen-house, and it began to rain. As the rain fell in a deluge outside, small groups of men and women danced (separately) in rows and chanted. With arms linked, they moved backwards for three steps with one line of the chant, and forward with the next. The stanzas of the chant were repeated until someone started a new one (Carole counted 43 repetitions of one). When someone shouted a new line, everyone chanted that one for a while. We set up the recorder and taped several songs, and then joined the dance.

Sometimes dancers formed a cluster, each person's hands on the shoulders of the person ahead, as they shuffled forward and back or around the room in a circle. There was a great deal of laughter and good-natured joking and frequent whooping that seemed to correspond roughly to clapping whenever somebody said or did something funny—when Bibängkä dropped a bowl full of *bïkï*, for example.

Among the dancers was Paä, perhaps the oldest living Waorani, another of the killers of the five missionaries, and the man who raised Wämönyï (who lay snakebitten in the next room) after his father was speared.

As darkness fell, most of the visitors (and they were mostly men) sat around the periphery of the kitchen, drinking, talking and laughing; occasionally someone would shout "*oweta!*" (bowl), and Bibängkä would come to refill the empty bowl. Periodically, she would stop and peel ripe plantains, which she put into a huge pot of water (at least five gallons) that sat on two old shotgun barrels laid across two logs that formed the sides of the hearth. Although her husband hauled water to make more drink as needed, she did all the work of serving and cooking. No one helped her hand out bowls, peel bananas, or keep the fire going. The drinking, singing, and dancing went on all night. Toward morning, we finally made our way, still in pitch-darkness, back down the trail, waded across the rain-swollen river, and went to bed.

We awoke about dawn, as the last of the visitors were leaving for home. Some were carrying plantains to eat on the trip. Two men came to our house and asked for fishhooks and line. We gave them some, but they really wanted big hooks—bigger than anything we had—to fish for the giant catfish that inhabit the larger rivers.

Shortly after they left we heard loud voices, then Mïngkaiyï shouted that Wämönyï was dying. We put on our wet jeans from the night before, and crossed the river to his house. He was sitting up, and Gämï said he had a terrible pain in his head. He had apparently told her that he did not think he could live any longer because of the pain. Someone heard him, and that was when people began shouting that he was dying. Gämï was crying and rubbing his neck and shoulders.

Carole asked if there was blood in his urine. Gämï said it had been red, but now it was only pink, so the internal bleeding seemed to be lessening. Because of the terrible headache he was suffering, we were afraid that disintegrating blood cells might be clogging the capillaries in his brain (which we had seen happen to malaria victims in Malaysia) and could precipitate a stroke. Cathy was able to contact MAF by shortwave radio, and the pilots said they would try to come in the afternoon if the strip dried out enough for them to land.

It did, and around three o'clock Clay and several of the men carried Wämönyï, in a hammock, down to the plane. He spent about a week in the hospital in Shell, and returned only a little weaker for his ordeal.

All of the *ëëmë* we attended followed a similar pattern, although the tone seemed to vary (at least from our perspective). At some, sexual attractions were more obvious. At others, such as the one we have just described, the sexual element was less apparent.

At an *ëëmë* at Ongkayï and Näntowë's house, Näntowë's relatives from Damöïntarö, a settlement a half-day's walk downriver on the Tïwënö, talked and made jokes about spearing Oyngkayï's mother (old Dyiko) and the *kowudï* (us). People laughed and hooted and Dyiko began to look more and more anxious as the night wore on. Knowing that several years before some of these same men had speared Gämï and Dïtë's mother in her garden just outside this settlement, we didn't feel any too secure either.

SOCCER

Every day, unless it is pouring rain, people gather in the late afternoon on the upriver end of the airstrip, in front of our house. By this time, the hard work of the day has been done and everyone has bathed in the river and put on clean clothes. It is time to play soccer or sit and chat.

The game seems to have been introduced by young men who learned it while working for The Company. Nearly everyone plays: men, women, children, and even fairly old people. It is not at all unusual to see a young woman carrying a baby in a sling across her breasts and running full-speed after the ball.

The players assort themselves into two roughly equal groups, and the goals are marked by sticking two poles in the ground. The enjoyment of the playing itself—driving with the ball, stealing it, blocking it, tripping others, and so on—is the real object, so there are few rules and usually no one keeps score.

Play goes on until dark, usually for at least two hours, and is exuberant with much laughing and hooting at falls and mistakes. Some of the young men who have been out working for the oil companies shout Spanish words, seemingly at random: "*mañana,*" "*Miercoles,*" "*muchacho,*" "*hermano,*" "*libré*" ("tomorrow," "Wednesday," "boy," "brother," "free"). English numbers are shouted at random too: "one," "two," "tree," "fo." Nothing is taken seriously; no one gets angry; the entire atmosphere is purely one of enjoyment, having fun, laughing at jokes made at one's own and others' expense.

This is another occasion when the whole community comes together. Some of the older women never play, but they bring along their string fibers or the net bag they are currently working on, and sit and talk. It is a time to pick lice out of each other's hair, gossip, pass on news of what happened during the course of the day, discuss illnesses, and air mild grievances. At dark, people headed back to their houses or came and sat in ours.

HOMOSEXUALITY

It was at one of these evening soccer games that we first became aware of the homosexual aspect of Waorani men's relationships. A group of young men from Damöïntarö and Tzapino were visiting, and that evening they joined in the free-for-all soccer game. At one point, Nängkä and one of the visitors (his cross cousin) were rolling around and wrestling in the grass, and it was apparent that they both had erections. This kind of horseplay continued until dusk, when the two went off, arm in arm, to one of the houses.

The next morning was Sunday, and in church during the recitations of Old Testament stories the two men could not keep their hands off one another. All through the service the young man from Damöïntarö maintained close body contact with Nängkä and, grinning uncontrollably, was clearly enthralled with him. This was a source of obvious amusement to the young women, including Nängkä's wife, who whispered and giggled as they watched the two fondle each other.

We had already discovered while collecting genealogies that asking someone to say the kin term ("*kï* ") of a cross cousin of the opposite sex reduces him or her to embarrassed speechlessness. We were also already aware that sex between male and female cross cousins was expected. What we had not realized was that sex between male cross cousins was also common.

We were probably slow in recognizing this because most people, most of the time, restrained any overt expressions of sexuality, either heterosexual or homosexual, in our presence. This may have been due, at least in part, to the influence of

Rachael Saint, one of the missionaries who made the first contact. She deplored any expression of sexuality outside monogamous marriage and, although she lived in another settlement, her influence on Omënï, the elder of the primary kindred in our settlement, was strong. Moreover, many people seemed to assume that, since we were *kowudï* and had come to live with them, we must be some kind of missionaries.

Once we became aware of the acceptability of sexual attraction between men, however, we began to see it often, especially at the soccer games and at *ëëmë*. It nearly always involved men who were real or classificatory cross cousins.

One evening, for example, Kogi and Tuka, who are cross cousins, were standing in the middle of the airstrip as the soccer game was winding down. Tuka bent over from the waist to tie his shoes, and Kogi laid across Tuka's back and put his arms around him. Tuka looked toward us with an embarrassed grin. The two spoke softly, and we caught the word "*kowudï*" as they straightened up. They proceeded down the airstrip, with Kogi keeping his arm around Tuka's neck.

DOMESTIC RELATIONS

The relationship between husbands and wives appears, for the most part, to be comfortable, cooperative, and affectionate. Even Bibängkä, Wänï's errant young wife who gave the *ëëmë* in 1987, had settled down in the five years between our two studies. In 1993, she had a two-year-old child, and she seemed to have developed into a mature and responsible wife.

We saw no violence between spouses. In fact, one of the things that Waorani find most disturbing about the Quichua is that men are said to beat their wives.

There is also no rigid sexual division of labor. Husbands and wives sometimes go off together on fishing and hunting trips lasting several days. Men are the primary hunters, but women are mainly responsible for carrying large game back to the settlement. They also chase down and kill small game with their machetes when the opportunity presents itself.

Husbands and wives also often work in the gardens together. Women have primary responsibility for planting, weeding, and harvesting, and for carrying chonta, manioc, and bananas from the gardens, but men often help in all of these tasks.

Children are treated with kindness and affection by everyone in the kindred. Infants and toddlers are never left alone; babies have unrestricted access to the breast and are the objects of everyone's attention. Children are carried by their mothers until they are able to walk. If a new infant is born before a child can walk, the older sibling is carried by an aunt or an older sister or cousin. Children of all ages have a great deal of close body contact with their parents and with each other. Fathers also hold babies and toddlers and spend time grooming them.

Children, like adults, are autonomous and independent. No one, even a parent or grandparent, can force a child to do anything. If someone does try to order a child to do something he or she doesn't want to do, the child's response is likely to be "*ba*" (refuse), and that ends the matter. Not surprisingly, children have few responsibilities. Young children spend most of their time playing, but they also regularly accompany and assist their parents, grandparents, aunts, and uncles in gardening,

Children carry home an agouti killed by one of their mothers with her machete.

hunting, gathering, and building activities. We never saw a child punished or disciplined in any way.

The only overt violence that we saw during both of our field trips was one instance of a child attacking his brother, an incident we observed from inside our house when no one else was present. A boy, about nine years old, had eaten all the pieces of *äüng*, a fruit that grows in segments inside a long pod, and his four-year-old brother was enraged. Crying and screaming, the younger child pulled on his brother's clothes and pounded him with his fists. Finally he picked up the long, empty pod and chased his older brother, trying to hit him with it. The older boy did not retaliate in any way but just ran away.

THE KILLINGS OF FATHER ALEJANDRO AND SISTER INEZ

One morning, about six months into our first project, a rumor swept through the settlement that the Yasuní River band had speared to death a priest from Coca who had maintained intermittent contact with them for a number of years. The story, as it was passed to us, was that the priest had taken a boy from that band out to go to school but, when the boy's father asked for his return, he could not be found. When the priest told the child's father that his son had disappeared, the father became en-

A child plays while his pet night monkey, holding its eyes tightly closed against the glare of daylight, clutches his hair.

raged and speared the priest in retaliation. "For only that reason," we were told, "they became angry."

That evening, Dïtë, the woman whose grandchild we were providing with milk, stopped Carole on her way to the river. "You don't have any children, do you?" she demanded. "On the Cononaco River, *kowudï* like you two came and gave food, and in return they took a child. The Waorani got angry and speared them and they two died. Tell me again; why have you two come here?"

Recognizing the implications of the questions in light of what had just happened, Carole went to great lengths to assure her that our children were grown and that we most certainly did not want any more. Still, we went to bed a bit uneasy again that night.

Over the next few days, more information showed the original account to have been wildly inaccurate. Two people had, in fact, been speared by Waorani: Father Alejandro Labaca, a bishop in the Capuchin order, and a nun, Sister Inés Arango, and they had not been killed by the Yasuní River band, but by the still "wild" Tagëiri.

After the relocation of Waorani bands onto the reserve came to an end, oil camps in the eastern portion of Waorani territory and outside the Protectorate continued to be attacked and harassed by raiders from uncontacted groups. As early as 1965, Father Labaca had made several excursions from the mission in Pañacocha on the north bank of the Napo to try to locate these Waorani, but without success.

In 1976, he was called by an oil exploration company to assist them because their camps were being looted by "Aucas." It was at one of these camps that he made his first contact with the Yasuní River band in December of that year. Assisted by the oil companies in locating settlement sites, Labaca and his Capuchin colleagues made several trips by canoe and helicopter to visit Waorani who lived on the upper reaches of the Yasuní River. By 1980, several of these Waorani had visited the missions at Nuevo Rocafuerte, Pañacocha, and Coca.

Sporadic attacks on oil camps by Waorani continued over the next few years. One group in particular, the Tagëiri (Tage's group), continued to kill anyone they encountered in their territory. They were also reportedly still at war with the group on the Yasuní. In 1977, three petroleum workers were speared, presumably by the Tagëiri, and in December of 1984 there was another bloody attack, again attributed to the Tagëiri. In 1987, a Waorani man returning from a stint with The Company told us that the Tagëiri had killed three Quichua workers.

After oil company pilots located a Tagëiri hamlet from the air, Labaca and Sister Inés Arango, were flown to the hamlet in a company helicopter. Their purpose was to initiate peaceful contacts, to warn the Tagëiri about the exploration that was moving into their territory and, they hoped, to forestall further violence. When the helicopter returned the following day, the crew found the two, naked and dead, pinned to the ground by more than 20 Tagëiri spears.

FIELDWORK, 1993

In 1993 we returned to assess the changes that were taking place and to visit groups living off the Protectorate. We found that a number of significant things had happened since our previous visit. Most of these centered around Waorani attempts to come to grips with the increasing salience of *kowudï*, especially other Indians, colonists, and oil companies.

The essence of these changes can perhaps best be seen in two new institutions that had come into being in the five years since our first study: soccer tournaments and the *Organización de las Nación Huaorani de la Amazonia Ecuatoriana (ONHAE):* (Organization of the Waorani Nation of Ecuatorial Amazonia).

The following ethnographic sketches are primarily intended to exemplify Waorani concerns and to convey something of the scope of the changes that are transforming the lives of these people, many of whom grew to adulthood, quite literally in the stone age.

Many of these changes are centered in the village of Tönyëmpadï. With a population of more than 200 Waorani, a number of other Indians and a few white schoolteachers, it is by far the largest settlement. This is where Rachael Saint made her home after severing relations with the SIL over their contention that she was interfering excessively with Waorani life and culture. This is also where she was buried after her death in 1994.

This settlement was named for our language informant's father Tönyë, the early convert who was killed trying to persuade the Ridge group to give up their vendettas. Tönyëmpadɨ has become the center for increasing acculturation and for political intrigue among Waorani factions, missionaries, non-Waorani indigenous political groups, national and state-level politicians, oil companies, and everyone else who sees political, economic, or other gain to be made from the Waorani.

Rachael Saint's lifelong friend, Wɨba, also lives in Tönyëmpadɨ with her husband and children. She was one of those who, as a young woman, had fled to the Quichua. It was she who taught Rachael the language and who accompanied her and Elisabeth Elliot to make the first contact.

In the intervening years, Wɨba has become arguably the most powerful and certainly the most widely known Wao. This situation derives from several sources: her friendship with Rachael Saint (who had numerous powerful friends and admirers in government, business, and missionary circles); her contacts with the *kowudɨ*, deriving from her years living on a hacienda and from an early marriage to a Quichua; the marriages of all of her daughters to *kowudɨ*; and from several books written by missionaries that depict her as the "savior" who rescued her people from savagery.

Last, but assuredly not least, is the need, in a headless and decentralized society such as this, for a "leader" with whom the government, oil companies, and other outsiders can deal, in order to give at least the appearance that the Waorani have some voice in the "agreements" that are transforming their homeland and their lives. In this capacity, Wɨba is frequently referred to in the Ecuadorian media as "The Auca Queen."

SOCCER TOURNAMENTS

The evening soccer games continue to provide the daily social interaction that helps to integrate individual communities, but there have been important changes in the scope of that integration. Individual settlements now invite other settlements for inter-village soccer tournaments, spiced with feasting and sex. These are called by the Spanish term *"carnaval,"* and are very much like traditional *ëëmë*, except that the soccer competition takes center stage, and that both the hosts and the guests are *communities*, rather than households or kindreds.

On one occasion, men from another settlement who had been invited to Tɨwënö for a *carnaval* arrived on a Sunday morning while everyone was in church. Some of them came in to sit with the Tɨwënö people. As the last person finished speaking, all the visiting men suddenly began seizing young women and smearing their faces with red paint made from *achiote* seeds. There was instant pandemonium as the young women tried, shrieking and laughing, to avoid being caught. This involved some serious struggling and roughhousing, since both the men and women are physically very strong, but it was all lighthearted and everyone was laughing and enjoying the struggle and the spectacle. The rest of the day had a strongly sexual tinge; the soccer game that evening was even more exhuberant than usual, with more body contact and sexual joking.

Hosts and visitors at a carnaval *smear each others' faces with red pigment, an indication of their sexual intentions.*

Several people told us later that, in the old days, young men who came to an *ëëmë* would paint the faces of the women they wanted to sleep with, using some of the mash made for drinks. "In former times," we were told, "they painted the faces of their proper cross cousins; nowdays they paint falsely, painting the faces of their 'siblings' too."

On occasion, even larger soccer meets are held. In January 1993, we attended one of these at Tönyëmpadɨ. It was sponsored by Maxus Ecuador, a subsidiary of Maxus Energy, the Texas-based company that is developing the infrastructure for extracting oil from the Waorani heartland. It was organized by Wɨba's son-in-law, a Quichua who is in charge of the schools in Tönyëmpadɨ. In addition to the soccer tournament, there were to be meetings with and speeches by officials from the Ministries of Education and Energy, and by other national and provincial politicians.

The soccer meet involved Waorani teams from each settlement and Quichua teams from Ahuano and Arajuno, villages near the western boundary of the Protectorate. Quichua from these settlements had traditionally come into Waorani territory to hunt and fish, and were often attacked when they did so.

In recent years, there have been a number of marriages between Waorani, primarily from Tönyëmpadɨ but from a few other settlements as well, and Quichua from these two settlements. There is intense resentment on the part of many other Waorani, however, because these Quichua spouses now bring their kin to fish and hunt in Waorani territory.

Around 9:30 A.M., as the games were in progress, a plane arrived, bringing the American head of Maxus Ecuador, his son, and an Ecuadorian sociologist who works for Maxus and whose job is to facilitate relations with the Waorani. Next, a huge army helicopter landed, bringing the minister of Energy and Mines and his wife, the undersecretary of the Environmental Department, the minister of Education, the head of the

Department of Education in the province of Pastaza, and a flock of video and still photographers. As the helicopter was landing, Carole asked a man standing beside her why all these outsiders were coming. "When we behave well, they come; when we behave badly, they don't come," he explained patiently.

The officials were seated on chairs arranged on the dirt in front of one of the school buildings along with the helicopter pilots and some armed soldiers. Video and still cameras started to roll. Wɨba was called forward and seated, and the minister's wife presented her with three dozen red roses. (It is difficult to imagine a more useless and pointless gesture than this but, of course, the gesture was not directed at Wɨba, or even at the Waorani. It was directed at the Ecuadorians who would see it on the evening television news or in tomorrow's newspaper [see chapter 10]).

Wɨba's Quichua son-in-law, who is trying to become a power broker and "spokesman" for the Waorani, had gathered together eight of the older Waorani men who had the large holes in their earlobes; they came forward wearing feathered headbands and carrying small made-for-tourists spears. It began to rain.

Each of the officials stood and made a short speech in Spanish, the essence of which was that they were going to work for and with the Waorani. Wɨba's son-in-law translated these into Waorani. When the speeches were finished, he told the Waorani men to dance for the visitors. They got up and started chanting and shuffling in a circular dance.

A man from the Ridge group shouted in Waorani, telling them to dance as if they were all drunk. They all grinned and began to stagger, singing: "drunk, we are singing for the *kowudɨ*." Then they presented their headdresses and spears to the visitors amid shouts from the crowd to kiss them. Old Omënɨ from Tɨwënö grinned and kissed the wife of the minister of Energy and Mines. The crowd hooted; the cameras rolled.

By then, it was raining quite hard. The helicopter took the minister's wife and several of the others away, and the rest went into a school building to talk about education. The people from Tɨwënö had been given to understand they would have a chance to voice their wants to these government officials, but the meeting was monopolized by Wɨba's son-in-law, and our group was left standing outside, all of us watching and listening through chain-link mesh from a veranda on the front of the building.

Although the young president of ONHAE, the Waorani organization, was inside, he did not say a word. Nor did the head of Maxus; he apparently did not speak Spanish. The self-appointed spokesman for the Waorani at this meeting was Wɨba's Quichua son-in-law. He asked for more buildings, dormitories for the high school, and more teachers (most or all of which would be in Tönyëmpadɨ, under his control). The Ecuadorian representative of Maxus assured everyone that Maxus would work through the existing infrastructure under the Department of Education.

The helicopter returned and the soldiers came onto the veranda carrying plastic bags of cheap clothing, candy, and trinkets. They threw these randomly into the crowd that quickly gathered. Later we would hear Waorani complain bitterly that the Quichua got most of those things that the *kowudɨ* had brought for them. Many were furious about it.

The inequitable distribution, among Waorani themselves, of goods from the *kowudɨ* was also apparent in the fact that the soccer players from Tönyëmpadɨ and

Waorani men dance for officials of the government and The Company.

Kiwarö, the two largest settlements, had real matching uniforms—shirts, shorts, socks—but those from the smaller settlements did not. These are potentially danger-ous situations in a society where, as we shall see, envy is seen as a motive for sor-cery, and such accusations are often the precursors of spearing raids.

THE ONHAE CONGRESO

The Organization of the Waorani Nation of Ecuatorial Amazonia (ONHAE) was or-ganized in 1990 by a small group of young men, mostly from Tönyëmpadï, who were still schoolboys in Puyo at the time of our first study. We attended a three-day *congreso* (congress) held in Tönyëmpadï February 16–18, 1993, the purpose of which was to allow the Waorani "nation" to elect officers to represent it, and to dis-cuss and make decisions on a number of issues.

Among the issues scheduled to be discussed were: marking the boundaries of Waorani territory to prevent colonists from other groups from encroaching; the extraction of oil from Waorani territory by Maxus; requests to Maxus regarding schools, health, and tourists.

More than 300 people attended, nearly one-quarter of all Waorani. They came from virtually every settlement, some by canoe, others by trail, and others on flights paid for by Maxus. Food contributed by Maxus was cooked outside in big pots: a stew of rice, onions, boullion cubes, tuna, and canned mackerel. Flavored fruit drink mixes were also prepared.

For the meeting itself, 168 adults crammed themselves into a tin-roofed school building, sitting on backless benches in stifling heat. Members from each community sat together. Others stood outside, watching and listening through the wire-mesh walls.

The agenda was typed in Spanish (by whom, we were never able to acertain) and the current ONHAE president read it and translated it into Waorani. He told people that they had not come to an *ëëmë*, that there would be no "playing" here. "Here we are going to talk about all the things that make us angry." Wiba's son-in-law repeated all of this, obviously intending to take control of the discussion as he had during the soccer meet. The officials for the congress were elected; they represented Tönyëmpadi and Kiwarö (the two largest settlements), and the small Cononaco and Shiripuno settlements. There was only one man among them who was over 25, and he was the only one who could not read Spanish. We estimated that more than 60% of those attending were under 30.

The young chairman of the congress addressed the assembly: "You will only speak if I tell you. Don't get angry, we are choosing our paths now. You are meeting for your land, food, houses, and schools. Don't get up and leave if you are hot or hungry; and don't just sit there like toads and snakes; tell us what you think."

The new officials then restricted participation in the discussions to Waorani, by fiat, preventing Wiba's son-in-law from attempting to seize a leadership role. This also excluded Rachael Saint, who was in attendance as well, from active participation.

Boundary Demarcation

A growing problem facing the Waorani is the invasion of their territory by colonists and others who want to exploit its resources. An organization known as the Rainforest Information Center has been raising funds, mostly in Europe, to provide supplies to support Waorani volunteers who are sporadically engaged in cutting a boundary zone around the most vulnerable areas of their territory and planting several species of palm trees to mark the boundary.

The issues discussed included the lack of Waorani volunteers on this project. Said one man, "We all say we are going to do it but we don't. On the day, we say 'I'm going hunting' or 'I'm clearing fields,' and we don't come. This will not do the job; if you say you are coming, then don't lie, come!" Several people voiced support for the project, but wondered how the contributed money was spent. This turned out to be a recurrent theme in many of the discussions: the suspicion that some were enriching themselves while others got less or nothing.

A government representative from the Institute of Agrarian Reform and Colonization told them, in Spanish, that at the end of the following month, a plan for the protection of ethnic minorities would be presented to the Ecuadorian Congress. He said he wanted both input from the Waorani and a representative of them to attend meetings in Quito.

He told them that he was aware of the problem of colonists settling in their territory and that he was speaking to the heads of the Quichua and Shuar organizations about a plan to move those people out. Then he said, "Your marrying with Quichua is another issue. That is your decision." That statement provoked a discussion and angry responses from two *kowudi* teachers who are married to Waorani.

The ONHAE president also addressed the issue: "On all the edges people are marrying out. Soon they will be *kowudɨ* living in town and only visiting here. We are destroying ourselves by marrying out."

Another officer said "No person should get angry. We are all expressing our opinions; we are not getting angry here."

As the Congress took a mid-morning break, one of the oldest men spoke: "My grandfather lived on the other side of the Akarö River and I have always protected our territory. When *kowudɨ* came in we killed them and I will kill them now." Another old man and an old woman then stood with him, and the three sang a song about decorating spears as they prepare to kill *kowudɨ*. The younger people first smiled indulgently, then began to pay attention. At the end, they applauded.

Oil Companies

This discussion centered on what the Waorani should get in return for the damage done by the oil industry to their land, their health, and their way of life. It showed clearly that they have no conception of the magnitude of the wealth that is being extracted from beneath their homeland. They are happy to get the twentieth century equivalent of beads and trinkets: an outboard motor and some gasoline, a few bags of rice, a visit from a company doctor, perhaps a set of false teeth, and a few clapboard school buildings.

A young man: "The government takes all our things, they come from far and do not give us anything. I get furious! If they come and tear our land apart, then they should give us *lots* of money. We need motors for our canoes, planes, schools, drinkable water, and we do not have them."

An old man: "We came here by foot, step by step, not in a plane. We came fast when they called. Without teeth, how can I eat?"

A middle-aged woman: "We don't have good houses or schools; they say they will give them to us, but they don't give."

A young man: "They charge us lots of money for pills; how can we live? We need money for hospitals."

A young man: "These companies are foreign and big. One comes with one project, then another comes with another. We should tell them 'no' and not just agree for a bag of rice."

A middle-aged man: "They have drilled right where we live. Our water isn't fit to drink and our fish . . . where have they gone? Where will we grow our food?"

The tenor of the discussion began to change from negative to predominantly positive, however, as people recounted the gifts (mostly consumables) received from Maxus.

A young woman: "The head of Maxus came to the Yasuní; I have never seen the leaders of the other companies. Maxus has given us a motor and gasoline."

A young man: "They are buying the pipe to drain the end of our airstrip; they are helping us."

A young man: "How many flights did they pay for to fly in this food for us and to fly in those who live far away? Maxus is trying to help us. They have given paper, books, and volleyballs for the schools, and they pay for flights for the teachers."

A young man: "Maxus sends the doctor here; his name should be *Mïngkayï* (Wasp), because he stings (gives injections)."

After two hours, a vote was taken on a resolution approving Maxus' operations in Waorani territory (operations that would have continued in any case, regardless of the outcome of the vote; oil comprises the bulk of Ecuador's exports). It passed overwhelmingly.

Health

A health worker from Petroecuador, the Ecuadorian national oil company, addressed the assembly, saying they were concerned about health problems among the Waorani. "After you decide what you want, then tell us and we can discuss it."

A Quichua man married to a Wao woman said, "We need medicine in each community. Petroecuador has not given us very much. The communities have health workers but no medicine."

The woman from Petroecuador answered, "I can't make the decisions. You write down what you want and send it to be discussed in Quito."

The chairman: "Why does she say this? I reject it."

Another young man: "Petroecuador doesn't give us pills, and we are angry."

An older woman: "Why does she refuse when she is taking oil out? Why don't they send her bosses here to talk?"

A young woman: "We live like chickens. Petroecuador worked here before I was born. What do we have? Nothing. Maxus is here only a short time and they are doing a lot."

A middle-aged man: "The leaders (politicians) do badly. Do we understand them? They are like dogs barking out there."

The ONHAE president: "Talk about health, but first about oil pollution and all the trash they have thrown out."

A young man: "I will talk about health. How many oil companies have taken things from us? How big is the debt all of the Waorani owe the hospital and how much money have they helped us with?"

The president (in Spanish): "Petroecuador has taken out lots of oil and wasn't regulated, and we have lost lots of land to this."

A young man: "We went to Araba's land (the Yasuní area) and we worked for The Company. They did *not* build the schools and health center they promised, *no*! You all keep saying Maxus and Petroecuador, but it's all of them."

A *kowudï* who has married in: "In 1987, they promised us a doctor. I haven't seen one yet."

A woman from the Shiripuno: "They say we have agreed to let them take the oil. How can my signature be on their piece of paper? We live in the forest. I don't know how to read and write. I didn't grow up with school. . . . We have no school and no medical care."

A young woman: "We suffer. We can only weave bags to sell for money for medical care. We have trained health promoters; we don't have money. How many health promoters do we have?" (The missionary hospital in Shell has trained Indian health promoters from many communities to assess illnesses, dispense medications, and give first aid. They are sold medicine at cost, which they, in turn, sell to those who need it.) "We have no money for medicine."

An old man: "We don't have any pills at my living place. We have to call a plane and it costs *lots* of money. We can only make lots of spears and dart quivers to pay for the doctors. If we take these things and they don't buy them, we have nothing."

A man from the Shiripuno: "On the Shiripuno River, we don't have any money [from The Company], just our own. The most important thing is for planes to get us out when we are really sick or when snakes bite us."

Wïba's Quichua son-in-law: "You are not looking at the community of Tönyëmpadï, but at a nation of Waorani. . . . How many Waorani are in hospitals, but can't pay for this care? We need to make a resolution so all the companies will help us."

TOURISM

In the past several years, some tour guides have begun bringing tourists to some of the more accessible settlements. Two issues were discussed: whether people want to permit tourism, and who will profit from it.

An old man: "I am old. I just lie in my hammock and *kowudï* want to come into my house."

Another man: "They show up and say they have 'permission.' Whose permission is this?"

A woman from Tzapino: "We have it at our living place too. The tourists come and our children get colds. How many tourists have paid 30,000 sucres to a guide, and then they come into our living place and dirty everything? Who will pay for the medicine for our children?" (1,800 sucres = $1 in 1993.)

A man from Tzapino: "A tourist guide told us that they do not have to pay us anything because they had already paid ONHAE. Why? *We* should get the money, it is *our* houses they come to!"

The president of ONHAE then stood up and denied that either he or the vice president had received any money from tourist guides.

Another man stood to say that a tourist guide once brought tourists to his settlement for five days. "Once he gave a little sugar. One time he paid 8,000 sucres, another time 20,000. Then he did not pay at all. I saw a tourist pay him 200,000 sucres in my house. Why do we not have this money?"

Another man: "They came and gave us machetes. We now have 10 machetes. We need the money. How much to charge them? We don't know."

A man from the Yasuní said that 50,000 sucres ($28) should be charged to each tourist who comes into a settlement.

Another man, vehemently: "*We* built this airstrip. *We* cut down the trees and carried the rocks. We worked together and contributed the food to do this. It was *hard* work! Now they want to come and use it, so they have to pay a lot."

The chairman: "They come to look at all these things and we don't get the money. Missionaries also come to look [referring to missionaries and their supporters who come to see where the five missionary pilots were "martyred" and to see the "progress" being made in Tönyëmpadɨ. Wɨba's husband usually has a monopoly on taking them to the spearing site by canoe.] This is not good. Don't let them take photos unless they pay lots of sucres. Get the money at the door."

Wɨba's husband: "Why are you angry? I take the missionaries and they pay me. Why are you mad? They don't give me a lot."

A woman from Tzapino: "Wɨba just left, angry; I don't care."

A woman from the Yasuní: "Where are the sucres coming from to pay for the pills when our children get sick from tourists' colds?" She becomes more and more agitated as she repeats this question in various ways, standing in one spot, her infant in a sling across her chest, waving her free hand back and forth. By the end of her tirade, she is trembling with rage. (We had seen this progression before, as people quite deliberately worked themselves into a raging fury.)

The vice president suggested that, since tourist guides are officially licensed by the government, they ask Maxus to provide courses in tourism so that they can act as their own guides. No one addressed an earlier suggestion that the various tourist guides be forced to pay a flat fee to come into Waorani territory. Everyone knows that the money would wind up in the pockets of the relatives of the ONHAE officers who had access to it, because they would not be able to resist the demands of their kindreds.

On the last day of the congress, the outgoing president complained about the difficulty of conducting the necessary business of the organization. "ONHAE doesn't even have an office," he said. "We are like birds with no nest. We have no place to work and no typewriter." The outgoing secretary stood, weeping, to say that his term was over and that, during it, they had lost Amö (a young ONHAE officer who had recently been killed in an accident; universally, Waorani believe he was murdered by *kowudɨ* colonists; see chapter 10).

A young woman, Amö's sister, said, "*He* cries! *My* brother was killed and I am afraid. There are so many colonists!" Another of her brothers then threatened retaliation against the *kowudɨ* who killed their brother.

At that point, Omënɨ, our neighbor from Tɨwënö, rose and voiced his concern over these threats of violence. He told a story of a raid he made years ago against the *kowudɨ*, when he himself was shot and wounded. "I have let go of my anger; I do not spear any more," he said. "We must all live right and let it go."

PART 2

THE CONTEXTS OF WAR

4 / The Material Context: Environment and Technology

THE PHYSICAL ENVIRONMENT

Ecuador, as its name implies, lies directly on the equator. In the high Andean valleys, where the Inca empire flourished at elevations of 8,000 feet and more, the climatic result is a dry, cool Mediterranean-like landscape basking in a glorious permanent springtime. Fewer than a hundred miles to the east, and 7,000 feet down, is the Oriente, and the heat and humidity that we usually associate with equatorial climates.

At an altitude of around 1,600 feet, several unpaved roads skirt the Andean foothills, and along them lie the frontier towns of the Oriente: Puyo, Tena, Mishahuallí, and the muddy oil boomtown, grandly and officially named Puerto Francisco de Orellana, but known everywhere in the Oriente only as Coca. Dirt tracks branch off and creep into the jungle for a few miles, linking a scattering of Lowland Quichua villages to the national economy.

Still farther to the east and south, far beyond the last of these tracks, lies the traditional homeland of the Waorani. It stretches from near the headwaters of the Curaray River, along the south bank of the immense Napo River (which, 400 miles downstream, joins with the Marañon River to become the Amazon), to the Peruvian border and beyond.

Much of the western (upriver) portion of the region is a low plateau, slowly rising with the Andes and simultaneously eroded by swift-running streams and broad rivers. The result is a deeply dissected terrain composed of generally east-west trending valleys of innumerable rivers and streams separated by steep ridges.

On the valley floors the rivers are constantly changing course, creating new channels and abandoning old ones in a cycle that begins when a loop of the channel is cut off to form an oxbow lake that slowly fills with silt and vegetation to become first a swamp; then a bog, treacherous with mud and quicksand; and finally, dry land through which the river will eventually cut a new channel and begin the cycle again. To the east are vast swamps and blackwater rivers. And blanketing all of this is the dense and seemingly endless tropical rainforest stretching to the horizon.

Unlike many tropical rainforests, including those in Malaysia, Waorani territory is rich in game. The trees are home to numerous species of primates, ranging from tiny marmosets to troops of howler monkeys. Brightly colored birds flash through the treetops, a riotous variety of toucans and parrots, including the spectacular red-and-blue macaws that are always seen in mated pairs. Still more birds frequent the understory or live on the forest floor.

Terrestrial game animals range from agoutis to "wild pigs"—white-lipped and -collared peccaries, the latter scavenging the forest floor in herds of up to 50 or more—to deer and tapir, the last remaining New World relative of the elephant and rhinoceros.

Competing for this bounty are the jungle predators—ocelots, pumas, and, especially, jaguars—with whom the Waorani identify, and from whose teeth and claws they make necklaces to decorate themselves and their children. Jaguars are surprisingly common here, another indication of the region's abundant animal life and its remoteness and isolation.

The rivers are similarly rich in fish, from some that were familiar to us from living room aquariums, to schools of piranha, to giant catfish that weigh 100 pounds or more. There are also stingrays, turtles, and caymans (South American alligators). Downstream on the Napo, Curaray, Cononaco, and Yasuní rivers there are manatees and freshwater dolphins. Also lurking in the rivers' depths—sometimes killed for their skins, but never eaten—are giant anacondas, the world's largest snakes. They can reach lengths of nearly 40 feet, and to them are attributed all Waorani deaths by drowning.

And there are venomous creatures, especially snakes, in profusion. Perhaps most dangerous, due to their sheer size—up to 10 feet—and the quantity of venom they can inject, are the bushmasters, pit vipers related to the North American rattlesnakes. Fortunately, they are also relatively rare and seldom encountered.

Much more common, and almost as dangerous, is the fer-de-lance. Known in Ecuador as *"equis"* (X) in reference to the X-shaped markings on its back, it is another pit viper, but one with a particularly potent venom and an aggressive disposition. A number of other vipers and coral snakes (related to the old-world cobras) inhabit the forest floor and, occasionally, the branches of the trees. Seldom does a day pass without someone in a settlement having a close call with a venomous snake. Every adult that we know has been bitten at least once, and some a half-dozen or more times.

There are also scorpions, venomous spiders, stinging caterpillars, congas (inch-long ants that bite and sting simultaneously), and huge tarantulas covered with tiny hairlike spines that cause a painful burning rash on contact with human skin.

In striking contrast with our experience in Malaysia, there was a much lower incidence of serious disease among the Waorani. Malaria is becoming a problem in some areas, but this appears to be a relatively recent introduction. Hookworms and other intestinal parasites are present, but seldom cause serious problems.

THE WAORANI ECOLOGICAL ADAPTATION

Waorani society is well adapted to this rich environment. The traditional settlement pattern was one of widely dispersed hamlets, each an extended family band consisting of one or more multifamily households occupying one or two large houses. These were usually oval in outline, built directly on the ground and thatched to the

A fer-de-lance killed in the settlement. The man who discovered it used it for target practice, killing it with curare-tipped darts shot from his blowgun.

ground with leaves, although some were walled with chonta planks for protection from raiders and, occasionally, elevated on pilings for the same reason.

Most households have a second residence with adjacent gardens, usually located in another valley a half-day to a day's walk away. This serves as a base camp for occasional hunting and fishing forays and, in the past, was also a refuge to flee to when raiders descended on the primary habitation. Related hamlets were scattered over a region, separated by distances ranging from an hour's walk or so to one of a day or more. Beyond that lay regions occupied by even more distantly related or unrelated bands.

This pattern still largely persists, although there have been some significant modifications in recent years. The large extended family house is being replaced by

A traditional extended family house form, now being abandoned in favor of nuclear family houses and households.

smaller rectangular Quichua-style houses, each with a nuclear family sleeping-house raised 3–4 feet off the ground and an adjacent kitchen-house built on the ground. The traditional residence pattern still survives as clusters of these nuclear family households of married siblings, or of parents and their married and unmarried children.

In the past, these settlements moved frequently to exploit new hunting and gardening territories and, especially, to escape retaliatory raids. As raiding has decreased, settlements have tended to become larger and more nearly permanent, although individual houses are rebuilt and relocated within them as termites and insect infestations make old houses uninhabitable. Growth and stability have also been fostered by the clearing of airstrips where the planes of the MAF can land. There are now several settlements with such strips, and these have become gateways for interaction with the wider world: people seek treatment for illnesses, injuries, and snakebites; hammocks and other handicrafts are sent out for sale; shotguns and other exotic goods arrive, along with missionaries, government officials, health teams, and schoolteachers to staff the increasing number of schools.

The traditional subsistence system based on hunting and swidden gardening remains fully intact, however. Outside of the one large settlement at Tönyëmpadï, where soils and game have been heavily overexploited, it still provides virtually all the food consumed.

Gardening

Waorani life and subsistence is rooted—literally and figuratively—in the manioc gardens. Waorani are classic tropical horticulturalists, and their gardening follows, with some minor variations, the typical swidden pattern. This cycle, typical of rainforest gardeners everywhere, usually involves cutting a patch of forest, burning the debris or allowing it to rot, planting, harvesting, and then moving on to repeat the cycle elsewhere.

Contrary to what the lush vegetation would seem to imply, most tropical forest soils are extremely poor, since all the available nutrients are tied up in the living vegetation. With little reserve of fertility in the soil, successful cultivation is possible only by making the trapped nutrients available to the growing crops, usually by cutting and burning the standing vegetation. This usually provides enough soil fertility to produce crops for a year or two. Then the process must be repeated in another area, and the previous field is left to be reclaimed by the forest for a fallow period of up to 40 years.

Waorani gardening follows this general pattern, but the soils, derived at least in part from the volcanic debris of the Andes, are much more fertile than is typical of tropical forest soils. Thus burning is not essential, and Waorani seldom burn the cut vegetation. This is, we suspect, at least in part because, in the past, the rising column of smoke would have immediately betrayed the location of a hamlet to its enemies.

Linguistic analysis gives some clues to the centrality of gardening in Waorani life: the linguistic root for both the verbs "to live/be alive" and "to reside" (*kïwï-*) is the same as the root for "manioc garden" (*kïwïnï*). Significantly, the verb "to eat" (*kë-*) and the noun "food" (*këngï*) have the same root as the word for "manioc" (*kënë*). Even the standard metaphorical construction used to describe a period of normal, tranquil life is premised on gardening; it translates "Chopping and drinking, chopping and drinking, like that, well we lived."

As this metaphor makes clear, the first step in gardening is the clearing of a patch of forest so that the sunlight can penetrate to the ground. Crops are then planted among the fallen trees. Both men and women work at clearing the undergrowth from fields, but men do most of the heaviest work of cutting trees. Today they use steel axes and machetes, but many people still remember using stone axes.

Surprisingly, they did not know how to make the ground-stone axe heads they used, but found them in the river gravels, an archaeological legacy of earlier societies. One morning while clearing a place for a hearth outside our house, Clay found a fragment of a stone axe and asked a friend if he recognized what it was. He did, and that afternoon he returned with a newly hafted stone axe. He had found the axe head some years before, he said, and had hafted it to show us how he had done it when he was younger.

After the cut vegetation has dried, women plant among the fallen trunks. The unusually high soil fertility allows fields to be cultivated for two years or more, and the necessary fallow period is much reduced. The primary food crops planted in the

After clearing the undergrowth from a new garden site, a man chops down the large trees to allow sunlight to penetrate to the ground.

swiddens are manioc (also known in Spanish-speaking regions as cassava or yuca) and plantains. Both are propagated from cuttings, plantains from "suckers" that emerge from the roots of mature plants, and manioc from cut segments of the plant's woody stem that are thrust at an angle into the moist soil.

Manioc, a starchy tuber now grown in tropical areas around the world, is native to lowland South America, where there are two major types, usually referred to as "bitter" and "sweet" manioc. Bitter manioc is poisonous and it must undergo an elaborate leaching process before it can be safely consumed. It is the more productive of the two types, and, because it is poisonous, is more resistant to field pests such as peccaries and agouti. Waorani grow only "sweet" manioc (*kënë*), but of a dozen or so varieties, all of which are processed into the drink *tipë*, as described in chapter 3.

Tipë is the archetypal food for Waorani and, in general, where we would talk about eating, Waorani talk about drinking. To be without food, for example, is *"bïkï dee ä"* (drink, there is none). To be starving is *"gïï bïti"* (thin [from lack of] drinking), and a period of tranquil plenty is, as we noted previously: "chopping and drinking, well we lived."

Plantains, or "cooking bananas" (*pëënë*) are a second staple and, along with several other varieties of bananas, are grown and consumed in large quantities. Plantains are harvested green, then hung in the house to ripen. When thoroughly ripe, they are peeled, boiled and mashed in the water in which they were cooked, producing a delicious drink that is rich in carbohydrates and potassium.

While plantains and manioc are available year-round, a third staple—chonta palm fruit—is seasonal. *Dagёngga* is the fruit of the chonta palm (*tïwё*). These trees, though privately owned, are scattered through the forest and concentrated around old dwelling sites. The ripe fruit is egg-sized and bright red-orange with an oily orange flesh, somewhat squash-like in flavor and texture, around a large hard seed. It is boiled and, like manioc, often mashed, pre-chewed, fermented, mixed with water, and drunk.

A number of lesser crops are also planted in the swiddens, including maize, sugar cane, peanuts, pineapples, sweet potatoes, and several varieties of bananas. The three drinks, made from manioc (*tipё*), plantains (*pёёnёmё*), and chonta (*dagёngapё*) (the -pё/-mё morpheme designates a fluid), however, form the core of Waorani subsistence, and provide the bulk of the calories consumed.

Fishing

Prior to the 1960s and 1970s, Waorani did not live on or heavily exploit the resources of the major rivers such as the Napo and Curaray, which they saw as the domain of the *kowudï*. They raided along these rivers, but lived high on the ridges above their upper tributaries.

Their technology was, and is, fully adequate for the exploitation of the resources of these smaller streams. Long, thin chonta wood fishing spears are used to take fish and stingrays in clear, shallow streams, and at least three different plants are utilized as fish poisons.

The leaves, stems, and/or roots of these plants are crushed with a stone to release the toxic juice, and then placed in a basket which is swished through the water in a stream or oxbow lake. Almost immediately, fish begin to float to the surface, where they are scooped up by hand or with small nets or baskets. When streams are high, women will often work their way, in waist-deep water, along the banks with small circular hand nets, scooping up the small fish hiding in the submerged weeds and branches.

Modern technologies now supplement, but have by no means replaced, these traditional methods. Fishhooks and commercial line are now widely used, and were welcome gifts that we brought whenever we visited a community.

A somewhat more spectacular innovation is the use of explosives acquired by breaking up the plastic explosive charges used by oil companies for seismic testing. These are stolen from oil camps or purchased in the frontier towns. On Clay's first fishing trip with a group of Waorani to a neighboring river valley, they stopped on a sandbar at a bend in the river. He sat down and was preparing a hand line when, suddenly, one of the young men lit a fuse and threw a baseball-sized, leaf-wrapped bundle of explosive into the pool off the sandbar.

The blast threw a column of water 20 feet into the air and, almost before it had fallen back, everyone was in the river, throwing stunned fish out onto the sand. When all the fish were out of the water, each person collected and stowed in a carrying bag every fish that he or she had personally thrown onto the bank. Within

A woman pounds kompago root to release the toxic juice used to poison fish.

In a rain-swollen stream, a woman nets a small fish.

minutes, they had collected some 25 pounds of fish and started upstream to repeat the process. Clay never did get a line in the water.

Hunting

While gardening is primarily the province of women, men are hunters. For most, it is a passionate preoccupation and a prime topic of conversation; they will spend hours discussing a hunt, one that may have taken place the previous morning or a decade before. The call of an animal from deep in the forest brings all conversation to a halt as men speculate on its location and behavior.

Hunting is typically a solitary endeavor. Generally, a man goes out alone in the morning with his shotgun or blowgun and spears. If he manages to kill more game than he can carry, two peccaries perhaps, or a tapir, he submerges the remainder in a small stream so that scavengers are not attracted by the scent, and returns to the settlement with what he can carry. That evening, or perhaps the next morning, depending on the distance, the women of his household go and retrieve the rest.

The hunting of collared peccaries is an exception to this pattern. Since they travel in large herds, it is much more productive for a group of men to hunt them. Typically, when a lone hunter comes across the tracks of a herd of peccaries (or smells them; their stench is detectable over long distances), he passes the word to the other men in his band and, armed with spears and/or shotguns, they go as a group to track them.

When they find them, they charge into the midst of the herd, shooting and spearing in all directions. In such a melee, a hunter with a bundle of spears is often more effective than one with a single-shot shotgun. It is not uncommon for a group of hunters to kill a dozen or more animals in one such hunt. Each one belongs to the man who killed it.

These animals can also be quite dangerous. Occasionally, a peccary will turn on its attacker, and we have seen the scars of terrible slashing wounds inflicted by their long tusks.

The traditional hunting technology of palmwood spears and blowpipes and curare-tipped darts is so effective that it is still in widespread use even today. Both blowguns and spears are made from the extremely hard and dense wood of the chonta palm. They are roughly shaped with axe and machete, then carefully shaved, smoothed, and finished with a sharp, usually unhafted blade made from a fragment of an old knife or machete.

Blowguns are crafted from two narrow, 9-foot staves of chonta, each grooved lengthwise down the center and carefully smoothed so that the halves fit perfectly together. The seam is sealed with beeswax and the full length of the blowgun is wrapped with a thin, flexible strip of bark peeled from a vine. The ¼-inch bore is then painstakingly smoothed and polished with a wooden ramrod and fine sand.

Darts are 15-inch slivers of palm frond midrib, carefully split and sharpened to a needle-like point. The tips are coated with curare, a paralytic poison derived

One family's yield from a peccary hunt.

from the *Curarea tecunarum* vine. To prepare the poison, the outer bark of the vine is shredded and placed in a cone made of leaves, and water is trickled through it. The dark fluid that drips out of the cone is collected in a clay pot and heated, cooled, and reheated until a scum forms on the surface. The dart tips are coated with this varnish-like substance and carefully arranged with the tips placed near a bed of hot coals to dry thoroughly.

When a monkey, a toucan, or other small game is sighted, the hunter draws a dart from his bamboo quiver and gives it a quick twist between the teeth of a piranha jaw that hangs by a string from his quiver. The teeth cut a fine groove about 1½ inches from the tip of the dart so that when the prey tries to dislodge the dart, the poisoned tip will break off and remain in the wound.

Finally, before inserting the dart into the blowpipe, the hunter draws a pinch of kapok fibers from a small round gourd that hangs from his quiver, and twists it around the base of the dart. This creates an air seal in the bore of the blowgun and also acts aerodynamically like the feathers on an arrow to provide the drag that keeps the dart heading in a straight line toward the target.

Curare is a powerful muscle relaxant that acts quickly to paralyze the muscles of the prey. Death is by suffocation resulting from paralysis of the diaphragm. Contrary to the impression fostered by innumerable Hollywood adventure films, however, a single curare-tipped dart does not mean swift and certain death for a human being. While the amount of poison delivered by one or two darts can kill a good-sized monkey within a few minutes, it is certainly inadequate to kill or immobilize a person or a large animal such as a deer, tapir, or even a peccary. As a consequence, blowguns are employed solely in the hunting of birds, monkeys, and

The tip of each dart is carefully coated with curare poison.

other relatively small game. Spears are the weapons of choice for hunting large
game and for killing people.

The double-pointed Waorani spear is a formidable and deadly weapon.
Roughly 9 feet long and ¾ inch in diameter, spears are made from staves split from
the trunk of the chonta palm. The wood is without grain and thus resists warping,
and it is extremely hard. The last 18 inches or so at each end is triangular in cross-
section and tapers to a needle-sharp point.

The shaft is decorated with feathers and, if the spear is intended for a human
victim, is painted red with *kaka*, the pigment made from the same *achiote* seeds
as are used for face paint. One end is barbed so that when the spear is imbedded,
it is almost impossible to withdraw. The victim of the recent clash with the
Tagëiri mentioned in chapter 1 was speared through the abdomen. He survived

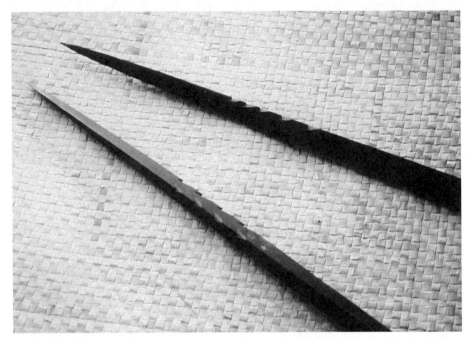

These barbed nine-foot chonta wood spears remain the preferred weapons for killing people.

the initial attack, but his companions had to cut the spear off so that they could carry him out.

In recent years, cheap, locally made single-shot shotguns have become available in the frontier towns, and most adult men now own one. Of the two types—muzzle-loaders and those that take shells—the former are ordinarily cheaper to buy, since their construction is simpler, and to use, since they are hand-loaded with powder and shot and detonated with percussion caps. Reloading is slow, however, and the hand-loads are erratic in their quantities of powder and shot. Manufactured shells are more consistent and much faster to load, but more expensive than powder and shot. Also, the cheapest 16-gauge shells available in the frontier towns are unreliable, and many misfire. Both kinds of firearms are poorly made, poorly maintained, and as a result they are rusty, unreliable, and frequently unusable. For all these reasons, and because one shot fired at a howler monkey sets the entire troop to flight and alerts all the other game within a mile or two, spears and blowguns, which are highly effective, continue to be widely used.

5 / The Historical Context

THE FIFTEENTH–NINETEENTH CENTURIES

The western Amazon basin has been a violent place for a very long time. The ultimate roots of this widespread culture of war are lost in antiquity, but the devastatingly destabilizing impacts of Spanish and later internal colonialism must certainly have contributed to its continuation and intensification. Still, the earliest accounts, even prior to the colonial period, describe the bellicosity of the region's inhabitants. The Incas attempted to colonize the eastern foothills, but their armies were repelled by the indigenous peoples. Early incursions by the Spanish were similarly repulsed, and resistance continued even after the establishment of Spanish control.

In 1538, Gonzalo Pizarro, brother of Francisco Pizarro, the conquerer of the Inca Empire, set out for the Oriente in search of El Dorado, the fabled land of gold. He traveled as far as what is now Coca, where his party's progress was halted by hardship and disease. From there, one of his lieutenants, Francisco Orellana, set out to reconnoiter downstream on the Napo River. Finding it impossible to return (or simply deciding not to), he continued downstream. He arrived, in 1541, at the mouth of the Amazon, becoming the first European to traverse the continent. His probably fanciful tales of fierce women warriors gave the name "Amazon" to the great river that he is credited with discovering.

Pizarro was forced to retreat to the highlands, but, by the middle of the sixteenth century, Spanish colonists were established in the foothills of the region, brutally exploiting the indigenous peoples in their insatiable hunger for gold.

In 1599, a temporary union of indigenous groups drove all colonists from the region, sacked the colonial cities, and killed all the inhabitants except the young women, whom they carried off. The Spanish governor of Macas was taken prisoner and the leader of the revolt is said to have told him that they wanted to see if he could finally get enough gold, whereupon the Indians set up a forge, melted the gold that had been collected for tribute, forced open the governor's jaws and poured the molten metal down his throat (Harner, 1972).

The region was a baffling mosaic of cultural and linguistic diversity. Linguistic evidence seems to suggest a succession of migrations pushing ever farther upstream along the tributaries of the Amazon. A survey of early mission records and other sources led one researcher to conclude that, in the mission province of Maynas, which included the Napo River region, "there were not less than fifty tribes with distinguishable languages, cultures and territories at the time of the first European contact" (Sweet, 1969, p. 37).

Most of these groups seem simply to have disappeared without leaving a trace when their refuge was at last breached by the emissaries of the Western world who brought with them those four horsemen of the colonial apocalypse: slavery, displacement, disease, and depopulation.

Plagues of introduced diseases caused massive mortality. There were few infectious diseases in Amazonia prior to European penetration, and native peoples had very little resistence to European diseases such as measles and, especially, smallpox.

In 1589, an exceptionally severe epidemic of smallpox spread from Cartagena on the Caribbean through most of South America. As many as 40,000 people died in Quito alone, and "In the province of Quijos at the headwaters of the Napo (from which some slave-raiding in the Amazon forests may already have been underway by that time), it wiped out several towns entirely" (Sweet, 1969, p. 126).

In 1660, an epidemic reportedly killed 44% of the mission-dwelling population in Maynas Province. In another epidemic nine years later, 20,000 out of a population of 80,000 native people reportedly died. Further epidemics of smallpox followed in 1749, 1756, 1762, and periodically throughout the nineteenth century (Sweet, 1969).

New social groupings were also emerging, apparently being formed out of the scattered remnants of decimated groups. The people known as Lowland Quichua, now the most populous of the groups neighboring the Waorani, are believed by anthropologists who have studied them to have coalesced from the remnants of a number of different societies that were destroyed by the colonial horrors that climaxed with the rubber boom. The Quichua language of the highlands had been the common trade language, and it became a *lingua franca* that united the survivors into what are now the Lowland Quichua (Whitten, 1981).

The "civilizing" of most of the indigenous peoples of the Oriente resulted in the transformation of those who survived from independent and self-sufficient hunters and gardeners to peons and peasants. Two institutions in particular shaped that transformation: the missions and the haciendas.

Missions

Catholic missionaries have been active in the Oriente for more than 400 years. Jesuits first entered the region in 1560, founding a mission at Archidona (Orton, 1876). In 1605, the first Jesuit missionary on the Napo estimated that there were 50,000 Indians in 10 different tribes living along the river. Several early missions were established on the fringes of what is now Waorani territory.

In the early seventeenth century, the Franciscans claimed to have established three missions among the "Avijiras," who reportedly lived in what is now Waorani territory near the headwaters of the Curaray (Sweet, 1969), but it is impossible to acertain precisely who these people were.

Missionization required the resettlement of populations into mission stations or *reducciones*, permanent settlements where they could be "civilized" and taught Christianity, and where their labor could be mobilized for mission projects. This process of resettlement continued throughout the eighteenth and nineteenth centuries, but was frequently disrupted by the epidemics that struck these settled groups with alarming regularity. Headlong flight, the only possible escape from these periodic plagues, spread the diseases to the most remote areas. These settled populations also made easy targets for slavers who raided upriver from bases in Peru or down from the Andean foothills.

Conflict among the missionaries and the slavers, rubber traders, *hacendados,* and local officials over treatment of the Indians and control of their labor was common, and several times the Jesuits were expelled from the country as a result of complaints to Quito from the local *blancos* (whites). Spiller, a priest writing a history of the Josephina Mission in Tena, described the aftermath of one such expulsion:

> After the Jesuits left, the missionary lands were at the disposition of adventurers who, like hyenas, invaded with the name of "caucheros" [rubber collectors] and hunters of cascaria [another jungle product]. They were men of no conscience. . . . With their arrival began the unfolding of the tragic drama of the Indians who, in order to avoid the lash of the patron, were obliged to look for the quantity of bark and latex required by the master under the penalty of beatings and death. Constantly heard was the . . . crack of the whip from the lashes that fell on the shoulders of the Indian who could not bring in his ration. The lashes fell, the blood fell, the tears fell. . . . For this ignoble cause, the natives of Archidona died in distant rivers of Ucayali [in Peru] or on the edges of the Madre de Dios in Bolivia. . . . 1,000 families looked for refuge in the most entangled parts of the jungle. In this manner, the populations disappeared . . . they fled from the caucheros. (Spiller, 1974, p. 17)

However well-intentioned and self-sacrificing these early missionaries may have been (and a good many of them were killed attempting to carry out what they perceived as their missions), the inevitable result of their efforts to "civilize" and "Christianize" the Indians was massive depopulation by epidemic disease and the utter destruction of most of the indigenous societies with which they had come into contact.

Haciendas

The hacienda system began with the granting of *encomiendas*—grants of land and its indigenous inhabitants—by the colonial government. By the late sixteenth century, encomiendas had been granted and haciendas established on the eastern slopes of the Andes, and the resident Indians had been set to working the alluvial gold deposits in the rivers. The key to the haciendas' success was the Indian labor force under their control, and securing that labor was a priority from the very beginning.

> As the Indians originally assigned to these enterprises died or withdrew to remote places, the settlers turned increasingly to the recruitment of labor by force from the Amazon forests. Slave-raiding was from the start one of the functions of military reconnaissance from Peru, and from the Portuguese establishments at the mouth of the Amazon as well. (Sweet, 1969, p. 9)

As the system evolved, the serfdom and outright slavery of the encomiendas was replaced in the nineteenth and twentieth centuries by a system that gained and maintained control over local Indian populations through a system of debt-peonage.

Cloth, machetes, axes, and other manufactured goods were sold to the Indians on credit and at enormously inflated prices. In order to pay these "debts," the Indians worked to produce the commodities that the *hacendados* would buy (at prices that they set, of course). Or they worked as laborers or servants for wages set by the *patron*, wages that were always insufficient to satisfy the debtors' needs and obligations.

At the center of the hacienda system was the *patron* (or, not infrequently, *patrona,* since some of the most rapacious and successful haciendas were under the control of women), who had, through one or another means, acquired control of desirable land after dispossessing its indigenous occupants.

The difficulty of getting to the Oriente from the highlands or from Peruvian ports far downriver on the Napo made it possible for the *patron* to monopolize the importation and sale of manufactured goods to the local Indians. In a very short time, most Indians were so deeply in debt that a lifetime of work for the *patron* could not erase their obligations.

The exports from these haciendas varied in response to world market demands: fiber, cotton, gold, and rubber. Since it was the Indians' labor that was essential in extracting or producing these exports, hacienda owners continued to go to great lengths to acquire it. In some cases, capture and outright slavery were employed. In others, Indians would be forced to accept the *patron's* goods—and the resulting debt servitude—whether they wanted them or not.

The goods given and the days of work received were required to be recorded in a ledger, but this was often not available for inspection by the debtors, and most were unable to read it in any case. Once enmeshed, a debtor was not likely ever to escape, nor were his descendents; when a man died his debt passed on to his widow and children. The law also gave the *patron* the right to control the movements of his peons, so that they could be returned to the hacienda by force if they fled to escape their debts.

> The wealth of these [*patrons*] was valued by the number of their debtors, so all procured the greatest number possible, including winning those of other patrons. This generated serious disputes between patrons and frequent claims before the civil authorities. In reality, the Indian debtors were truly slaves, for when a patron decided to trade, deed or sell a hacienda, he included among the items all of his personal debtors. To attend the church, to send his children to school, and even to marry his sons, the Indian had to gain the authorization of his patron. (Spiller, 1974, p. 85)

The haciendas also supported and encouraged raiding against the Waorani. In one raid described to us by a survivor, Quichuas surrounded a Waorani house where a drinking and dancing feast was under way. They opened fire on the house, and killed or wounded most of the inhabitants.

Sra. Josefina Torres de Peñaherrera, an Ecuadorian friend of ours now living in Quito, spent her early life in the Oriente on haciendas owned by her father and her husband. She described to us an incident that occurred—probably in the late 1930s or early 1940s—when she was a young woman.

A young Wao boy had been captured in a raid by Indians working on her husband's hacienda. After church one Sunday morning, she found the boy, who was about 12 years old, cowering in a tree and surrounded by angry Quichuas. They had decided he was too old to be safely "tamed," so they were going to kill him. She intervened and took him into her house as a servant, where he lived for some time, long enough for her to learn a few words of Waorani which, a half-century later, she still remembered. We asked what happened to him. "He died," she recalled, adding, "those Auca children always died of colds very soon."

The Rubber Boom

We have several times made reference to rubber collectors and to the "rubber boom." This was a castastrophe that descended on the indigenous people of Amazonia in the mid-nineteenth century as industrialization in Europe and North America generated a rapidly increasing demand for rubber. At that time, the primary sources of rubber were several wild species of latex-producing trees native to the new world tropical forests, the greatest of which lay in the Amazon basin.

By the end of the nineteenth century, immense fortunes had been made in the rubber trade. The Brazilian city of Manaus, a deepwater port far upriver on the Amazon near the mouth of the Rio Negro, was the center for the export of rubber. It boasted lavish mansions and an opera house featuring the stellar attractions of the day, imported directly from the capitals of Europe.

The processes for extracting the latex were labor-intensive so, ultimately, all of this too depended on the labor of Amazonian Indians. Extending the search for rubber into the remote western hinterlands in Ecuador required an endless supply of Indian labor, much of it slave labor. There was a flourishing slave market downriver on the Napo in Iquitos, Peru, and slavers raided the upstream tributaries relentlessly.

Catholic missionaries returned in the late nineteenth century, in time to bear witness to the savagery of the *caucheros* (rubber collectors) and the Peruvian slave raiders who fed their insatiable demand for labor. One account unearthed and translated by Blomberg (1957), described their depradations in the upper Napo region:

> Many caucheros who penetrated into these regions were lawless and totally devoid of moral sense: their insatiable greed led them to enslave the people of the jungle and set them to the hardest forced labor. They overran the Indian settlements, murdering and burning. The luckless victims who endeavored to defend themselves were cut down, likewise the women, old men and children who were of no use as slaves. If any wretched prisoner tried to escape from his slave-drivers, he was hunted into the remote fastness of the forest. The rubber, says the Colombian author Eustaquio Rivera in his gripping book *La Vorgaine*, was stained with blood, mostly that of these defenceless [sic] children of the jungle. No mercy was shown. Is it strange that many tribes are filled with a vehement longing for revenge and hatred of the whites and all who do not belong to their own people? For Indians from other tribes were willing tools in the hands of the whites and, faithless to their own race, took place in the rubber gatherers' correrias ["round-ups"].
>
> The remnants of these hunted tribes now inhabit the region around the upper course of the Curaray, while other groups are spread over the area between the lower course of the Curaray and the Napo. In the rubber era they were called Shiripunos (after the Shiripuno River, a tributary of the Tiputini, which in its turn is a tributary of the Napo), but their real name is Aushiris or Avishiris. The Yumbo [Quichua] Indians call them *lucho Aucas*, the naked savages. (Blomberg, 1957, pp. 84–85).

How all this impacted the Waorani or, for that matter, whether they were even there during the fifteenth–nineteenth centuries, we can only speculate, since there are no references to any group that can conclusively be identified as Waorani prior to the early years of this century.

In 1948, the *Handbook of South American Indians*, a multi-volume compendium of the current state of anthropological knowledge of the indigenous peoples of South America at the time, was published. It contains no reference to Waorani, although it does make sketchy reference to several shadowy "groups"— Ssabela, Avishiiri, Aushiri, Oa—about which little was known, and who are believed by some to have been Waorani. The evidence is, in most cases, equivocal at best.[1]

A case in point are the "Orejones." Accounts from the 1870s mention a tribe of "savages" living on the north side of the Napo River who were referred to locally as *"Orejones"* (big ears) because of their practice of stretching their ears by inserting large wooden plugs into holes in the lobes, a practice abandoned by most Waorani only since contact.

There is a Waorani story that recounts how they came to be in their present location. It recalls that their numbers were dwindling as they were captured and eaten by the cannibalistic *kowudï*. They fled farther and farther upriver, but some returned and were captured by the cannibals. They were taken to the *kowudï* camp where, one by one, they were killed, their flesh eaten, and their blood painted on a magic "thing" that made a loud noise. A few survivors escaped and fled even farther upstream, to where they live today.

Rachael Saint, who first recorded this story, recalled that when some Waorani were taken to the Summer Institute of Linguistics compound at Limoncocha, they identified the generating plant as matching the descriptions of the *kowudï* "thing" to which so many had been sacrificed (Saint, 1964).

It takes only a little imagination to see in this story a subjective account by Stone Age people of being captured and taken as slaves to a jungle rubber processing operation where they encountered their first industrial machinery (perhaps red with rust, or painted red with rust-inhibiting paint), where many of them died, and from which the survivors fled. Some such flight from genocide in a distant region may explain why the Waorani language is apparently unrelated to any of the surrounding languages and, perhaps, to any other surviving language.

The lack of direct historical evidence notwithstanding, we are certainly safe in assuming that the Waorani, like other Amazonian peoples, have long suffered the effects, both direct and indirect, of European incursions. While it is clear that warfare in the region predates the period of initial European contact, the level of violence was almost certainly intensified by the penetration of Europeans and by their exploitation of the region and its inhabitants. Further, alliances between outsiders and some indigenes gave groups differential access to Western technology—especially firearms—altered power relationships, and exacerbated the conflicts among indigenous groups.

---

[1]A word list identified as having been collected from Ssabela Indians is clearly Waorani, but the name *Ssabella* cannot be, since the Waorani language has no sibilants.

It also provided an additional motive for raiding, as disadvantaged groups sought to acquire the new weapons and other tools. In the Waorani case, their hostility to all outsiders blocked their acquisition of iron tools and other goods by peaceful means. Our neighbors recalled raids launched solely to acquire tools.

Predatory slave raiding and introduced diseases weakened and depopulated—in some cases annihilated—some groups so that others were able to expand into and occupy their traditional territories. This also may explain the presence of the linguistically isolated Waorani. In any case, whoever and wherever the Waorani may have been in the nineteenth century, it is clear that, by the early years of this century, they were established in the territory they still occupy.

THE TWENTIETH CENTURY

The catastrophes of the sixteenth through nineteenth centuries dramatically simplified the ethnic composition of the Oriente. Some groups simply vanished, wiped out by disease and slave raiders. Others were so weakened that they were displaced from their traditional homelands by haciendas, civil governments, missionaries, and other indigenes. Survivors assimilated into other groups or were left as tiny enclaves of a few hundred people. The Cofan, Siona, Secoya, and Waorani are among those whose sociocultural survival hangs by a thread.

A dramatic example of the effects of this period is provided by the case of the Záparoans, who at one time numbered, according to some accounts, 100,000 or more. Although that estimate is undoubtedly an enormous exaggeration, it does serve to indicate that this was a large and powerful group. They reportedly occupied a territory that stretched from the Marañon River in the south to the Napo in the north, an area encompassing much of what is now the Waorani homeland.

From the sixteenth through nineteenth centuries, however, they suffered massive depopulation—95% or more—from enslavement, mission resettlement, and disease. A final attempt, made in the 1930s, to concentrate the survivors in a mission settlement led to yet another epidemic and further depopulation. The result is that there are no remaining Záparo settlements in Ecuador today. Only a few scattered individuals and families retaining some elements of Záparo culture and language exist within some Quichua communities (Whitten, 1981). The two men from one of these communities who, during our first field project, walked for two days through the jungle to bring Clay two broken shotguns to repair, were the only Záparo we met.

By the mid-twentieth century, only two major indigenous cultural/linguistic groups remained in the region immediately adjacent to Waorani territory. To the southwest are the Jivaroan speakers, the Shuar and Achuar and, immediately adjacent to the Waorani on the north, south, and west, are the Lowland Quichua.

Shuar

The Shuar (Jivaro) are known outside Ecuador primarily for their taking and shrinking of human heads, a practice that continued well into the twentieth century. They were the leaders of the revolt that expelled the Spanish in 1599, and from then until the arrival of the first missionaries in the 1870s, they had little direct contact with the outside world. Over the next 30 years, missions were established by the Jesuits and Dominicans and by one Protestant group, but all were soon abandoned.

The rubber boom had little impact on the Shuar, since there were few rubber trees in their territory and no truly navigable rivers by which to export what little rubber there was. Not until the mid-1930s, when a minor gold rush was ignited by the rediscovery of the gold deposits that had originally drawn the Spanish, did outsiders begin colonizing their lands (Harner, 1972).

Initially, the Shuar did not resist the colonists. They saw them as a source of tools and shotguns that could be acquired by clearing areas of forest for pasture for the colonists' cattle. As the numbers of colonists increased, however, the epidemic diseases that they introduced devastated Shuar communities and left them unable to resist when colonists, now supported by military and police, began appropriating their garden clearings to pasture cattle.

Catholic and Protestant missions established in the late 1940s and early 1950s began sending Shuar children to boarding schools with the explicit goal of forcing acculturation and assimilation (Harner, 1972).

Quichua

The indigenous people with whom the Waorani have had the most direct contact in this century are those called the Lowland or "Jungle" Quichua. Whitten (1981), on the basis of his long-term research, sees their origins as a sociocultural group in the chaos and depopulation of the nineteenth century.

He argues that the modern Lowland Quichua are the result of an amalgamation of other devastated groups that occurred in a context where Quichua, the language of the highlands, was a *lingua franca,* a common trade language permitting access to foreign goods. In the south, this amalgamation was "a merger of Záparoan and Jivaroan peoples, the culture being spread by Quichua speakers. . . ." In the north, the origins lay in the Montaña (Whitten, 1981, p. 128).

Now referring to themselves as "Runa" (people), these Quichua speakers occupy the north bank of the Napo River and abut Waorani territory on the south, west, and north. For much of this century, the two peoples have raided each other relentlessly.

Blancos (Non-Indigenes)

Until relatively recently, the government in Quito exercised only minimal direct control over the Oriente. The politicians and bureaucrats of the capital were occupied with the political intrigues and power struggles that were played out in the highlands and in the coastal economic powerhouse of Guayaquil. The Oriente was peripheral to these interests in almost every sense, and few resources were made available for its "development."

Into this political vacuum were drawn missionaries, minor bureaucrats, adventurers, and entrepreneurs. With the approval of a government that lacked other resources for exploiting the Oriente, they established churches and schools, organized local and regional governments, searched for gold and rubber, and established ranches, farms, and haciendas. With only sporadic interruptions, actual political and economic power in the Oriente was vested in local officials, *hacendados,* missionaries, and occasionally the military.

With the exception of the military, all the others were dependent for their success, indeed for their very survival, on their ability to exploit the lands and labor of the indigenous inhabitants. All along the Napo and other major rivers, Indian land was seized by white colonists and converted into towns, missions, farms, ranches, and haciendas.

Haciendas

Although their economic activities changed in response to changing conditions in the world economy to which they were linked, many of the haciendas persisted and prospered into the twentieth century. In terms of their direct influence on the indigenous population, they continued to be the most important institutions in the region.

At the turn of the century they participated in the rubber boom, and Indian laborers were sent into the forests to collect latex. As the profits from the sale of rubber began to dwindle, the patrons in the Oriente began to turn to cattle raising and to the cultivation of cash crops, including cotton, coffee, and rice. In addition, they planted plantains and manioc for their own subsistence and that of the indebted Indians. Cotton and coffee were carried up the Andes to Ambato or Quito on the backs of Indians, while cattle were exported by river to Peru. Sugar cane was grown and processed into molasses and rum.

In the 1930s, during the worldwide depression, the price of gold rose on the world market, and the patrons once again set their peons to panning for gold in the streams of the Andean foothills (Muratorio, 1991, pp. 144–145). The one constant, regardless of the economic activity they pursued, was the absolute dependence of the haciendas on the labor of the indigenous people.

By the 1920s, white settlements were scattered at intervals all along the Napo River. Two geologists exploring the region in 1921 described the situation:

> In Napo, as in other settlements of Eastern Ecuador, no Indians are resident except as servants and laborers for the white families. They are to be found living in small clearings, hidden in the jungles along the streams where they raise yuca and plantain, fish a little, and also pan for gold from the gravels along the bed of the river. Each white family has under its patronage a number of Indians whose gold is taken in exchange for cloth and other commodities obtained from Quito, an eight days' journey northward over a rough trail. (Sinclair & Wasson, 1923, p. 192)

Such settlements extended all the way into what is now Peru. The power of the haciendas finally began to wane with the arrivals of Protestant missionaries in Tena in 1927 and of the Shell Oil Company in 1937. When they began offering the Indians wage labor, the patrons of the haciendas began to lose their place as the only source of trade goods, and with it, their control over Indian labor (Muratorio, 1991, pp. 164–166). A resident of the town of Napo summed up the *hacendados'* view for Blomberg in 1947:

> "I don't know which has spoilt the Indians most, Shell or the Protestant missionaries—Shell with its high wages and eight hours' day and all those new lunacies and the missionaries with their damned fawning ways. It's no longer we who rule the Indians, but they us. Impudent and lacking in respect, that's what they've become. . . ." (Blomberg, 1957, p. 151).

The final blow to the debt system and to the patrons' control in the Upper Napo region came with the building of roads, especially the road between Tena and Puyo, and the arrival of traders who bought cacao, coffee, and gold, and paid in cash. It was not until 1973, however, that Mrs. Esther Sevilla, one of the last of the *patronas,* was forced by the courts to "liberate" her "peons" (Muratorio, 1991, p. 177).

Civil Government

There was another class of Indians who were not indebted to *patrones;* unfortunately, their economic and political situation was little better. They were under the control of the civil government and were divided into groups according to the precinct where they lived. Each precinct had a mayor and other officials whose responsibility was to mobilize the labor of the members for public works.

If a colonist wanted to hire an Indian to work for him, he could not negotiate with the person directly, but had to contract for his labor with the civil authority. On Thursdays and Sundays, all of the "free" Indians had to present themselves to do the work that had been contracted by the civil authority.

They were also responsible for public works projects, such as clearing and widening roads, projects which might last for weeks. The workers had to provide their own food and tools, and they were not paid for their labor. Anyone who fled in an attempt to evade such service was hunted down by trackers hired by the civil authority, and jailed or put in stocks (Spiller, 1974).

Missions

Missions continued to be an important component of the national government's strategy for colonizing, governing, and exploiting the resources of the Oriente. The government chartered missions that were given the responsibility of spreading Christianity, providing schools and medical care, and generally "civilizing" the indigenous population.

The Catholic missions had to be largely self-supporting and, like the civil governments and the haciendas, were dependent on Indian labor for their success. This put them in direct competition with these other interests. Moreover, the priests were charged with "improving" (in their view) the lot of the Indians, and this frequently led them to rail against the exploitation of the indigenes by the haciendas and by local officials.

Fairly typical is the assessment made in 1928 by an Italian priest from the Josephina Mission in Tena:

> Some patrons who ought to be the bearers of civilization are, on the contrary, elements of obstruction and the return of barbarism. . . . The whites are the "patrones," and the Indians "the slaves." From the Napo to the Marañon, there is not a single free indigenous family. (Spiller, 1974, p. 116)

Friction between the missionaries and local whites was, consequently, a constant, and both sides carried their complaints to Quito.

In 1922, the Padres Josefinas arrived in Ecuador, and in 1925 established a mission and school at Tena. In 1926 the first protestant missionaries arrived to explore the possibility of establishing a mission in Tena. The Protestants were well received by local whites eager to drive a wedge between the Catholic missions and the Indians, and in 1927, they established a mission with "patronage provided by a committee of blancos" (Spiller, 1974, p. 107).

Some of the haciendas offered land and other material support to the Protestants, and over the next few years missions and schools were established on various haciendas along the upper Napo River and elsewhere. The *patrona* of one of the most prosperous of the Napo haciendas was even publicly baptized as a Protestant in the Napo River, although the account of the event notes, "her daughters remained Catholic" (Spiller, 1974, p. 109).

In the late 1930s exploration for oil was begun by the Royal Dutch Shell oil company, and in 1939 an airstrip was constructed near the town of Mera to aid exploration and mapping. Soon the Missionary Aviation Fellowship began operations. This presented the possibility of rapid transportation to remote and otherwise nearly inaccessible sites, a possibility that was quickly exploited by the Protestants.

Within a few years, primitive airstrips were being cleared near many of their missionary outposts among the Quichua and Shuar, and small planes were ferrying missionaries to remote locations and transporting sick and injured Indians out of the jungle for medical care.

With this new ease of accessibility to some of the most remote parts of the Oriente, the pace of acculturation began to increase rapidly, and the airstrip and the ramshackle town called "Shell-Mera" that grew up around it soon became the hub of Protestant missionary activities in the Oriente. This included the group that launched the ill-fated flight that brought worldwide attention to the Waorani and that ultimately breached their isolation.

In 1941, while the rest of the world was occupied with World War II, Peru seized and annexed a huge area of Amazonian Ecuador, including the remote frontier town of Rocafuerte on the Napo. An armistice brokered by the United States established a new boundary line between Ecuador and Peru, crossing the Napo River just east of the mouth of the Yasuní River. In an attempt to reestablish a national presence in this remote part of the country, a new town, Nuevo Rocafuerte, was established on the north side of the Napo, across from the mouth of the Yasuní.

In 1954, Capuchin missionaries arrived to found a new parish and to establish missions at Nueva Rocafuerte and Coca. In later years these missions became the center for Catholic attempts to contact the Waorani of the Yasuní region. Still later, these towns became the hubs of the petroleum industry's efforts to extract the oil riches that lay beneath it.

Oil

The search for oil begun in 1937 by Shell Oil eventually included forays by heavily armed exploration teams into Waorani territory in the region of the upper Curaray. The results were predictable. A Waorani attack in 1942 on a Shell oil camp near the Quichua village of Arajuno was described in a letter from a company executive:

"We regret to have to inform you that a most unfortunate incident occurred on Wednesday, January 7th last, in our camp at Arajuno. A group of hostile Indians attacked a gang of our laborers working near our camp and our foreman and two other Ecuadorian laborers were killed with spears. This attack caused some panic among our laborers which was aggravated when these Indians made another appearance and seemed to be surrounding the camp. . . . We fear it will become more difficult than before to engage an adequate number of laborers for our camp at Arajuno." (Elliot, 1957, p. 98)

More than a decade of exploration by Shell resulted in nearly a dozen workers killed by Waorani spears and an unknown number of Waorani casualties, but yielded no evidence of significant amounts of oil. Shell abandoned the search in 1950. More than a decade later, a second round of exploration was begun by Texaco, resulting in the discovery of major oil resources north of the Waorani homeland near the town of Lago Agrio. This sparked an oil boom and a rush of exploration that eventually revealed a vast pool of oil beneath the heart of traditional Waorani territory.

Colonists

As the Oriente became increasingly "civilized," as local government was established and routinized, as transportation improved, as towns grew up, and as the region was progressively integrated into the national and international economies, Ecuador came to see the "underpopulated" Oriente as the solution to crowding, land shortage, and poverty in the highlands. Immigration was encouraged, and it increased dramatically. Improvements in public health and medical care brought a decline in infant and other mortality rates, and populations grew. All this added to the pressure on the lands of the Shuar, the Quichua, and others directly or indirectly adjoining Waorani territory.

"Civilization" brought ideological changes in the region as well. As acculturation progressed among other indigenous groups, the universal native ethnocentrism was undermined. Groups might still call themselves "people," but they were increasingly aware that that they were not the only "true" people. New identities were being forged, one of which was an "indigenous" identity formed in opposition to the increasing flood of immigrants and colonists from the highlands.

But the Waorani continued to resist violently all attempts at colonization, missionization, and the establishment of haciendas within and on the fringes of their territory. Any hunter, colonist, or missionary who ventured across the Napo did so at risk of his or her life.

Missionaries continued to make occasional and sporadic attempts to contact them. In 1957 a British missionary built a hut on the Curaray River from which he hoped to make contact. Fortunately for him, when the hut was discovered by a Waorani raiding party, he was visiting elsewhere. The raiders ripped the door off, destroyed his belongings, and carried off his machetes and pots and pans. Outside the door, they left two crossed spears, a sign that, then as today, meant "death to anyone who passes beyond this point."

6 / The Social/Cultural Context

THE HUMAN WORLD: KOWUDÏ AND WAORANI

For Waorani, the human world consists of Waorani and *kowudï*. As is often the case in societies at this level of social complexity, the Waorani word for themselves translates literally "people": *wao-* (person) + *-räni* (3rd person plural). It includes only those who were born into Waorani society. All others are *kowudï* (foreigners).

For Waorani, unlike Semai, that division is absolute and uncrossable. After we had lived with the Semai for some months, they began shifting from the use of the exclusive "we" ("we-all, not including you") when they spoke to us, to the use of the inclusive form ("we-all, including you"). Among the Waorani, that shift never occurred. Even Quichua spouses who have married in, lived as Waorani, and produced Waorani children, are still *kowudï*.

Kowudï

Kowudï were, until the most recent generation, seen as enemies and eaters of human flesh who were to be killed on sight. In truth, we are not sure just how literally most Waorani took this conventional view of outsiders as cannibals. It is certain that most people felt, at least on some occasions, that *kowudï* were capable of being cannibals, and there are stories, told and believed as true accounts, of Waorani encounters with them.

Although allegations of cannibalism are notoriously unreliable, some *kowudï* may, in fact, have eaten human flesh. Farabee (1922) reports that the Witoto, who lived between the Putomayo and Napo rivers, just north of Waorani territory, practiced at least ritual cannibalism on captured enemies, eating the flesh of the head and making flutes from arm bones. In any case, it is abundantly clear that the Waorani attribution of cannibalism to *kowudï* was a part of a conventional cultural definition of them as subhuman.

But it is also clear that, on other occasions, *kowudï* could be perceived as human (or almost human). The *kowudï* who have been most relevant to the Waorani in this century are the people now called "Lowland Quichua," the people Waorani call *"Oruna."* We know several Waorani women who fled to the *Oruna* to escape the internecine killing.

Some, such as one woman who went to the *kowudï* immediately after her young daughter died, may have, in effect, been seeking to commit suicide. That was certainly not an unrealistic expectation; "naked Aucas," both men and women, were routinely shot on sight on the presumption that they were members of a raiding party. One of our informants, when she was a young teenager, fled to Quichua territory along the Napo following the spearing of her grandmother. She was shot and seriously wounded by the first *kowudï* that she encountered. Other women who fled, however, told us that they saw their chances of survival as better with the *kowudï* than at home.

Kowudï women were also occasionally taken prisoner, kidnapped to be wives. In at least one instance that we know of, a raid on the Quichua was mounted with the specific intent of capturing a woman to replace a wife who had fled to the *Oruna*. Although the prospects of long-term survival for these captured women were not great (they were usually killed within a few months), for a time, at least, they were incorporated into Waorani households.

In any event, *kowudï* were, without question, unpredictable and dangerous enemies who continually tried to encroach on Waorani territory, who raided Waorani settlements for captives, and who killed Waorani at every opportunity. As we will see in chapter 10, these historically derived conceptions continue to inform Waorani perceptions of *kowudï* and to influence relations with them.

The *kowudï,* for their part, saw the Waorani as "Aucas," a Quichua word that, as Taussig (1987, p. 97) deconstructs it, connotes "the unrepentantly 'other' world of savagery down there in the jungles of the *oriente,* a world quintessentially pagan, without Christ, Spanish words, or salt, inhabited by naked, incestuous, violent, magical and monstrous people, even wilder, perhaps, than the *tigre mojano*—animal, but also human, and unreal." Instantly recognizable by their nakedness and by the large balsa wood plugs through their distended earlobes, they were murderous savages to be shot on sight.

Waorani

There were at least three major territorially localized groups of Waorani when peaceful relations were first established in the 1950s. How long these had existed and occupied these territories we can only guess, but the groupings are still evident today.

Within these are subgroups designated by the name of an important elder plus the suffix *-iri* ("type, kind, group, bunch"); thus, the Upriver band that we first lived with is called the Gïkitairi, or "Gïkita's group," whose territory was, and is, on the Upper Curaray and its tributaries, now the "Auca Protectorate."

The Baiwäiri, then and now, were located off the Protectorate, originally on the upper Tiguino and Shiripuno rivers and now on the upper Cuchiyacu River. The Wïpïiri, formerly on the Upper Nashiño and Yasuní rivers, are now split, with some members living on the Protectorate and others on the lower and middle Yasuní and Cononaco rivers. The Piyëmöiri, who occupied the lower Tiputini and Tivacuno rivers, are now mostly living on the Protectorate. The Babëiri once lived on the Tiguino, Shiripuno, and Tivacuno Rivers but are now located on the Tiguino River at the end of the oil company road leading south from Coca.

To the east, between the Shiripuno and the Cuchiyacu, are the still uncontacted Tagëiri and, during our last project, we heard reports of yet another uncontacted group known only as the Tarömïnäni ("they who go across-country") living somewhere near the Peruvian border between the Nashiño and Cononaco rivers. There are also rumors that another one or more small bands may still be living in that remote and disputed border region.

In the pre-contact period, relations among these groups were typically hostile and marked by vendettas rooted in a history of raids in previous generations. Although the vendettas have nearly been extinguished, at least one remains active today. Some years ago, men from the Yasuní band raided the Tagëiri, killing at least two people. The Tagëiri soon retaliated and severely wounded two Yasuní men (Smith, 1993). That vendetta remains active today.

More recently, the repeated incursions by the Babëiri into Tagëiri territory in 1994 that provoked an ambush by the Tagëiri in which one of the Babëiri was speared to death threaten to ignite another feud.[1]

KINSHIP AND MARRIAGE

As a consequence of these kinds of vendettas, and the pattern of prescriptive cross cousin marriage—a requirement that one must marry a person classed as "father's sister's child" or "mother's brother's child"—these regional groups have tended strongly toward endogamy (marriage within the groups). Still, they are all linked by kin ties flowing from marriages that took place in the past, some of which resulted from the kidnapping of women during raids.

Within each of these regions, local settlements are, as we have seen, linked by bonds of kinship and affinity, but these bonds can be sources of conflict as well as amity. One potential source of such conflict derives from the practice of prescriptive cross cousin marriage itself. To understand this conflict potential, we must first understand how Waorani think about kinship and marriage relations.

Waorani descent, like that of Euro-American society, is bilateral, traced equally through male and female lines. The way kin are grouped and perceived, however, is very different from our categories (See figure 6.1). The all-encompassing term for kinsmen or relatives, members of one's bilateral kindred, is *girï-* (*girïngä*: kinsman; *girïnäni:* kinsmen). As in the English usage of "relative," the term is not ordinarily used for those kin with whom one lives or whom one visits often; these genealogically and spatially close relatives are referred to by their specific kin terms: brother, mother, potential spouse, and so on.

Waorani kinship classification, coupled with prescriptive cross cousin marriage, results in a social world that is composed of two kinds of *girïnäni*. Parallel cousins (father's brothers' children and mother's sisters' children) are classed as siblings, and their mothers are addressed by the same term as ego's own mother.

Their fathers, although addressed by a term (*mäapo*) different from the one used for ego's own father (*mëmpo*), are often referred to by the same term (*wëmpo*); (the "proper" reference term for father's brother is *wäapo*).

Cross cousins (father's sisters' children and mother's brothers' children) of the opposite sex are classed as *"kï"* (potential spouses), and their parents as potential mothers-in-law and fathers-in-law.

[1]Randy Smith, personal communication.

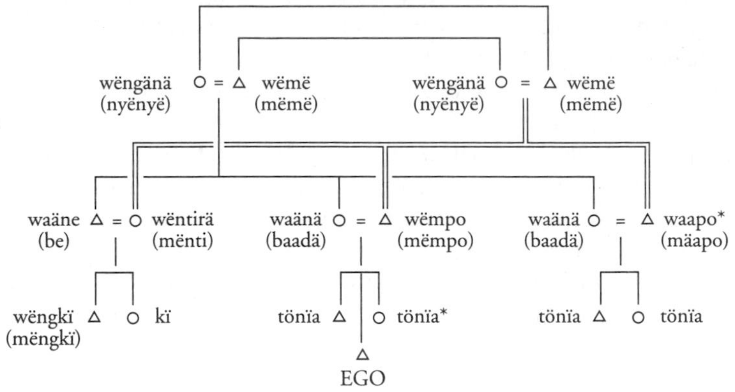

Figure 6.1   Waorani Kinship Terminology
1. Reference terms are given first; address terms in parentheses.
* Siblings are further distinguished by sex and relative age: younger brother *(biwï)*, younger sister *(biwïngkɨ)*, older brother *(mïmö)*, and older sister *(mëngä)*.

People outside these groups are *waräni* (different people) or *wakabo* (different group), with whom there is no preexisting basis for any relations at all (unless, as was usually the case in the past, old vendettas remained active).

Marriages are arranged by parents, often without the knowledge of the children, and sometimes by one parent without the knowledge or consent of the other. They are formalized at the drinking feasts *(ëëmë)* that are hosted periodically by individual households. Runners are sent to invite neighboring kindreds for several days and nights of visiting, feasting, singing, dancing, and sex with classificatory cross cousins.

If a marriage is to be formalized, at some point during the feast a group of relatives will suddenly seize the couple (who may or may not know in advance), forcibly seat them side-by-side in a hammock, and link or tie their arms together. With that, they are married.

The potential for conflict arises from the conflicting interests of the father's and mother's kindreds. For example, a father may have agreed to marry his daughter to his sister's son. At some point during the feast, he may go outside to urinate and, when he returns, he finds that, in his absence, the girl has been married to his wife's brother's son.

The stakes in such conflicts over marriage rights were further intensified by the ongoing vendettas in which many potential spouses were killed. This also caused groups to disperse widely as they sought to hide from their enemies. All of this progressively limited the numbers of potential spouses available to each group. In some bands, in fact, most or all of their classificatory cross cousins were members of bands with whom vendettas were raging. The effect was that virtually every marriage left some group of "siblings" enraged, feeling cheated of a spouse that should have come to one of their kin.

RESIDENCE

Within these territorial/kinship groupings, settlements are widely dispersed. In the past, a typical hamlet consisted of one or two houses occupied by an extended family, usually consisting of a married couple, their unmarried children, and some of their married children (especially daughters), with their spouses and children. These kin/residence groupings still exist, sometimes as large extended family households, although they are now more likely to be represented by a cluster of nuclear family households.

Within a walk of an hour or two will be another similarly constituted household, occupied by a brother or cousin and his family. Lying farther out, perhaps a day's walk away, would be another, more distantly related, residence cluster, and so on. Individual families may shift residence among these hamlets over time, but these extended family clusters remain the primary units of social, political, and economic organization.

Since contact, settlements have tended to become larger and more permanent. When the first two Protestant missionaries arrived, they established their residence in a hamlet on the Tiwënö River, a headwater tributary of the Curaray. A clearing was soon made for an airstrip, and from here they launched their efforts to contact other bands.

As other groups were contacted, they were convinced to relocate to Tiwënö, where gardens had been prepared by earlier immigrants to support them until they could plant their own. Through the 1970s, groups continued to migrate to the reserve, leaving only a few scattered kindreds outside the reserve on the Cononaco, the lower Shiripuno, and the Yasuní rivers. That process soon began to reverse itself, however.

The danger in concentrating so vulnerable a population became apparent in 1969 when a polio epidemic swept the settlement at Tiwënö. The relatives of one victim blamed a suspected sorcerer and sought revenge. The intended victim was not at home when they raided his house, however, so they killed his son. On this occasion, the missionaries and other Waorani were able to convince the dead man's relatives not to take revenge and reignite the vendettas, which no one really wanted. Polio vaccine was quickly flown in from the United States and the epidemic soon ended, although it left 16 Waorani dead and a number of others with varying degrees of paralysis.

The dispersal out of Tiwënö was actually precipitated by a shooting. Wiba, one of the Waorani women who had lived on the outside and also one of the original converts to Christianity, became enraged over her husband's affair with another woman. When another man tried to intervene, she shot him, wounding him in the neck.

Since it was she who had been instrumental in bringing other bands to the reserve, beseeching them to abandon their vendettas, and assuring them that the violence was over, her resort to violence led other groups to fear that her people, the Upriver group, in whose traditional territory they were all living, might resume its vendettas against them. As it was explained to us,

> After this, Kiwa became afraid, now that Wiba had become angry again, that she and her group would kill him for his past spearings of her family members. Kiwa and his group made rafts and went to Wamönö. Then Dabeta went to Daiyönö and Kupë went

to Kiwarö. Old Paä stayed in Tïwënö until after his sister Akawo was speared and beaten to death, then he retreated to Kïrïmïnenö rather than retaliate.

After this incident, people began to disperse, establishing settlements that roughly recreated the traditional regional groupings. At the time of our most recent fieldwork in 1993, groups were reestablishing themselves in their traditional territories off the Protectorate on the Tiguino, the Shiripuno, and elsewhere.

Although many of those returning to their territories are the same people who left two decades ago, the intervening years have wrought some important changes: many of the men have worked for oil companies and some know how to operate outboard motors and chain saws. Most people have learned to handle money; many of their children have been to school. They have been proselytized by Christian missionaries and by Marxist politicians from other indigenous groups and other organizations, and some have married *kowudï*. Although they still may not understand the *kowudï,* they are no longer ignorant of their ways.

POLITICS: AUTHORITY AND SOCIAL CONTROL

Waorani society is egalitarian in the extreme and every residence group is completely autonomous. Within these groups, there are no headmen and no formal councils. Even within households and settlements there is no authority beyond individuals' powers of persuasion or coercion. There are no communal religious rituals or obligations and no clubs or other associations that might confer on some individuals authority over the actions of others.

Several women who had fled the vendettas and who returned after contact have been able to garner some influence by virtue of their roles as intermediaries between Waorani and the *kowudï,* and, as we saw in chapter 3, very recently there has been an attempt to organize a Waorani "tribal" government. (This incipient organization is discussed at greater length in chapter 10.) With these minimal exceptions, however, there are no institutional structures of any sort that confer on any person more authority than another, or authority over another.

Even within the extended family and residence group, individual autonomy is the norm. The authority of elders is limited to their ability to cajole and coerce. Even parents have little control over the actions of their children and cannot force them to do what they do not want to do.

One of our informants described to us the killing of her grandmother, to which she was a witness. Three young men, two brothers and a parallel cousin, speared the old woman, who was also *their* grandmother, as she lay in her hammock. According to our informant, the killers' father (who was the dead woman's son) was furious at the killing of his mother. "What did he do?" we asked. "Nothing," she replied, "What could he do? They are his sons" (in other words, his only recourse was homicide, and he couldn't kill his own sons).

In many societies lacking centralized authority, there are other institutions that cross-cut kindreds and limit autonomy by linking individuals into wider networks of obligations and responsibilities. Here, there are such no cross-cutting ties. With bilateral descent, there are no lineages or clans to provide a framework for wider social ties.

Since Waorani society lacks any pronounced gender dichotomy, there are none of the men's clubs that structure social relations in many Amazonian societies. Nor are there tutelary spirits, ancestor cults, or other religious beliefs to engender ritual obligations that could bond individuals into interdependent groups. In the final analysis, any individual's freedom of action is limited only by what others will tolerate.

ECONOMIC RELATIONS

There are also few economic obligations to limit individuals' freedom of action. In theory, and to a large extent in practice, one has a commonality of interest with *girïnäni,* the bilateral kindred, especially parents, siblings and classificatory siblings, and children. This core group of kin is also likely to constitute the residence group, within which cooperation and generalized reciprocity are the norm. In essence, day-to-day obligations, economic and otherwise, are limited to resident members of this group.

But even within the kindred, autonomy is the rule and active cooperation is minimal. Several years after her first contact, Elliot made a similar observation:

> Gikita was building a large house, requiring many heavy palm poles and tons of roof leaf. He had a strapping teen-age son, Kumi, who I noticed spent most of his time teasing and chasing younger boys, or simply sitting in the house. I asked Gikita why Kumi didn't share the work with him. "I told him to, but he said *'Bah!'* [I refuse]," was the reply. I never saw one man help another in any task unless it was something that would benefit both. If two men planned to live in the same house, then of course both men worked on it. Women, likewise, were responsible for their own families and had no community projects equivalent to the quilting party, where the work of all would benefit only one. They of course went together on fishing trips, and caught their own fish, but when they returned, each usually shared her catch with some of those who had not gone. (Elliot, 1961, p. 144)

Such sharing, however, encompasses only those in the immediate kindred; outside the household or house cluster, little or no sharing or cooperation takes place. Waorani assume that every person is capable of providing for himself or herself through hard work (and anyone who is unwilling to work hard is openly disparaged).

Since people have few responsibilities for one another, economic or otherwise, material transactions outside the immediate family are explicitly balanced. During our first study, for example, a widow who was running out of manioc in her own garden made arrangements to help another woman weed hers in return for the right to harvest manioc, a straightforward exchange of labor for food. Waorani assume that a woman who has no husband or son to hunt for her can always go to the river with fish poison and a dip net and get a few minnows to eat with her manioc. In any case, if anyone does not have enough to eat, it is his or her own problem (or, at most, the problem of his/her immediate kindred).

There is not even a common claim on the produce of group hunting and fishing activities. Fish poisoning, for example, is often done by a group; one or two people pound the *kömpago* roots to release the poison, then swish baskets of crushed roots through the water. As the poison flows downstream, fish begin to rise to the surface. As the fish rise to the surface, everyone in the fishing party plunges into the water and begins throwing fish onto the bank or scooping them up in baskets. When all have been retrieved, each person claims all the fish that he or she personally scooped up or threw out of the water.

Similarly, on two occasions when large numbers of peccaries (more than 10) were killed at one time and brought back to the hamlet to be butchered, the carcasses belonged to the families of the men who had killed them and the women who had helped carry them home. No meat was given to unrelated families in the settlement who had not participated in the hunt.

Nor does one person have responsibilities for another's well-being, or even his/her survival. Each person is responsible for himself or herself. During our first study, a woman from a settlement where we lived for several weeks was bitten by a snake while she was on a fishing expedition to another valley with a number of other people from her settlement. The rest of the group went on and completed their fishing before bringing her back to the settlement for treatment, by which time her leg was already extremely swollen. She barely survived, and then only because she was evacuated by MAF to the hospital at Shell when her breathing began to fail.

With few obligations to (or responsibilities for) others, there is little to constrain autonomy, and each person's self-interest is his or her primary concern. With no institutions conferring authority or otherwise imposing social control, there are no mechanisms for resolving disputes or for containing conflict. Any dispute has the potential to escalate into a homicidal confrontation, a potential that is well recognized by Waorani and acknowleged in the prayers in Christian communities exhorting those embroiled in conflict to "let go of their anger" and to avoid violence.

For the most part, however, these interlocking self-interests generate relatively few serious disputes and, on a day-to-day basis, life is seldom troubled by conflict and strife. People are outgoing, gregarious, and quick to laugh. One of the things that most surprised us was the typically amicable tone of community life.

MEN, WOMEN, AND SEXUALITY

As we have seen, Waorani social life involves no marked gender dichotomy. Gender relations are egalitarian, and there is no rigid sexual division of labor. In general, men hunt and women garden, but men often work in the gardens, and women hunt opportunistically, running game down and killing it with their machetes when the opportunity presents itself. On one occasion, Dïtë killed an agouti with her machete while she was working in her garden. Omëni had gone fishing that day, but had not been very successful. That evening, in the kitchen-house, she "needled" him, saying, "If it weren't for me, we wouldn't have any meat at all to eat today."

Both men and women fish, although men are more likely to utilize spears and explosives, and women to use hand nets and poisons. Both use hooks and lines when they are available.

A woman carries home a peccary killed by her husband during a group hunt.

In contrast to many Amazonian societies, men and women are not seen as fundamentally different in character. There is no dichotomy in ideal personality or temperament. In many warring societies, there is a marked contrast in the ideals of masculinity and femininity, with masculinity often defined in terms of courage and aggressiveness and in contrast to a feminine ideal of passivity and submissiveness. Among Waorani, however, there is no such contrast between male and female. Both men and women are autonomous, independent, self-confident, and assertive. Both pride themselves on being capable, effective, and physically strong. Women are not, as is the case in many hunting societies, seen as polluting or defiling to men or to their activities, and there is no menstrual seclusion. Thus there is no ideological basis for the men's clubs or other kinds of physical or emotional separation of the sexes common elsewhere in Amazonia.

Men are more likely than women to be killers, but women often accompanied men on raids, and some women have killed. The women of the group we lived with actively took part in the killing of the missionaries on the Curaray, helping to hold them while the men speared them. Old Dyiko, the woman who named us, reportedly accompanied her brother on spearing raids when she was young. Both men and women are believed to kill with sorcery.

Both men and women are also exuberantly sexual. Rights of sexual access to spouse's siblings and to siblings' spouses (all of whom are *ki*) means that both men and women have the opportunity for robust and diverse sex lives. One of the attractions of the drinking feasts is the opportunities that they provide for sex with *kï* from other communities.

For men, at least, it doesn't really seem to matter whether the cross cousin is male or female since, as we saw in chapter 3, homosexual sex is acceptable and quite common. Several years after Fr. Labaca was killed, his diary, in which he had recorded his early contacts with the Yasuní River band, was published. He reported his first encounter with the Waorani, one that occurred when they invaded an oil camp where he had come in hopes of contacting them. The Waorani raiders forced the oil workers to perform fellatio on them. On other occasions, when he was sleeping in Waorani houses, he reported that the teenaged boys tried to "excite" him.

Although we can not say that female homosexuality does not occur, we saw no indication of it nor did we hear accounts of it. Among men, however, it seems that, when it comes to sex, the gender of the partner is largely irrelevant.

THE NONMATERIAL WORLD:
MAGIC, SORCERY, AND CHRISTIANITY

Religion does a great many things in societies, and one of them is to embody, in "concrete" form, abstract ideas about the nature of reality. Someone once said that "man creates God in his own image," meaning that people's conceptions of a nonmaterial world, a world they can never perceive and experience directly, must be based on what they already know about the everyday world. Thus, by examining a people's conceptions of the "supernatural" world, we can gain some insight into their understandings of the "natural" world.

One of the things that impressed us most strongly was the relative unimportance of the nonmaterial world to the Waorani, compared with the Semai. For Waorani, there is relatively little concern with "supernatural" beings and forces. Wëngöngï, the creator who originally set the world in motion, now has little role in human affairs, although among Christians he has been assimilated to the Christian God and is the object of prayers (see below). Human actions are not contingent upon or constrained by more powerful beings or forces. There are few animistic beliefs (i.e., beliefs in nature "spirits"), relatively little magic, and relatively few taboos.

The one notable exception to this focus on the mundane world is sorcery, but even there, although the sorcerer employs nonmaterial animal familiars to implement his evil intentions, the murderous hostility is entirely human and this-worldly.

The relative insignificance of "supernatural" beings beyond witches' familiars means that there is little in the way of communal rituals to link people together. Neighboring peoples use hallucinogenic drugs, especially *ayahuasca* (*Banisteriopsis muricata*), to communicate with the spirit world in public rituals for the benefit of the community, especially for treating illness. Among Waorani, however, the same drug (*mïï*) is said to be regularly consumed only by solitary sorcerers who use it to contact their familiars and to work their individual evil. Moreover, since only the sorcerer who caused an illness can cure it, even attempting a cure would be an admission of guilt.

Magic

The anthropologist Bronislaw Malinowski long ago recognized that the gap between the outcomes a people seek to achieve and the limits of their knowledge and technology is often bridged by magical rituals. The narrowness of the gap between means and ends in Waorani life is evidenced by the relative unimportance of magical practices on a day-to-day basis; there is little place for magic since, with relatively few exceptions, their knowledge and technology are adequate to their needs in a world that they see as largely under their control.

This is not to say that magic is entirely lacking. One ritual we witnessed occurred one afternoon when Mïngkaiyï returned from a hard day's work clearing his swidden, bringing with him a bundle of stinging nettles. He went directly to his mother-in-law's house, where he, his mother-in-law and his sister-in-law seized his young nephew, about eight years old, and switched him over his chest, back, and legs with the nettles.

The boy's skin was immediately covered with large stinging welts, and his screams were greeted with laughter from the adults. When we asked what was going on, he told us that switching the boy with the nettles after he himself had been working exceptionally hard, would transfer his capacity for hard work to his nephew.

Another day, a hunter killed a peccary and the women of his houschold took it down to the river to butcher. As the carcass lay half submerged in the water, Dïtë took both her infant grandson's hands in hers and pressed them against the pig's side. When we asked why she had done that, she said it was so that the child would grow up to be a good hunter and would not be afraid of peccaries.

It is worth noting that both these rituals have as their goal the development of an individual capacity for hard and dangerous work, a quality whose effect, in a society structured like this one, is to increase children's ability to achieve and manifest as adults the valued social traits of autonomy, independence, and self-reliance.

Another focus for magic is, as Malinowski might have predicted, snakebites. These are situations where indigenous technology *is* inadequate to control outcomes and, consequently, there are a number of rituals and taboos associated with them. Burying a bit of one's hair in the mud of the trail will ward off snakebite; when someone is bitten, close kin must not consume banana drink or the affected limb will turn black; close relatives must not hunt with blowpipes or the victim will die, and so on.

Hunting, on the other hand, is relatively unproblematic and there is little magic associated with it. One notable exception is hunting songs. These songs can call specific kinds of game to the hunter, and they are sometimes sung the night before a hunt, especially if there is a special need for that particular hunt to be successful, such as when a feast has been scheduled.

Taboos

In some societies, Semai being a case in point, the existence of taboos reflects a concern with warding off unseen dangers and placating powerful forces. Among the Waorani there are relatively few taboos, and those that do exist seem, for the most part, to be rather lightly held and easily abandoned.

After a day of hard work in his garden, a man and his mother-in-law whip his nephew with stinging nettles to transfer to the youngster his capacity for hard work and endurance.

Traditionally, there were taboos on eating a number of animals and fish; many of these, however, were creatures that could not have been consistently taken with the available technology. Deer, tapir, and white-lipped peccaries were all taboo, but these are all large solitary animals on which the blowgun is ineffective (and at least two of them—deer and tapir—are also believed to be sorcerers' familiars). Lacking bows and arrows or firearms to shoot them from a distance, or dogs to hold them at bay so they could be speared, it is unlikely that Waorani hunters would have been able consistently to take them with spears alone. When new technology—shotguns and dogs—made it practical to hunt them, the taboos were quickly abandoned (cf. Yost, 1981).

Similarly, the huge catfish was taboo, as were turtle eggs. These, however, are primarily resources of the major rivers, which Waorani tended to avoid. Like the taboos on some terrestrial animals, none of these taboos seem to be central to Waorani ideology or cosmology, since they too were abandoned rather readily once people began to exploit the resources of the larger rivers.

Another set of taboos seems to be more stable; all predators—jaguars, ocelots, birds of prey, snakes, and so on—are taboo to eat. We suspect that this is, at least in part, a reflection of a fundamental ordering of the Waorani world into predators and prey. Waorani clearly identify themselves with the former and not with the latter.

A conversation that Carole had with Dïtë brought this out clearly. We sorely missed green vegetables in our diet and, when we lived with the Semai, we got a significant portion of our vitamins and protein from the boiled young leaves of the manioc plant. One day Carole asked Dïtë if Waorani ever ate manioc leaves. "Leaves?" she said incredulously. "We don't eat leaves; *monkeys* eat leaves" [and, of course, we eat monkeys].

A baby boy's hands are pressed to a dead peccary so that he will not be afraid of peccaries and will grow up to be a good hunter.

Waorani do kill jaguars, ocelots, anacondas, and other predators for their skins, which they can sell in the frontier towns, and for their teeth and claws, with which, made into necklaces, they adorn themselves and their children. The flesh of these and other predators, however, is left to rot. Cannibalism, eating the flesh of those like oneself, was, of course, one of the most repulsive and feared characteristics of the hated *kowudï*.

Omens

The pragmatic focus on the mundane, on the here and now, is also indicated by the relative unimportance of omens, signs that can transcend time and space and foretell the future or indicate distant happenings. Omens, like magic, can indicate uncertainty and a lack of control. Significantly, most of the relatively few omens that we did encounter, are concerned with human malevolence and violence.

One afternoon, as we were talking with Ompudë and Dyiko, it began to thunder. Ompudë explained that "loud thunder, the *duuräni* [old ones] said, meant that somebody had been speared." Then she recalled that when her grandmother, Akawowodi (dead Akawo), was speared, it suddenly started to thunder and rain.

Dyiko pointed toward the east, where the thunder seemed to originate, and said maybe the Tagëiri were spearing. Ompudë said maybe they had killed somebody from The Company. Then she said that thunder in the east means *kowudï* have been killed and thunder in the west means Waorani have been speared. (People's accounts of specific spearing raids almost always recall the occurrence of a thunderstorm sometime during the raid.)

Jungle cats are killed for their skins and because they prey on the settlement's chickens and pets.

On another occasion, when there was a halo around the sun, someone said it was a sign that someone had been speared. Yet another evening, Dïtë and Carole were looking at a red sunset, and Dïtë said "Blood standing in the sky; tomorrow they will have died."

Certain animals and birds are omens of sorcery, the other primary manifestation of human malevolence. When the bird called *"pugëngga"* calls at night, other groups are angry and a snakebite or other attack by sorcery may soon follow.

Sorcery

If the creator and other supernatural beings are not very important to most Waorani most of the time, the same certainly cannot be said of sorcerers and sorcery. As we noted in chapter 2, there really are no "accidents" or "bad luck" and few, if any, "natural" deaths here. Serious illnesses, injuries, snakebites, and most deaths are all the consequences of human rage and malevolence deployed through the practice of sorcery.

A case of sorcery that occurred in our home settlement shortly before we arrived for our second project was recounted and explained to us by the sister and brother-in-law of the "victim." According to their account, Mïmä, whose garden was exhausted, asked Umï, daughter of Omënɨ and Dɨtë, to let her harvest manioc from her garden. Umï refused and the old woman, enraged at this refusal, went to Dyiko, who has long been suspected of sorcery, and asked her to bewitch the young woman.

Here, as in many societies, social divisions often become foci for accusations of sorcery. Recall that the two women accused in the account that follows are the two outsiders from the Downriver and Ridge groups; only their marriages to Gïngata link them and some of their descendants to the kindred in whose traditional territory they are all living. We present this account at length because it gives a sense of Waorani perceptions of the dynamics of sorcery and illustrates the internally consistent logic of sorcery accusations:

> Almost everyone in our families had gone to Akarö [an alternate settlement with swidden fields] except for Ompudë and her husband, Mïngkaiyɨ, and Ompudë's unmarried sisters, Umï and Gakämö. Umï was tending Dɨtë's fields, which were abundant. Mïmä's bunch had eaten her manioc while it was still immature and now they were all hungry. Mïmä was almost dead of hunger, and she asked Ompudë for some manioc and Ompudë gave it to her; then she asked Umï for manioc and Umï refused, saying that, since she had been sick, she had not made a field for herself and she would not give away food from her mother, Dɨtë's, field.
>
> So Mïmä, angry, went to Dyiko and asked her to do sorcery. The next morning, Umï felt a big sting, like a scorpion, while she was sound asleep. No scorpion was found but, by evening, she was very sick. That night the *togönömönyɨ*, a bird that is a sorcerer's familiar, came onto her blanket and pecked. Saturday and Sunday she was still sick. "Why is she so sick?" they wondered, when there was no sign of a sting or bite. Umï said, "I feel like *para* grubs are eating my heart and liver!"
>
> Mïngkaiyɨ said, "Go out to the hospital" and Umï agreed. So they called for a plane to come in and take her out to the hospital at Shell-Mera. At about this same time, little four- or five-year-old Kënto was reacting at Akarö just as if he had polio and had to be carried home by his grandmother, Dɨtë, [who is also Umï's mother]. When the plane came, Dɨtë, Umï and Kënto all went out. At the hospital, the doctors could find nothing wrong with Umï and gave her no medicine. The doctors said to Umï, "It is one of your people's illnesses; your witchcraft it is," they said. Kënto had a real illness and they gave him medicine and sent home pills with him and, after a while, he recovered.
>
> After they came back, Umï was still very sick, and she spent most of the time semi-conscious. Her parents notified Kuba in Tönyëmpadï on the radio. Kuba told Dyiko, his paternal grandmother, to stop her sorcery. Kawia, Kuba's father and Dyiko's son, came to get her and take her to Tönyëmpadï. [This was undoubtedly a prudent precaution, since she was now branded a witch, even by her own grandson.]
>
> For months Umï was still sick, so they took her to Duma, an Oruna sorcerer who lives on the edge of the headwaters of the Curaray. Mïngkaiyɨ told her to go. They gave Duma a canoe as payment for his services. They had to whip Umï with stinging nettles to get her up and walking to climb the ridge between the valley of the Tɨwënö and the valley of the Dyuuiwënö River [which feeds into the Curaray]. Her parents, Omënɨ and Dɨtë, took her to the sorcerer. Duma is a good sorcerer who always does well and doesn't become angry.
>
> Duma drank *mïï* [*ayahuasca*] to see who had bewitched Umï and said that it was Dyiko. Omënɨ and Dɨtë took Umï to Tönyëmpadï so that Dyiko could perform the ritual to release Umï from her spell [only the witch who has executed the witchcraft can undo the harm]. But when they arrived at Tönyëmpadï, Umï refused to enter Dyiko's presence because she was so afraid. So her parents brought her home.

Since she still wasn't well, her sister, Ompudë, and her brother-in-law, Mïngkaiyï, took her back to Tönyëmpadï to be cured by Dyiko. They did this in secret; no one else was there. They had to use Paä (Umï's grandmother's brother, an old man famous for spearing sorcerers) as a threat to get Dyiko to perform the ceremony. Everyone knew that Dyiko had done this before; before the missionaries had come, she had witched Mïnyïmöwodi [the dead Mïnyïmo] by sending a wasp to sting her; she died, and Dïtë's sister had to raise her toddler.

Mïngkaiyï told Dyiko that he knew she was a witch and Dyiko shook with fear. "Properly, properly do it," he ordered her, and she agreed. Umï took off her outer clothing and sat down in the doorway in her underpants. With special leaves, herbs, and mosses, Dyiko poured heated water over Umï and held her tight. Umï said that her heart felt like the grubs flew straight out of it; she felt released. This ceremony went on for three hours and then Dyiko told her that she had to do it once a day for a month. Mothers with babes in arms could not come near her at first, or she would die. Dyiko told her all the foods she couldn't eat. Even now, she cannot eat these foods; she ate a little fish called a *bidekata* and was very sick again.

Mïngkaiyï said, "Umï would be dead if it wasn't for me. I had been working for The Company and gave the Oruna witch, Duma, 60,000 sucres [about $30], an adze and lots of smoked meat and fish." Mïngkaiyï paid him after Umï was well again.

Dyiko tried to move back to Tïwënö after this incident, but her daughter, Ongkayï, refused, saying she was a witch and that she would not feed her. So another son living in Kiwarö came to get her to live with them. It is well that she moved away for good, because I am very afraid of her for my wife and children.

Jaguar Shamans

There is, at least in theory, a distinction between a jaguar shaman (*mïnyï mëmpo*) and a sorcerer (*irö*). A *mïnyï mëmpo* (literally, "jaguar father") is a shaman who can call jaguars to help locate herds of peccaries. He drinks *mïï* (*ayahuasca*) only once, when he is young. Thereafter, he can go into trance (*dyïwë mïnyï*, literally: "jaguar drunk/trance") to summon jaguars to find peccaries. The jaguar will locate peccaries and drive them toward the *mïnyï mëmpo's* hamlet, where the hunters will find them.

A sorcerer (*irö*), however, is one who uses magic to cause other people to be bitten by snakes or to sicken and die. He/she drinks *mïï* whenever he/she wants to do sorcery, and uses the trance to contact his/her spirit familiars (*wïnëiri*), animal spirits, of which there are many types. As Imäa explained it to us,

> The tapir, they say, causes abscesses. The tapir is a *wïnë*, a sorcerer's familiar. The deer is a sorcerer's familiar, they say. For example, this is how the deer is a familiar: when they get angry, those people [sorcerers] cook *mïï*; like the coffee you two drink, they boil it. Wanting another person to die, raging and wanting to do sorcery, they boil *mïï* and drink it. To that person's presence the deer goes and the person does not see it. The deer goes right to the person's back and touches it, and inside he is already dead. At dawn, when he wakes up, the person feels something and cries out: "Yeee." Even if he takes medicine, he will die, they say. Like that the deer is the sorcerer's familiar.

Other common *wïnëiri* are scorpions, snakes, and wasps; they bite or sting the victim. "The *irö*," we were told, "keeps *wïnëiri* like we keep our pet monkeys. We do not see the *wïnëiri*, but after drinking *mïï*, the *irö* sees them."

Although *wïnëiri* are the vehicles for sorcery, the anger and malevolence that motivate it are thoroughly human. In fact, the sorcerer stands between the material, human world and the nonmaterial world. With the help of *ayahuasca,* he bridges the gap between the two in order to perpetrate his evil.

Given that, it is not surprising to find that, while there may be a distinction in theory between shamans and sorcerers, in practice they seem to be indistinguishable. We know of only one person who openly claims to be a *mïnyï mëmpo,* and he is universally believed to be a sorcerer as well.

Christianity

The first modern sustained peaceful contacts were initiated by Protestant missionaries, and a good many Waorani, mostly on the Protectorate, now consider themselves to be Christians. Some of the beliefs and values promoted by the missionaries—especially the belief that there is a God and that he abhors killing—have been fairly widely accepted.

For some smaller number, Christianity has become the anchor for a new identity and a new value set premised on a commitment to nonviolence. The missionaries speak of "changed hearts," and for those who have truly internalized these new values, the metaphor seems wholly appropriate. Our nearest neighbor, Omënï, comes immediately to mind; although he has been involved in the killings of a number of people, including the missionaries on the Curaray, we find it impossible to imagine circumstances where he would kill again. He and some others have indeed foresworn the old ways. Constantly urging conciliation and the renunciation of anger and violence, he and others like him are an important moral force, especially on the Protectorate.

Even for most nominally Christian Waorani, however, Christian theology and ideology have not penetrated deeply, and they consist, for most, of little more than a few Bible stories and a belief in a God who deplores killing. Other beliefs and values promoted by the missionaries have had little impact: Charity is notably lacking, polygyny and infanticide persist (although at reduced levels), and extramarital sex remains a popular recreational activity. For many Waorani, however, being peaceful and being Christian are indissolubly linked; being Christian means, in the words of the patriarch of the Upriver band, a renowned killer, "we are not Aucas; we don't spear any more."

Several of the settlements hold regular Sunday church services. In all but Tönyëmpadï, where Rachael Saint, the only missionary living permanently on the Protectorate, made her home until her death in 1994, these were entirely under the control and direction of Waorani. Individuals, both men and women, lead prayers and recount Bible stories. If there have been rumors of a dispute somewhere, prayers are offered to keep it from turning violent. Prayers may also be offered for the recovery of victims of illness, injuries, and snakebites. As Yost (1981) also observed, however, the concern with violence is clearly the focus of the entire ritual.

The church service is one of the few events that bring the entire community together, and being Christian and attending the weekly services are powerful and public symbolic statements of a commitment to the new "civilized" identity. But this new identity is, even for most of these self-identified Christians, only a superficial veneer over the pre-contact consciousness, an overlay on the traditional value and belief system rather than a replacement of it (cf. Yost, 1981; Robarchek & Robarchek, 1990). Many others, especially in the generation that has grown to adulthood since contact, have completely rejected any identification with Christianity.

Culture: Information and World View

We argued at the outset that social behavior of the sorts that we have been examining—economic, political, religious, and so on—is organized and regulated by the information available to the members of society. This historically derived and socially transmitted information constitutes a more-or-less systematized body of knowledge about the world and how to live in it—what anthropologists call a society's "culture."

Culture is, in a very real sense, a society's theory about the world and how it works. Like a scientific theory, its ultimate "truth" is less important than its utility; it must serve the needs of the people who use it as both a map of the world and a plan for effective action in it. It defines the essential entities and processes in the world, specifies their characteristics, and describes how they are related. Just as physics defines the physical world in terms of atoms and molecules, charm and quarks, a culture theory defines a society's world in terms of human nature, sorcery, spirits, kinds of animals, heavenly bodies, and so on.

Unlike scientific theories, however, culture theories are all-encompassing. Where a scientific theory only explains some small part of the world, a culture theory explains everything: the movement of the moon and stars, the growth of plants and animals, the actions of human beings, good and bad luck, even life and death.

Within this complex and comprehensive knowledge structure, individual human lives take on meaning and comprehensibility. An individual's subjective experience is like a single piece of an enormous jigsaw puzzle—meaningless by itself, it takes on meaning and purpose from its relationship to the whole. Thus, people make sense of and attach meaning to their own experiences in terms of the cultural knowledge system in which those experiences are imbedded.

Organizing and giving structure to this vast body of knowledge is a set of underlying assumptions. If culture is a theory, these are its axioms. These fundamental assumptions and premises constitute a society's world view, which includes basic beliefs and values—core assumptions about what is and what should be—assumptions about the nature of human beings, the world around them, and the relations of one to the other.

A people's world view assumptions are seldom available to them for conscious reflection and contemplation; rather, they are implicit in their knowledge systems. Still, they inform and give structure to conscious thought and reflection; they comprise a kind of nonconscious knowledge. Like grammatical and phonological knowledge which, although ordinarily unavailable to conscious reflection, organizes and structures a people's linguistic behavior, so their world view assumptions organize and structure their social behavior.

Because it is implicit in thought and action, world view must be drawn out by the observer, abstracted from observations of people's behavior, from their voiced attitudes and values, their responses to situations, their religious beliefs, their medical practices, and so on. One of the central challenges for an ethnographer is the attempt to move from his or her world into the world of the people studied, to begin to understand it in terms of their concepts and assumptions, to come to see it through their eyes. This is when the method of participant observation begins to pay dividends—when, through participation in and contemplation of the experiences of daily life, the premises upon which it rests begin to emerge into consciousness.

As we immersed ourselves in the community, we began to realize that the world Waorani look out on is very different from what we had expected. On reflection, it seems that, because of the many similarities that *we* saw in the worlds of Semai and Waorani, we had, largely unconsciously, expected Waorani world view to be somewhat similar to what we had experienced living with the Semai, who saw themselves in a hostile and dangerous world that was largely beyond human control (Robarchek, 1980). Instead, we found a view of the world and human beings that is much more like our own Western, and especially American, conception.

We identified six fundamental clusters of Waorani world view presuppositions:

1. The world exists for humans to exploit. It is not inherently threatening, dangerous, or hostile to humans or human intentions. It offers few dangers beyond the human threats of sorcery and spearing.
2. People are powerful and effective. They are fully capable of controlling a world that is tractable to human purposes, and thus are able to control their own experiences and destinies.
3. People are independent and autonomous. A person should be self-reliant, and any person's survival and well-being are primarily his or her own responsibilities.
4. People are equal, politically and economically. No one can compel another to do anything, except through the threat or application of force. There are no rank distinctions on the basis of gender, kinship, group affiliation or wealth; therefore everyone should be equal in terms of *all* desired good, material or immaterial.
5. There are fundamental differences between Waorani and *kowudï* ("people" and "foreigners"), and between *girïnäni* ("kin") and *waräni* ("nonkin"). Only among a fairly restricted set of *girïnäni* are there obligations and responsibilities; all the rest are actual or potential enemies.
6. Since the world is under human control, all misfortune is the consequence of deliberate human actions growing out of rage, envy, and malevolence.

Waorani culture defines a world where people are not subject to stronger or more powerful beings and forces, a world that people can master and turn to their own ends. The vast forest poses little threat and evokes no fear; rather, it exists to be exploited for human purposes. Lone individuals and couples go off to hunt and fish, sometimes camping alone in the forest for days, something that would be unthinkable—a sign of lunacy, in fact—for a Semai.

Although the region abounds with venomous snakes, Waorani run heedlessly through the forest, even at dawn and dusk, knowing that sooner or later they will be bitten, but confident that they will survive. It is an environment over all of which, except the human component, they have mastery, and within which individuals are ultimately responsible for themselves.

The Waorani case is unusual, perhaps unique, in that, until their isolation was breached by missionaries, their cultural schema was insulated from significant inputs of new information. Isolated by both warfare and language, their cultural knowledge system was virtually closed to new information for a century or more. It fed only on itself, and on the experiences of Waorani individuals, experiences that could only occur and be interpreted and understood within the framework of that preexisting view of the world.

7 / The Individual/ Psychological Context

CULTURE, SELF, AND EMOTION

The collective repository of that body of information that we are calling "culture" is in the minds of the individual members of the society. Another way of saying the same thing is that the sum of the knowledge of a society's members constitutes the information that the society has at its disposal—its culture.

Societies are, of course, composed of *interacting* individuals, individuals who must know how to behave in accordance with other people's expectations. Unlike many other animals, however, we humans are born with little or no genetically encoded knowledge of how to behave. Compare the social insects that have so impressed sociobiologists: they come into the world fully equipped with a genetically encoded map of their social world and a plan for action in it; they require no training to know how to communicate, how to interact and cooperate to perform their tasks, when to reproduce or not reproduce, and so on.

We, however, come into the world with neither map nor plan, but we must rapidly acquire both because we will soon have to know and be able to perform the roles required by the sequence of social statuses that we quickly begin to assume: son or daughter, brother or sister, student, friend, hunter, gardener, husband, wife, and so on. We must, in short, incorporate within ourselves an individual schema that includes both a map of the world and a plan for action in it—what we earlier called a "personality."

Fortunately, since every human being is born into a preexisting social group with its own body of cultural knowledge, we do not have to discover all of that information for ourselves; we can simply learn the cultural information relevant to our particular social positions.

That learned information includes, of course, those world view assumptions and values that inform the cultural knowledge system. These become central components of individuals' knowledge systems, their personalities.

Although by definition there is a relatively high degree of congruence between most individuals' beliefs and feelings and society's cognitive and affective norms, the two are not identical: "culture" and "personality" are not the same things.

First of all, they exist on different analytical levels: culture is a society's map and plan for action; personality is an individual's map and plan.

Second, as we have seen, culture precedes any individual personality; all individuals are born into social worlds that are already culturally constituted. Thus, much of the information incorporated into an individual's schema comes from that preexisting body of cultural knowledge. Just as individuals enculturated in a particular linguistic context acquire the information and the behavioral habits that allow them to speak the language spoken around them, so also do they acquire other information about their world and habits of dealing with it. These socially shared aspects of individual knowledge systems—what some researchers have called "modal personality," "social personality," or "basic personality"—represent widely (but not necessarily universally) shared information about a particular culturally constituted reality, the people who inhabit it, and ways of dealing with it.

Thus, the cultural assumptions that we called "world view" (along with a great deal of additional cultural knowledge) are embodied in individuals' personalities, in their beliefs, attitudes, values, habits, expectations, motives, and goals. These represent individuals' assumptions about the nature of their reality and about how to deal with it. They tell us what people, including ourselves, are like, what the world is like, how we should feel about it, what is good and to be sought after, what is bad and to be avoided, and so on.

THE CULTURAL CONSTRUCTION OF SELF

A crucial part of the cultural construction of reality at the individual level is the cultural construction of self. Waorani cultural construction of self and personhood stresses, as we have seen, individualism, autonomy, self-reliance, and egalitarianism. Both men and women are expected to be, and for the most part are, independent, self-reliant and self-sufficient. While there is food sharing and cooperation between spouses, among parents and children, and among real and classificatory siblings, a person's well-being and survival are ultimately his or her own responsibility.

Even within these kindreds, support is conditional on one's own capacity to be self-reliant: The elderly, when they became a burden, were often allowed to starve or were even speared to death by their own kin. A man partially paralyzed during the polio epidemic that struck shortly after contact starved to death when his wife refused to feed him. Another woman allowed her grandmother, who had adopted and raised her after her parents were speared, to starve to death when she could no longer get food for herself. When raiders struck, men often abandoned their wives, and women their children, as they fled into the forest.

Our neighbor Omëni recounted his abandonment by his mother:

My mother now lives at Pavacachi [a Quichua village far downriver on the Curaray]. Oruga [a Quichua woman who married a Waorani] said she saw her there. She is married to an *Oruna*. She left after Kënto was speared by Möipa. She was angry and fearful over that; she said, "My brother is dead and I am going to go to the place of the *kowudï*." Having said that, she left permanently. She feared that she too would be speared. From her sleeping place, abandoning me when I was in my early childhood, she fled into the forest. She went empty-handed, taking nothing. She was pregnant when she fled.

As the foregoing makes clear, Waorani self-interest and self-reliance can take some extreme forms. For example, and in contrast to nearly every other society known, Waorani women typically give birth alone and unattended. When a woman goes into labor, she cuts a slit in an old hammock and hangs it in the house or at the edge of the forest. She places some banana leaves on the ground beneath the hammock and, straddling it, delivers the child herself.

During our first field project, Ompudë gave birth while her husband was out of the hamlet working for The Company. She and her young daughter had gathered firewood the day before and had cooked manioc and plantains. While she was in labor, her three children, aged about 8, 5, and 3, gathered breadfruit seeds and roasted them to eat. No mother, sister, or aunt—all of whom lived nearby—came with food or help of any other kind, and no such assistance was expected or needed.

As a young wife, she had given birth to her first child on a jungle trail as she and her kin were returning from their secondary homestead a day's walk from the main settlement. About midway along the trail home, she went into labor, and her grandmother, mother, aunts, and sisters continued on their way. Accompanied only by her young husband, she delivered the baby herself and then walked on to the main settlement.

Cultural values such as self-reliance are, of course, ideals and, as such, they are the standards against which individuals are judged, both by their neighbors and by themselves. People see themselves evaluated in the eyes of (and through the responses of) others, and they come to evaluate themselves in terms of how badly or well they approximate these ideals. Cultural ideals thus become individuals' ideals, defining central components of their self-images. Thus, Waorani individuals are typically autonomous, self-reliant, confident, and pragmatic; they see themselves living in a world they feel fully competent to control and exploit.

We were struck by our discovery that there is not, in fact, any simple linguistic expression for the concept of the inability to do something—for "I can't!" One can say *"ëëntï gorämaï ïmopa,"* which could be translated: "I can't carry [it]," but which literally means "carrying not I am," implying "I refuse to carry [it]," or "I don't want to carry [it]." Another common construction is of the sort *"eröng ketï ëëntï goboï,"* literally "how doing [it] could I carry [it]?"

Neither of these constructions, however, quite implies the sense of helplessness conveyed by "I can't!" While anthropologists have long been wary of drawing conclusions about culture from purely linguistic data (vocabulary, grammar, syntax, and so on), at the very least, it seems that, for Waorani, the idea of being helpless and unable to accomplish one's objectives is not one that often requires straightforward expression.

The Waorani egalitarian assumption, manifested socially in political and economic equality, also has implications at the individual level in relation to autonomy. Individuals are unwilling to concede authority to anyone, and no one can be forced to do anything. It can also be seen in the normative assumption that no one should have more of anything than anyone else. From the perspective of any individual, this implies: "No one should have anything that I don't have."

THE CULTURAL CONSTITUTION OF EMOTION: RAGE

A cultural knowledge system not only has implications for how individuals think about the world, it also influences how they *feel* about it. The cultural emphasis on egalitarianism and on the primacy, autonomy, and effectiveness of the self has psychological implications—both cognitive and affective—as well as implications for social action.

Such cultural assumptions, incorporated as individual ideals, not only describe how things *are,* they also, as we have seen, define how things *should* be. Their violation contradicts the natural, proper, moral order of things and calls into question the basic assumptions and values that give life its meaning, stability and coherence. For Waorani the appropriate emotional response to such violations is homicidal rage: *piïntï* —"angering"/"raging."

Autonomy

Where the autonomous self is paramount, any interference with that autonomy and effectiveness violates the image and expectation of a self that is in control of its own experience, and is likely to be felt as an assault on the self itself.

It is tempting to use the word "frustration" to label what we are describing, but that term carries too much theoretical baggage. In the Frustration-Aggression Theory of violence, "a frustration" is taken to be any interference with a goal-directed activity, a situation that triggers the emotion of anger, which generates an aggressive response.

Such a view of "frustration" is not very useful here, first, because it includes any sort of interference with a goal, and second, because it entails a conception of emotion, specifically of anger, as part of a "pre-packaged" response sequence that is triggered by, but otherwise independent of, the context in which it is elicited. Neither of those assumptions apply to the Waorani case.[1]

One of the things that most impressed us while we were living with the Waorani was their typically good humor, even in the face of what would usually be considered frustration. Many "frustrations," as we ordinarily think of them—a man has spent a week building the structure for a new house and a storm blows it down; a woman slips and falls and dumps the basket of plantains she has carried for a mile; a flood washes away half of a woman's manioc garden—provoked not anger, but laughter, both by bystanders and by the "victims."

Elisabeth Elliot made a similar observation shortly after the first peaceful contact:

> If the Auca is indifferent to the sufferings of others (and perhaps he is not so indifferent as he appears to us), he is also indifferent to his own. He can laugh when he hurts himself. He does not pity himself. To be free from self-pity is to be well on the way to adulthood. (Elliot, 1961, p. 129)

For Waorani, it seems, it is not simply the interference with a goal-directed activity that provokes rage. Rather, it is active *human* infringement of one's autonomy

---

[1]They do not apply in the Semai case either: see Robarchek, 1977, 1979.

and the resulting experience of helplessness and powerlessness, that is, the inability to be effective and in control of one's experiences. A sibling is shot and killed when a raid goes wrong; a sorcerer causes a child to die; a suitor's marriage plans are blocked when an old woman objects to the proposed marriage of her granddaughter—these kinds of situations are seen as deliberate assaults by another person on the autonomy of the self, and they are the kinds of incidents that precipitate homicidal rage (each of these, in fact, *did* result in one or more killings).

Questioning Ompudë about a fairly recent killing, we got the following explanation:

"In regard to Gämï, her grandchildren wanted to marry and Gämï refused. Angry, they speared her and she died. Her grandson said, 'Like that grandmother refuses, and I will kill her.' Her grandchildren wanting to marry, they speared Gämï."

"Why did the grandmother refuse?" we asked.

"The grandmother, why might she have refused? [meaning "who knows why?"] She told them: 'Do not marry!' For that reason they killed her and she died. Even though she was their own grandmother, they cut her head off and put it on a stake and threw her body into the river. Like that they did it."

On another occasion, we heard that a man in another settlement was angry and threatening to spear bystanders because his daughter had left and gone to the outside, probably to become a prostitute.

In all of these cases, the concept of "frustration" as it is typically understood would ignore the crucial feature for the Waorani—one person's deliberate infringement of another's autonomy. In so doing, it also ignores the crucial role of cultural and individual values and assumptions in giving such events their emotional and motivational power.

The conception of emotion implicit in the Frustration-Aggression Theory is similarly deficient. It sees emotion generally, and anger specifically, as something that exists, independent of the culturally defined contexts in which it occurs.

We found, in contrast, that the experience of an emotion, in this case of anger/rage, is a part of an individual's evaluation and definition of a situation in terms of a set of cultural values and assumptions. Emotion, then, is a function not only of the "objective" situation (e.g., of some "frustrating" event), but of the whole person—including his or her culturally structured history and learned response patterns—in interaction with an environment that is, itself, culturally constituted. The experience of emotion is among other things a part of the process of making experience comprehensible by assigning meaning to it. (See Robarchek, 1977, 1979 for further discussion of the biocultural construction of emotion.)

The relationship between the experience of emotion and the attribution of meaning can be seen clearly in situations where, for most Americans, the dominant and persistent emotion would be grief: one's child is bitten by a snake and dies; a sibling contracts polio and is dead in a few days; a man's wife is stung by a scorpion, goes into shock, and dies. In all of these cases, an almost immediate reaction on the part of the survivors was homicidal rage.

In situations such as these, the relationship between culture and emotion enters into the processes of definition and evaluation in at least two ways. First, all of these situations are *culturally defined* as the consequences of the actions of another person, specifically as acts of sorcery. Thus, each was defined and perceived as a human attack on the autonomy of the self. The response, in all of these cases, was rage and homicide.

Second, all of these situations violated the assumptions of the autonomous and effective self, and the *culturally appropriate* emotion was rage; and that is how the survivors defined their feelings. The felt emotion, defined and experienced as rage, in turn validates the cultural assumption that the situation is a result of the deliberate hostile action of another person. A human agent—a sorcerer—must be responsible.

In this case, the belief in the existence and malevolence of sorcerers—a part of the cultural knowledge system—provides a framework for individuals' understanding of and responding to misfortunes. At the same time, the belief in sorcery itself is subjectively validated: it is obviously truthful because it coincides with the emotional response; it "feels" true.

Curiously (to us), however, the rage and violence elicited in these kinds of situations are not necessarily directed at the "guilty" party; an innocent bystander may serve just as well as a target. Returning from a raid in which a sibling has been killed by *kowudï*, a man sees his elderly grandmother lying in her hammock. "Why should a worthless old woman like you be alive when my brother is dead?" he shouts, and drives a spear through her where she lies. (Had someone else speared her, of course, he would have been enraged and would have sought blood vengeance.) Or, (from our field notes) aroused to fury by the death of a child, a group of men spear two innocent women to death :

> Kupë said three of them were sitting in the house: Kupë, Boikä (her grandmother) and Wïnyä [who was about 30–40 years old]. Boikä was sitting in a hammock and Kupë was nearby. Three men, Boikä's grandsons, came in the morning and asked her to make tïpë for them. She mixed the tïpë, they drank and got up and took the spears of the household and speared Boikä and Wïnyä saying that she was old and still alive and Nïmo was dead.

When we asked why they speared their own grandmother, Kupë said a child, Nïmo, had died of an abscessed jaw and they became enraged and speared.

Much more recently, an American acquaintance of ours who was working on a project delimiting Waorani territorial boundaries encountered the group of Waorani returning from their foray (described in chapter 2) into the land of the *Tagëiri*. They were carrying their kinsman who had been mortally wounded by a Tagëiri spear. Our friend's immediate fear, he told us, was that the wounded man would die before they reached a town.[2] His anxiety was well-founded; as the only *kowudï* within reach, he would very likely have become the target for the rage of the dead man's kin.

This "displacement" is comprehensible if the rage is not so much a response to a specific act as it is an unfocused emotional reaction to a violation of autonomy and of the capacity to control events, that is, to the experience of powerlessness at the hands of another. Such unfocused rage may, it seems, be as easily directed at an innocent bystander.

Similarly, the difficulty that we encountered in eliciting what we considered to be coherent "reasons" for particular spearing raids—"they were raging" was the

---

[2]Randy Smith, personal communication.

standard answer—becomes comprehensible if the raiders' rage is a response to a violation of the existential and moral orders and to the subjective feelings of help-lessness and powerlessness as much as it is to a specific event. In the Waorani psy-chological map, the natural result of such rage, a reaction that restores a sense of autonomy and control, is homicide.

EGALITARIANISM

As we saw in chapter 6, Waorani society is highly egalitarian, both politically and economically, with virtually no rank distinctions on the basis of gender, kinship, group affiliation, or wealth. Traditionally, there was also little variation in material wealth, since the means of production were accessible to everyone. With contact and the influx of manufactured goods and the opportunity to work for The Com-pany, however, material differences have begun to appear, violating the egalitarian presumption. When people see themselves as materially deprived in relation to oth-ers, especially their kin, the result is malignant envy.

Envy necessarily indicates a violation of the egalitarian premise because, by definition, it entails the idea that "someone has something desirable that I do not have." This violates the assumptions that equality is the norm and that it is morally "right." Like the violation of autonomy, it is inherently rage-inducing. In the Wao-rani cultural schema, envy and rage on the part of others find their expression in at-tacks by sorcery.[3]

HOMICIDAL RAGE AND WAORANI ETHNOPSYCHOLOGY

If we rely on their own explanations for raiding and on their attributions of homici-dal rage to others, Waorani ethnopsychology seems consistent with the foregoing analysis. When we asked "Why did he go spearing?" the answer was almost always the same: *"piïntï bakändapa,"* roughly, "raging he became." From the perspective of our informants, that clearly was both reason enough and explanation enough for wholesale slaughter.

Seldom did people even mention the event that we would have seen as the pre-cipitating incident; it seemed irrelevant to the account and, if the fundamental cause of the rage is the challenge to the self posed by the perceived loss of autonomy and control, it *is* irrelevant.

We can see a similar scenario implicit in people's explanations of why sorcer-ers bewitch others, that is, in people's understandings of *others'* rage as these un-derstandings are revealed in accusations of sorcery. These explanations of others' motives for sorcery are felt to be true, we would argue, because they represent peo-ple's generalization and projection onto others of *their* understandings of *their own* feelings and motives.

---

[3]Schoeck (1966) has also argued for causal connections among an ideology of equality, envy, and violence. Meyers (1988) also saw a relationship between egalitarian values and anger. Rosaldo (1989) explored the conjunction of grief with rage in Ilongot headhunters and in himself. While explicitly rec-ognizing its culturally situated nature, he takes the conjunction itself as an irreducable given that is not amenable to further analysis or explanation.

Why do sorcerers bewitch people? They practice their evil because they are en-raged. Digging deeper into specific accounts of sorcery, we found two primary reasons for the rage that is believed to motivate it. Most commonly it was, again, because of someone's interference with the achievement of another's objectives.

The account in the previous chapter of the accusation of sorcery leveled at Mɨmä and Dyiko is entirely typical. The accepted explanation for Maria's illness, translated into the terms we have been using here, was that her interference with Mɨmä's ability to achieve her objectives (and, perhaps also Umï's perception of material inequality) generated murderous rage. This found its expression in her use of a woman already suspected of witchcraft—just as a man might use a spear—to kill the person who had thwarted her. It seems that rage and murder are the normal and expected results of interference with another's autonomy, with the achievement of his or her objectives.

In a Waorani community less committed to nonviolence than the one where this incident occurred, these two women, tried and convicted of sorcery by public opinion, would have been in great danger. Even here, it was the threat of spearing by Paä that finally forced Dyiko to remove the spell and, by so doing, to admit her "guilt."

The second kind of explanation for witchcraft sees it rooted in envy. One recent retaliatory raid was precipitated by the death of a woman who was believed to have been bewitched by her own kin because they were envious of the goods, especially the four gold teeth that her husband had purchased for her with money he earned working for The Company (see chapter 9).

In another case, what sounds like a stroke was attributed to sorcery inspired by envy. Omakä, an old man whom we had interviewed and whose songs we had recorded in his hamlet on the Tzapino River had, we heard, disappeared while hunting. "Maybe he was speared by the Tagëiri," people said.

Some time later, we met a young man from his group in Puyo; we asked if there was any news of Omakä. He told us that Omakä had gone into the forest and been attacked by jaguars sent by a sorcerer. He was missing for five days and, when he found his way home, he couldn't remember anything and he couldn't speak. His mouth and one arm were affected. For three days and nights his relatives gathered around him and prayed to God, and then he could speak, but not very well.

"Who did it?" we asked.

"People at Tönyëmpadɨ did it; they bewitched him."

"Why did they do sorcery?"

"They are angry because at Tzapino we have lots of food, lots of meat. They did very badly."

Inequities in material goods, however, are not the only source of envy, as is demonstrated by a witchcraft accusation that occurred some years ago. The accused witch is the same Dyiko who was accused of witching Umï. We recorded this account during our first project, four or five years before Umï's illness, thus the statement (below) "Now she behaves well."

We were talking with Ompudë one day about the deaths of her grandmother, Akawo, and Akawo's sister, Gämï, both of whom had been killed within the previous several years:

"Those two are witches," they said. After people become old, they always say that about old men and old women. Now they are saying the same thing about Dyiko because she is old. Now she behaves well, but in former times she was a witch. For example, she bewitched the child of her sister-in-law, Omëngkɨdɨ, and she died. The child, a girl, was very beautiful and Dyiko, seeing her, said "How can she be so beautiful? I will bewitch her and she is about to die!"

They lived in the same house at that time. One day Dyiko was swinging in her hammock back from the doorway and Omëngkɨdɨ's child came jumping into the house. Dyiko bewitched her, perhaps it was as if she was bitten by a snake, and the child cried out in pain. As Omëngkɨdɨ came in after her child, carrying her backbasket, she heard her child cry out, but there was nothing to be seen. As she set the basket down, the child cried out, then she died. She was about as old as my sister's child, Gïmari (about 4 years old).

[How did she do it?]

With *mïï (ayahuasca)* she did it. She drank; while drinking, she said, "She will not grow more beautiful, she is about to die!" After drinking the *mïï,* she went to the house where the child would be. She drank; then Omëngkɨdɨ's child came in through the door and "Yeee!" she cried out in pain. Omëngkɨdɨ, coming in, said, "Why does she cry out?" She cried out again and again, suffering, and finally died. Like that she did, Dyiko, in her youth.

[Why did she do it?]

After seeing this beautiful person, perhaps she thought, "She is growing so beautiful, everyone will want to marry/sleep with her," and she became enraged. "I don't have a child like that," she said. So saying, being enraged, Omëngkɨdɨ's child she bewitched, and she died.

The attribution of murderous rage—expressed through sorcery—to those who are presumed to be envious reflects Waorani perceptions of the psychodynamics of anger. Implicit in their explanations of sorcery is the assumption that inequality, like powerlessness, is inherently rage-producing. Envy is thus intrinsically hostile and, like powerlessness, the rage it generates finds its expression in sorcery.

8 / Waorani Warfare in Context

THE ANTHROPOLOGY OF VIOLENCE AND WAR

Although anthropologists have often reported the occurrence of group violence in "traditional" or "tribal" societies such as the Waorani, only in recent years has it become a major focus of anthropological theorizing. As these societies have been steadily brought under the political and military control of state systems, there has been a rapid decline in the incidence of warfare within and among them. They have been much more likely to be the victims of violence from the expanding states.

Almost paradoxically, as the incidence of warfare in traditional societies has declined, there has been an increase in interest on the part of anthropologists—especially American anthropologists—in explaining it. This is probably, at least in part, a consequence of the increasing concern in American society with violence and war, coupled with the hope that understanding the causes of warfare in these less complex societies may provide some insight into the dynamics of violence in our own.

This new interest was initially sparked by the appearance in the 1960s of several popular books that, in the sociopolitical climate of the times—especially the turmoil surrounding the Vietnam War—generated widespread interest and discussion outside the anthropological community. These works by biologists and ethologists found the causes of human violence and war in the genetic heritage of human beings, a product of biological adaptations for innate aggressiveness or territorial behavior made in the course of our species' evolutionary development. While this argument found little support among anthropologists, the resulting controversies fueled new research and theorizing by anthropologists on the subject of warfare in traditional societies.

Such field research has, not surprisingly, been concentrated in those few areas where pre-state (sometimes called "tribal") warfare persists or has only recently ceased, especially in New Guinea and, increasingly, in Amazonia. By the 1970s, ethnographic research and debate on the origins and persistence of tribal war was largely concentrated on Amazonian peoples such as the Yanomamo, the Jívaro, the Sharanahua, the Guahibo, and other similar groups.

The narrowing of the areal focus of anthropological research on warfare to Amazonia was accompanied by a shift in theoretical perspective. In the 1970s, an ecological approach emerged that saw warfare as a cultural adaptation to particular environmental conditions. In this framework, warfare is seen as an adaptive response to population pressure and limited resources; it functions to increase access to resources by limiting or dispersing populations.

Proponents of this ecological-functional approach have used it in attempts to explain other social institutions—religious beliefs, food taboos, and so on—as well, but it is their explanations of warfare that have generated the most controversy.

Biological explanations of warfare and violence soon reappeared in a more sophisticated form in the paradigm of sociobiology, to which the earlier ethological approach had given rise. Sociobiology sees the source of violence in men's evolutionarily selected strategies for what biologists call "maximizing inclusive fitness," in this case, fathering more children in order to pass more of their genes into the next generation.

From this perspective, conditions were such in the evolutionary past that men who engaged in violence gained sexual access to more women, enabling them to produce more children and, thus, to increase their inclusive fitness. Violence and war in present-day traditional societies are expressions of those evolved strategies by which men maximize their inclusive fitness.

As was the case with ecological explanations, proponents of sociobiology have attempted to apply it to the explanation of other human social behaviors: altruism, kinship behavior, and so on, but violence and warfare have been central issues in the development of the paradigm.

These two approaches, the ecological and the sociobiological, are the dominant models currently used by anthropologists in their attempts to explain violence and war. It will become apparent that, for a variety of reasons, we disagree fundamentally with both of these approaches as explanations, not only of violence and war, but of human behavior generally.

As we see it, there are two sorts of problems with these approaches: empirical and theoretical. On the empirical level, while these models may seem plausible in the abstract, they fail when we try to apply them to specific cases. The more closely we look at specific ethnographic data, the less relevant and explanatory these approaches seem to become.

The theoretical problem fundamental to both approaches is that they see human beings not as active goal-directed decision makers, but as reactive, as robots responding mechanically to biological or environmental determinants. These empirical and theorctical shortcomings are nowhere more apparent than when we attempt to apply the ecological and sociobiological models to the Waorani case.

Empirical Issues

Ecological Functionalism and Waorani Warfare   Many researchers have maintained that warfare in Amazonia is a complex adaptive cultural response whose primary function is to maintain a proper balance between population size and available resources.[1] This effect or "function" is, in turn, seen as the cause of the warfare complex. Logical problems with that argument aside,[2] numerous studies have shown that

[1]See, for example, Bennet Ross, 1980; Harris, 1971, 1974, 1979; Ferguson, 1992; Gross, 1975; and Ross, 1978, 1979.
[2]See Robarchek, 1989, 1990, for a discussion of these problems.

Amazonian soils and gardening techniques are capable of supporting vastly larger populations than they typically do and, therefore, that land scarcity or a generalized shortage of food are not limiting factors.

In view of that, proponents of the ecological approach argue that the crucial limiting resource is animal protein, and that warfare serves to regulate populations in relation to this resource. In one such proposition, Harris (1977) argues that it does so by (1) reducing the population directly through deaths in battle, (2) limiting population growth by reducing the numbers of potential mothers through the practice of female infanticide allegedly functionally associated with warfare, and (3) by creating "no-man's-lands" between warring groups where depleted prey species can recover.

The key to this entire argument, obviously, is the scarcity of protein. Unfortunately, more than two decades of research have found little empirical evidence of protein shortage in most Amazonian societies. On similar empirical grounds alone, it is clear that the theory is not relevant to the case of the Waorani.

In the late pre-contact period, when Waorani warfare was most intense, some 600 or so Waorani maintained effective control over a vast territory of some 8,000 square miles, giving a population density of approximately .075 persons per square mile. For comparative purposes, this is less than 1/50 the population density of the Semai.

The Waorani homeland is, moreover, one of the most diverse ecosystems on earth. More than 600 species of birds, 120 species of mammals, and 500 species of fish have been identified (Kimerling, 1991). Waorani traditional territory encompasses the 600,000-acre Yasuní National Park, which, because of its immense biological diversity, has been declared by UNESCO to be a "world biospheric reserve." Waorani technology—blowpipes, poisoned darts, and spears—was and is fully adequate to harvest this abundance.

Moreover, the smaller streams along which the Waorani traditionally live yield fish, turtles, turtle eggs, sting rays, and caiman, and their traditional technology—poisons, nets, and spears—allows them to harvest all of these. They do not even bother to collect the small rodents, lizards, snakes, amphibians, crustaceans, and other small animals that are critically important to many other tropical horticulturalists, including the Semai.

A detailed year-long survey of hunting productivity on the Waorani Protectorate—in an area where missionary activity had resulted in a population concentration 10 times the pre-contact density—showed that traditional hunting technology produced 190 grams of edible meat daily for every man, woman, and child in the community (Yost & Kelley, 1983). Assuming a standard 20% protein content, this yielded 38 grams of protein per person per day. This is roughly 25% above the estimated minimum daily requirement of 30 grams per day (cf. Milton, 1984). Maintaining this level of productivity required each man to spend only 4.5 days *per month* hunting (Yost & Kelley, 1983).

This is without taking into account *any* protein derived from vegetable sources. Although manioc and plantains, the carbohydrate staples, are low in protein, they are consumed in prodigious quantities. They are also complemented by a variety of wild and cultivated plant foods including maize (corn), peanuts, chonta palm fruit, a variety of other indigenous cultivated fruits, and numerous wild fruits of palms and other trees.

The sighting of a deer sent this man in pursuit with his spear.

Visiting parents relax in their son's kitchen-house after an extended hunting trip. Smoked monkeys are stacked like cordwood on the shelf behind them.

Finally, and most conclusively, a team of North American medical professionals examined all the Waorani living on the Protectorate in 1976—almost 60% of the total population—and found them to be in exceptionally good health, well nourished, and showing no evidence of dietary deficiencies (Larrick, Yost, & Kaplan, 1978).

In short, it is clear that Waorani have access to an abundance of animal protein and other foods far in excess of their nutritional needs, and that scarcity of protein or other subsistence resources cannot be a factor in any explanation of Waorani warfare.

Tapir meat is smoked on a rack to preserve it.

Sociobiology and Waorani Warfare   Sociobiological explanations of warfare and violence typically see homicide as the result of a competition among men that represents an evolved strategy for maximizing their reproductive success. As was the case with the ecological approach, the effect is then proposed as an explanation for the existence of violence and war (see Robarchek, 1989, 1990).

In this view, much of human behavior is the product of evolved "biological control mechanisms." In one such argument premised on the reproductive advantage allegedly conferred on violent men, Wilson and Daly hold that urban violence within the poorest segment of American society is the consequence of an evolved "willingness to participate in risky or violent competitive interactions" and that "both appetite for and aptitude in this milieu [violent conflict over status] should be basic evolved attributes of masculine psychology" (1985, p. 61).

In another widely cited paper published in the prestigious journal *Science,* Napoleon Chagnon (1988) proposed a "theory of tribal violence" based on data that he collected over a number of years of research among the Yanomamo of Venezuela and Brazil. The Yanomamo are another tropical horticultural and hunting society, similar in many ways to the Waorani, and who, like them, also suffer a high death rate resulting from intragroup raiding. Chagnon argues that participating in raids and becoming a killer increase a man's genetic fitness. He hypothesizes that, if this theory is correct and Yanomamo warfare is the product of men's competition to increase their fitness, then those men who are the most violent should have the most wives and children. The data he presents certainly seem to support the argument; they show that men who have killed clearly have more wives and children than those who have not.

Following from what he takes to be confirmation of his hypotheses, the author argues that competition to maximize reproductive success constitutes (at least in part) an explanation of the existence of Yanomamo warfare, and supports the socio-biological theory of violence, so that "reproductive variables must be included in explanations of tribal violence and warfare" (1988, p. 985).

Since the violence in Waorani society was even greater than it was among the Yanomamo, we tested these hypotheses against data derived from our field research. From our field notes and genealogies, we identified 128 killings where we had reliable data on the identities of the killers, their wives or children, and on their life careers. Forty-eight men were named at least once as participants in these killings.

Chagnon, in analyzing his Yanomamo data, divided his sample into killers and nonkillers. That was not possible for us since, when a residence group staged a raid, all the teenaged boys and adult men typically took part; thus, until the most recent generation, virtually all men were killers. Asked who was responsible for a particular raid, our informants' typical response was to name the leaders of the raid, often senior men in a residence group of close genetic relatives consisting primarily of siblings and parallel cousins, their spouses (who are their cross cousins), and their children.

We divided our sample of killers into three groups: those who had been named as killers in five or fewer killings, those who had been named six to ten times, and those who had been named more than ten times. We then calculated the numbers of wives and children of the men in each category, and derived tables 8.1 and 8.2.

At first glance, the data were markedly similar to those presented by Chagnon, and they certainly seemed to support the sociobiological hypothesis. Still, we were uneasy, since there seemed to be a good deal of cultural information relevant to both raiding and procreation that was left unaddressed. We suspected that these qualitative data might alter the interpretation of the quantitative data. These included things such as the following:

1. There is, for all practical purposes, no such thing as a "natural" or "accidental" death among the Waorani. Until recently, most deaths were homicides, and cultural values demanded blood vengeance. Sickness, and deaths from illness, accidents, snakebites, and so on, are culturally defined as homicides—the result of sorcery—and such deaths also demand vengeance. Raiding was thus an ongoing fact of life and the longer a man lived, the more raids he would participate in, and the more killings in which he would be complicit.

2. In order to minimize future retaliation against themselves, raiders targeted not only the primary victims(s), but also all the other members of the household, including women and children. Since the adults, both men and women, would most likely be related as siblings and cousins, a man who became embroiled in vendettas imperiled not only himself, but also his closest genetic relatives including, especially, his siblings and his children. Since half his genes are also theirs, the effect of their deaths is to decrease the number of "his" genes in the next generation, in other words, to reduce his own inclusive fitness.

3. Since both men and women were killed when raiders struck, the astronomically high homicide rate assured that there were many widows and widowers, virtually all of whom remarried.

4. While polygyny and occasionally polyandry do occur, multiple marriages are much more likely to be consecutive than concurrent.

TABLE 8.1   KILLERS' WIVES/KILLINGS

	Number of Killings Attributed		
	1–5	*6–10*	*11 +*
Number of Killers	31	13	4
Number of Wives	42	26	9
Range	0–4	0–7	0–5
Mean Number of Wives	1.35	2.00	2.25

TABLE 8.2   KILLERS' CHILDREN/KILLINGS

	Number of Killings Attributed		
	1–5	*6–10*	*11 +*
Number of Killers*	27	13	4
Number of Children	118	79	33
Range	0–20	0–17	0–20
Mean Number of Children	4.37	6.08	8.25

*Killers number 44 in this table; data were lacking on children for four men (each with one killing to his credit).

5. Sexual access to women is seldom a problem, since men can have sex with their spouse's siblings and with their siblings' spouses, all of whom are their own cross cousins. The principle governing such sexual access, however, is not status and prestige as presumed by sociobiology, but kinship.

We decided that the quantitative date merited a closer examination. What that examination revealed was that the appearance of correlations among numbers of a man's killings, the number of his wives, and the number of his children results from the fact that all three are functions of two other variables: when a man lived and how long he lived.

Moreover, the latter was heavily influenced by the former: If a man lived out his entire life in the pre-contact period, he might continue fathering children as long as he lived, but his life was likely to be significantly shorter than was the case for those who were still alive when the large-scale killing ceased.

We have no way of reliably estimating the ages at death of most of our sample of killers, but it seems reasonable to assume that those whose lives were not cut short by spears would have lived longer, on the average, than those who were killed. Of the 48 killers in our sample, only 18 survived into the post-contact period. Two of these died in a polio epidemic soon after contact, and we lacked information on children for four others. We identified 12 men who were able to live out their lives, continuing to father children *after* the vendettas had come to an end.

The result, shown in table 8.3, is clear: they averaged more than 50% more children than did those whose careers in paternity were cut short by spears. In other words, the longer a man lived, the more children he had, and the *cessation* of warfare dramatically increased killers' inclusive fitness.

It was *not* the case, however, that those who survived into the contact period were those who were the most proficient killers. In fact, precisely the opposite was the case: the more killings a man had been involved in, the more likely he was to be a homicide victim (table 8.4).

Every raid generated or perpetuated a vendetta and produced a set of enemies who were committed to avenging the deaths of their kinsmen. Of those with three or more killings to their credit, nearly 70% were killed. Of those with two or fewer killings, 32% were killed (table 8.5).

One of the indicators often taken by sociobiologists as evidence that genetic fitness is at the root of raiding and war ("male competition over female reproductive capacity," is the kidnapping of women during raids) (cf. Daly & Wilson, 1987). Such kidnappings did occasionally occur here, but in Waorani raids, women were much more likely to be killed than kidnapped. Of the 63 wives of killers in this sample whose fates are known, 19 were killed in raids and two fled to other Indian groups. Only two had, at some time in their lives, been kidnapped (table 8.6).

Furthermore, the accounts that we collected indicate that the women kidnapped from non-Waorani groups were often killed within a short time.

The high rate of homicide for women is the primary reason why men who survived had more wives: the longer a man lived, the more killings he would participate in, the more likely it was that his group would be raided in retaliation, that he and/or his wife would be killed and that, if *he* survived, he would remarry (see table 8.7).

In other words, a man with three or more killings to his credit was nearly three times as likely to have his wife killed (and thus to remarry if he survived) than was a man who had been involved in two or fewer killings. Just as was the case with the number of children sired, the number of a man's wives was also a function of his longevity, given that his reproductive life was lived in the context of this warfare complex.

Finally, and perhaps most inexplicable from a sociobiological perspective, was infanticide, and especially the not uncommon practice of burying children alive with their dying fathers. Waorani have a horror of having their bodies left on the surface of the ground to rot or be eaten by animals, and people who were mortally wounded would sometimes ask their relatives to bury them alive.

We have several accounts of raids where men, grievously wounded, asked for one of their children to be buried with them. In one case described to us, as the wounded man lay at the bottom of his shallow grave, he looked up at his kinsmen and cried, "How can I die here all alone? Give me one of my children." As our informant recalled it, "We grabbed his son, tied the [two- to three-year-old] boy's wrists and ankles and laid him on his father's chest. His father wrapped his arms around him and we covered them up. We could hear that child down there for two or three days; sometimes you could hear them for a week."

TABLE 8.3   NUMBER OF CHILDREN/LIFESPAN

	Number of Killers*	Number of Children	Mean Number of Children
Killed pre-contact	24	99	4.13
Survived to contact	12	82	6.83

*These numbers do not include six men who died from causes other than homicide, four men about whom information on children was lacking, and two men who barely survived the pre-contact period and died in the polio epidemic that swept the protectorate.

TABLE 8.4   NUMBER OF KILLINGS/SURVIVAL

	Number of Killers*	Number of Killings	Mean Number of Killings
Killed pre-contact	24	138	5.75
Survived to contact	18	61	3.38

*Does not include the six non-homicide deaths mentioned above.

TABLE 8.5   KILLERS' DEATHS BY HOMICIDE

Number of Killings	Number of Killers	Number Killed	Percent Killed
2 or fewer	25	8	36.0%
3 or more	23	16	69.6%

TABLE 8.6   FATES OF KILLERS' WIVES

Outcome	Number	Percent
Fled Out	2	3.2%
Kidnapped	2	3.2%
Killed by Husband	1	1.6%
Killed in Raids	19	30.2%

The point of all this is, we hope, clear: ecological functionalism and sociobiology, the dominant theoretical approaches that have been put forward as offering explanations for warfare and violence in precisely these kinds of societies, turn out to

TABLE 8.7   HOMICIDE OF KILLERS' WIVES

Number of Killings	Number of Killers*	Number of Wives Killed	Mean Number of Wives Killed
2 or less	20	5	.25
3 or more	20	14	.70

*Not counted are five unmarried men and three men whose wives' fates are unknown.

tell us absolutely nothing about the causes of warfare in this, the most violent "tribal" society known.

The ecological-functional approach, premised on the need to regulate the relationship of population to protein resources, is entirely irrelevant in this context of abundant animal life. The apparent covariation among numbers of wives, children, and killings—precisely the kinds of data offered in support of the sociobiological paradigm—are seen here to be incidental consequences of an entirely different set of causal relationships that derive from the sociocultural context and are entirely irrelevant to sociobiological assumptions.

Moreover, since both of these approaches see warfare and violence to be a determined result—either of ecological relationships or biologically programmed fitness-maximizing strategies—neither can offer any insight into the dynamics of the warfare complex itself or of culture change. Neither can address how it was possible, in the absence of significant changes in population biology or in ecological relationships, for the Waorani to abandon warfare almost overnight, or how this abandonment led directly and immediately to a dramatic *increase,* both in total population and in killers' genetic fitness.

Theoretical Issues

The second problem we see with these approaches is that both share a conception of human beings, not as intrinsically active, but as *reactive,* and of their behavior as more-or-less mechanical responses to forces outside themselves. In neither of these approaches is there a place for human consciousness, or for beliefs, values, goals, or intentions—the very stuff and substance of *human* life. Rather, people's actions are seen to be determined by factors and forces entirely irrelevant to their intentions, goals, and purposes.

Much of the controversy surrounding attempts to explain and understand human violence and war (and human behavior generally) is rooted in these two differing conceptions of the nature of human beings. On the one hand are the sorts of explanations we have just been examining, those that see human beings as primarily reactive, responding to external forces. These responses may be direct and mechanical as in behaviorist (stimulus-response) psychology, or mediated by cultural evolution as in the ecological-functional approach, or mediated by biological evolution as in the ethological and sociobiological approaches.

Human behavior, such as warfare and violence, is, from such a perspective, determined by simpler factors and processes. The goal of explanation is to reduce these complex social and psychological phenomena to the biological or ecological processes that determine them, that is, to explain them in terms of environmental conditions or biological propensities.

On the other hand are approaches that take human activity for granted and view people not as passive machines pushed this way and that by ecological, biological, sociological, or even cultural determinants, but as thinking decision makers. From this perspective, people are active participants in the creation of their own destinies, making their ways through fields of options and constraints in pursuit of individually and culturally defined goals in a reality that they themselves are continuously constructing and reconstructing. It is to this view of human beings and human action that we subscribe.

WAORANI WARFARE IN CONTEXT

In the previous chapters, we have been defining and describing the various contexts—material, historical, cultural, social, and psychological—that ultimately constitute the experienced reality within which Waorani social behavior, including violence and warfare, is enacted. This behavioral environment presents its own options, possibilities, and constraints. Individuals weigh their options, make decisions, and direct their actions on the basis of the information—the cultural and psychological maps and plans—that they have available to them. How they act in a given situation depends on how they perceive and understand it and on what they are seeking to achieve in it.

We want to make it clear that we are *not* arguing that human behavior is independent of or unconstrained by the environment or by human biology. We are simply insisting that human beings do not respond, either automatically or otherwise, to some "objective" environment, to "nature in the raw" whose "reality" is imprinted on passive minds. The worlds that people inhabit and interact with are worlds whose characteristics, meanings, and implications are attributed to them *by* human minds.

This was one of the things that immediately struck us when we undertook our first fieldwork among the Semai more than 20 years ago. We quickly realized that, although our nearest neighbors lived only a few feet away, although we were eating the same food and living in the same kinds of houses, the worlds we inhabited could hardly have been more different.

Our world was filled with malarial parasites, amoebas, hepatitis viruses, tubercle bacilli, and other pathogenic microorganisms whose presence constrained and shaped our behavior in important ways: we boiled our water, got injections of gamma globulin, took weekly doses of chloroquine phosphate, and so on. Of this reality, our neighbors had not a clue.

Their world, on the other hand, was filled with a vast array of "spirits," powers and forces—nearly all of which were hostile—associated with aspects of the natural world—mountains, waterfalls, boulders, and many others. These powers had to be avoided or appeased or they would bring disaster and death. This reality constrained their behavior in important—but very different—ways: They could not mix food containing different classes of animals; they must not laugh at butterflies or dragonflies; they must keep their emotions under control; and so on. Until we learned the nature of their world, much of their behavior was as bizarre and incomprehensible to us as ours must have been to them.

And this is always and everywhere the case; the environments with which human beings actually interact are always culturally constituted. In causal explanations of human behavior, these environments cannot be defined and specified apart from the cultural and psychological contexts in which they are experienced, and through which they are both constructed and understood.[3]

The Material Context

To assert that Waorani warfare is not the determined result of protein scarcity or a drive to maximize inclusive fitness is not to say that either the natural environment or the biology of sex is irrelevant to the Waorani warfare complex. Quite the contrary, they constitute important parameters of action.

The sex drive, whose reward—sexual pleasure—constitutes nature's reinforcement of behavior (sex) that tends to increase inclusive fitness, often leads to conflict. In the Waorani sociocultural context, one that included a prescriptive cross cousin marriage rule and a pattern of active vendettas that often constituted a state of war between related bands, the result could be a shortage of potential spouses. This shortage of spouses was sometimes, as we have seen, a motive for raiding.

But it is important to remember that the sex drive is a constant in all human societies; it is the sociocultural context—in this case of marriage rules and ongoing vendettas—in which it is embedded that gives it the potential to generate conflict and violence. It is also important to remember that Waorani culture provided numerous other avenues for sexual expression, including sex with the spouses of real and classificatory siblings, and homosexuality; the lack of a spouse did not necessarily entail a lack of sex. Our analysis of the data on biological reproduction in terms of the sociocultural context in which it occurs showed that success in marriage and procreation are *dependent* rather than *independent* variables in the warfare complex; they are effects, not causes.

In regard to the ecological context and the "protein scarcity" argument, while it is certainly true that Waorani tried their best to kill all those who entered their territory, defense of scarce resources does not seem to have been the issue. Waorani traditionally preferred to occupy the ridges and the smaller river valleys rather than live on the large rivers where the surrounding groups lived. Given the low population density of the region, they and others could, in principle, have shared it without overstressing the environment or coming into conflict over its resources.

Their homeland is suffering no population pressure; indeed it has, for most or all of this century, been underpopulated. Their technology for resource exploitation is efficient and effective, game is plentiful, soils are fertile in comparison with those available to most tropical horticulturalists, the crops are well adapted, and their yields are reliable.

By all measures, the Waorani adaptation to their material environment is remarkably successful: their diet is more than adequate, disease morbidity and mortality are low, and their technology is fully adequate to the challenges they face. In short, there was no "ecological" necessity for territorial defense; the character of

---

[3]This should not be confused with the view, currently fashionable in some postmodernist circles, that there is no reality independent of how people think about it (for example, Watson, 1991). We firmly reject that notion, believing, for example, that the dinosaurs existed and did rather well for a good many millions of years when there were no people around to think about them at all.

the environment and the Waorani adaptation to it did not require warfare, either against surrounding groups or within Waorani society, as a functional prerequisite for survival.

This is not to say that the natural environment is irrelevant to the issues we are considering; far from it. It too defined a set of parameters and presented a range of options and constraints that clearly influenced the viability of warring societies. As more socially and technologically advanced societies—beginning with the Incas—attempted to project their power into the region, the advantages conferred by technology and complex social organization were counterbalanced by, among other things, the natural environment; it afforded some protection to the more remote groups such as the Waorani.

The dense forest, steep ridges, flood-prone rivers, and vast swamps all made invasions of hostile territory immensely difficult. The problems of maintaining extended supply lines when all supplies had to be carried overland made long-term incursions difficult to sustain. Only with the advent of industrial technology has it been possible to extend military power into the Waorani heartland readily. And even today, as we have seen, several remote groups continue to resist contact with the modern world successfully.

Other aspects of the material environment undoubtedly helped shape world view and the ideological context. This is a highly productive environment whose challenges are effectively met by an efficient body of cultural knowledge and technology that leaves few intractable problems. This is likely a contributing factor to the world view that sees people as competent, self-sufficient, and in control of their lives.

Many societies at this technological level place a great deal of emphasis on magical rituals in an attempt to ensure success in activities such as hunting, gardening, fishing, and warfare in a world that is largely beyond the control of their technology. Among Waorani, as we have seen, there is relatively little emphasis on magic; there is little need for it since they see their cultural knowledge and skills as adequate to their tasks in a world that they see as largely under their control.

Disease, or rather its relative rarity in the Waorani environment, probably contributes, along with the relative ease of making a living, to this perception of mastery and self-sufficiency. Among the Waorani, serious illnesses are relatively infrequent and account for only a fraction of mortality. This is in striking contrast to our experience among the Semai, where virtually every disease known to medical science is endemic, and where everyone can expect to suffer illness and incapacitation and to require the assistance of others just to survive.

One indication of the magnitude of this difference: In the six years between our first and second field studies among the Semai, 10% of the population of our home hamlet, people of all ages, died from a variety of diseases; in the five years between our two trips to the Waorani, not a single death occurred in a community of roughly equal size.

In such a context, Waorani individuals are much less dependent upon a supportive community and, consequently, there is much less concern with maintaining group ties, with suppressing conflict, with resolving disputes, or with promoting interdependence.

The high incidence of poisonous snakes and the frequency of snakebites is probably also relevant here. Since 100% of the population suffer snakebites, most people several times, but only around 1–2% of bites result in deaths, a death from snakebite is not a "normal" occurrence, either statistically or psychologically. It is an "unnatural" event that, in the context of the cultural knowledge system that we have been describing, regularly proves the power and malevolence of sorcerers and gives direct empirical evidence of the truth of the belief in them.

We hope it is clear that we are not proposing that Waorani world view, their beliefs about the "supernatural" or other aspects of culture are caused or determined by some set of environmental variables. Rather, those beliefs are both shaped and validated by people's *perceptions* of their environment and their experiences with it, all seen through the lenses of the information and control systems (cultures and personalities) that they have at their disposal.

The Historical Context

We have also sketched the historical context of Waorani warfare, but it is well to remember that history becomes relevant to people's behavior only to the extent that it becomes a context for human action. The extinction of the dinosaurs, for example, is a historical fact, but it is probably not terribly relevant to an understanding of most people's day-to-day behavior, other than the fact of its having cleared the ecological space for the evolution of mammals, of which we are one species.

History becomes context in at least two ways. On one hand, it defines many of the parameters—ecological (as in the dinosaur example above), demographic, sociopolitical, technological, and so on—within which action occurs. This is primarily how we have been looking at history up to this point.

Beyond shaping parameters, however, a people's history also informs their daily experiences. It helps to define their current reality by providing much of the informational context within which they make their choices and live their lives.

Anthropologist Melford Spiro pointed out some years ago that to ask why some social behavior (such as, in this case, organized violence and warfare) exists is actually to ask two very different kinds of questions (Spiro, 1967). One is a historical question: "How and why did the behavior in question originate?" The other is a question of psychological and sociocultural dynamics: "What are the factors influencing people's actions such that the pattern of behavior is maintained and perpetuated (or changed) over time?"

Our exploration, in chapter 5, of the historical context of Waorani warfare was directed primarily toward the first of these questions, the question of origins. The culture of war and the social contexts that it defines—described in chapter 6—are the end results of a series of historical events and, even in the absence of specific historical accounts of Waorani society, the general outlines of the historical context are clear enough.

The western margin of the Amazon Basin has, as we have seen, been a violent region for a very long time. Assaults by the Inca Empire failed to subdue the region's inhabitants. The following 300 years of colonial rule in the highlands was marked by outbreaks of spectacular violence such as the 1599 revolt in the *montaña* but, until the nineteenth century, outside influences penetrated the lowlands slowly and often indirectly. Indigenous warfare was undoubtedly affected and probably intensified as a result of these indirect influences, but the earliest historical accounts show that raiding was long a part of the cultures of the region, as evidenced by the famous headhunting and "shrunken head" complex of the neighboring Shuar (Jívaro).

The fact that the language of the Waorani is apparently unrelated to those of any of the groups that surround them, together with the lack of any significant borrowings from those languages, suggests that they may be relatively recent intruders into a region where warfare has long been endemic, a situation to which they would have had to adapt violently to survive.

Missions and haciendas established during the colonial period subjugated many groups. Their activities exacerbated the effects of the epidemics that periodically swept the region, resulting in massive depopulation in the sixteenth through nineteenth centuries.

Slave raiding was widespread, with some indigenous groups collaborating in the enslavement of others. But not until the catastrophe of the rubber boom at the end of the nineteenth century did the outside world successfully dominate much of the region. Even then the resistance of the native peoples was characteristically violent, and those groups that were subdued were often defeated as much by introduced diseases as by force of arms.

Throughout this period, alliances with outsiders and differential access to Western technology, especially firearms, intensified conflicts and altered power relations among indigenous groups, allowing some to expand at the expense of others; some disappeared entirely as other groups pressed their advantage. The new technology also provided a further stimulus to raiding, as disadvantaged groups such as the Waorani raided to acquire the new tools and weapons. Immigration, colonization, the establishment of haciendas, missions, and towns put pressure on the territories of some groups, often displacing them into territories claimed by others.

With the nineteenth and twentieth centuries came the expansion of missions, civil government, and haciendas in the lower Andean foothills, and with those institutions came "civilization" and the imposition of a system of debt peonage on the indigenous people of the *montaña*. Still, endemic warfare between the "civilized" Indians and the "savages" continued. The Waorani attacked Quichua and Záparo who invaded their territory and raided surrounding settlements for machetes and axes, women, and excitement. They were raided in retaliation and for women and children who were taken, essentially as slaves, to work and usually to die on the haciendas.

This, then, is at least an approximation of the historical context within which the Waorani culture of war developed. While the specific details may be lost to us, the long-term pattern of endemic violence is undeniable.

When warfare is endemic, as has long been the case in the Oriente, the options available to any given group are rather limited: they can flee into the hinterlands if there are unoccupied hinterlands available (which may have been the initial Waorani response that accounts for their linguistic isolation); they can refuse to flee or to fight (and almost certainly be destroyed or absorbed by their more bellicose neighbors); or they can fight aggressively to resist or retaliate for incursions. Under such conditions, warfare is contagious; when one group takes up warfare as a means of advancing its objectives, their neighbors must either adopt it or be destroyed.

In the context of the culture of war that permeated the Oriente for at least the past several hundred years, where no group had the absolute technological and organizational superiority to defeat conclusively both its enemies and the forest, the result is predictable and precisely what we have seen: a balance of terror with constant warfare among the various social groups. Given the sociocultural environment of the region, and with no safe refuge available, engaging in at least defensive warfare would have been a functional prerequisite for the survival of any group.

While a historical contextualization of warfare such as the one we have just offered, premised in part on the existence of a regional "culture of war," may in some sense "explain" the existence of warfare between the Waorani and surrounding groups, it tells us little of relevance to Spiro's second question; it does not explain the maintenance and perpetuation of warfare from generation to generation as conditions changed, nor does it explain the violence that raged within Waorani society, or the recent dramatic decline of violence. Addressing those issues requires an explanation rooted in the ongoing, contemporary, and probably changing psychological and sociocultural dynamics of action within the shifting contexts whose parameters we have been defining.

This brings us to the second way that history becomes a context for action: A people's history informs their daily experiences, and thus shapes the behavioral environment within which they make their choices and live their lives. History, as it is distilled and distorted in myths, legends, stories, and memories, is incorporated into social and individual knowledge systems—into cultures and personalities—and thus helps to define the current reality.

This is history as it is transmitted through enculturation and as it is experienced directly by individuals. This is the history to which people are actively responding and which they are continually recreating. In the Waorani case it includes, among other things, the stories of previous killings (real or imagined) by *kowudï* and by Waorani: the experience of taking part in raids; being the victims of raids; spearing men, women, and children to death; watching relatives and friends die in agony; finding others dead and mutilated; and so on.

Distilled in folklore, accounts, and memories, and filtered through contemporary cultural beliefs and understandings, this cognized history helps to define the current context of action. It provides a major part of the framework of knowledge and feelings that people use in making sense out of their everyday experiences and in deciding how to act in regard to them.

The case of the Waorani construction of history was clearly an extreme one. Their almost complete isolation meant that, since they had no other points of reference and no experience with or access to a non-Waorani reality, their understanding of the world fed almost entirely on itself, on this culturally constituted history and on the contemporary experiences that it informed.

Still, this merely represents one extreme on a continuum since, for all people, the events that comprise daily life are experienced and understood in terms of culturally and historically constituted frames of reference. Lacking such a frame of reference, we wouldn't know what to think or how to feel about what happens to us.

The explanatory and transformative power of such a frame of reference can be seen in incidents surrounding the killings of the two Catholic missionaries described in chapter 2. Recall that, according to the first account we heard, a priest had been killed by the Yasuní band because a child that he had taken away to school had disappeared. A few days later, new information showed that account to be wildly inaccurate, and that two people had been killed while trying to make contact with the still hostile Tagëiri. The original account, although it turned out to be almost entirely wrong, was wrong in some revealing ways.

The people we were living with interpreted the news that a *kowudɨ* had been killed by Waorani in terms that made cultural and personal sense of it *to them.* For generations they had been raided by *kowudɨ* who, when they could, kidnapped Waorani children for their own, unknown, purposes. That history, embodied in cultural memory (and in personal memories), provides a ready framework for understanding and interpreting new events such as this. It also defines the appropriate emotional experiences—how people should feel about them.

In this case, judging from people's comments, the dominant feelings about this incident did not appear to be horror, revulsion, or even sadness; rather, our neighbors speculated about the accuracy of the account of the events that reportedly had triggered the killing. One young man even said that he hoped the story about the missing child was true because (he implied) then the killings would have been justified.

Had strong disconfirmatory evidence not been forthcoming, this account would likely have continued to be the culturally constituted and validated "truth" of the matter (see, for example, the story of the "killing" of Amö in chapter 10). The continuing salience of that framework for interpreting the actions of *kowudɨ* became even clearer to us later that same day, when Dɨtë accosted Carole with the barely veiled accusation that we, too, had come to kidnap Waorani children.

The point of all of this is that (1) Waorani perceptions, understandings, and expectations of the events and experiences of daily life, including social interactions, depend upon the information that they have available to them, and (2) that much of that information is derived from the historical context as it is encoded, transformed, and transmitted in myths, legends, stories, and autobiographical accounts and embodied in individual and cultural memory.

This information includes, among other things, both the abstract underlying assumptions of world view, and the more specific, generations-old cultural complex that stresses vendettas, blood vengeance, the malevolence of *kowudɨ,* and so on. Each new generation is born into a world already suffused with warfare and violence. Social relations, both with other Waorani and with *kowudɨ,* are thereby historically grounded and culturally legitimized.

The Social/Cultural Context

Implicit in all social relations are conceptions of reality: of human beings, the relations among them, and the world they inhabit. Here, as we have seen, social behavior is premised on autonomy, self-reliance, and egalitarianism in a world that is tractable to human action and control. Every aspect of Waorani social life—economic, political, and religious—reflects this conception of human beings and human relations. The net effect is the generation of a social world where every kindred, every household and, in the final analysis, every individual is independent and autonomous.

Waorani social organization is leaderless and decentralized, with few limits on individual autonomy and few social obligations. With no institutions conferring authority or otherwise imposing social control, there are no mechanisms for resolving disputes or for containing conflict. Any dispute has the potential to escalate into a homicidal confrontation, a potential that is well recognized by Waorani and acknowledged in the prayers in Christian communities exhorting those embroiled in conflict to "let go of their anger" and to forego violence.

The only political structure is the structure of kinship, expressed in localized kindreds, each of which is entirely autonomous. With bilateral descent, there are no lineages or clans to provide a ready framework for mutual obligations and support. Within kindreds, individual autonomy was the norm: no one has authority over the actions of another. Even the influence of elders over their younger kin is minimal. A radical dichotomy of kin/nonkin leaves relations with those outside the kindred prone to hostility.

Here, as everywhere, economic exchanges are the enactment of social relations in material terms and within particular constructions of reality. In this reality, premised on autonomy and self-reliance, we found few economic obligations or responsibilities and little cooperation. There is little functional differentiation, and thus no specialization or division of labor (not even a strong sexual division of labor) to foster reciprocity, interdependence, or integration beyond the immediate kindred.

Even marriage promotes conflict as well as solidarity. The system of prescriptive bilateral cross-cousin marriage should, in theory, knit kindreds together through time into networks of kinship and affinity, as those who call each other "brother" and "sister" marry their children to one another.

In practice, as we have seen, the system is prone to potentially deadly conflict. The classification of all same-generation kin into siblings and potential affines immediately excludes half of those who might be eligible marriage partners. Different kindreds thus found themselves in competition for genealogically appropriate spouses.

These conflicts over marriage were, until recently, exacerbated by the raiding and vendettas, as the high mortality rate from raiding further reduced the absolute numbers of potential mates. Further, the low population density and the residence pattern of widely scattered settlements meant that only a fraction of those potential mates were actually accessible.

Finally, the ongoing vendettas precluded peaceful contacts and marriages among many kindreds, often even closely related ones. Thus virtually every marriage was likely to generate conflict with some kindred that saw its members deprived of a potential spouse.

The shortage of eligible spouses also increased the pressure toward unions that were technically "incestuous" or otherwise genealogically inappropriate (cross-generational, for example). This, in turn, generated conflict *within* kindreds, conflict among those who should unconditionally support one another. The hostility that ultimately led our friend Omenï to kill his father's brother, Nëngkiwi, for example, had its origin, at least in part, in Nëngkiwi's insistence on marrying Gïmari, a woman he called "daughter" who had been promised to Omenï (see chapter 9).

Social organization beyond kinship was, until very recently, nonexistent. With no strongly marked gender dichotomy, no strict sexual division of labor, and no contrastive conception of men and women, there are no gender-based clubs or associations. Nor are there age grades or other associations that might cross-cut kinship and enmesh people in a wider network of social relations or confer on some individuals authority over the actions of others.

With the exception of Christian Waorani, there is little concern with nonmaterial beings and forces other than sorcerers and sorcery. With no tutelary "spirits," there are no cults or ritual responsibilities to generate social ties. With the exception of Christian services, ritual, including magic and sorcery, is individualistic rather than communal in both its performance and its objectives.

One important additional implication of the empowered and optimistic construction of reality that sees a world under human control is the perception that misfortune is likewise the product of purposive human action—of sorcery. Evil and danger thus have their origins in the human rather than the "supernatural" worlds; they are rooted in the all-too-human anger and envy of sorcerers.

Unlike the case in some societies, here the belief in sorcery does not promote social control by encouraging proper behavior (i.e., Waorani do not constrain their behavior either out of fear of being victimized by sorcerers or being accused of practicing sorcery). Here, the belief in sorcery motivates killings and generates vendettas.

Except in the case of committed Christians, there is no intrinsic value placed on nonviolence (although many others recognize its pragmatic value in avoiding a regeneration of the vendettas). Even among many nominal Christians, the new ideology and values are merely an overlay on the traditional consciousness, and not a replacement of it.

This is perhaps most dramatically evidenced by the case of Wɨba, one of the first Christian converts and one of the women who was instrumental in spreading the Christian message and in bringing the vendettas to an end. Yet, a few years later, she shot a man, a more or less innocent bystander who tried to intervene when she became enraged over her husband's affair with another woman.

These conceptions of social reality are, of course, cultural constructions and historical products, both creations of and creating the society that must make its life within them. In many societies where there is intense external warfare, there are social mechanisms that restrain internal conflict and promote social solidarity so that a strong and united front can be presented to the outside. Here, however, no such mechanisms exist. With no value placed on conciliation or cooperation, nearly all social relations carry a strong potential for conflict and for violence.

The result is a social world with no institutional framework for the imposition of authority or social control, resolving the inevitable conflicts arising from the pursuit of self-interest, settling disputes, preventing conflict from escalating into violence, or limiting or resolving conflict and violence once it has begun.

The Individual/Psychological Context

Social relations, and the assumptions and values implicit in them, comprise the context of enculturation for each new generation. Culturally structured experiences shape the very core of developing individual personalities as those assumptions and values are embodied in individual beliefs, attitudes, values, habits, expectations, motives, and goals. At the most fundamental levels—the construction and perceptions of self and of the world around oneself—the processes are culturally informed.

Moreover, given that individual personalities are premised on these values and assumptions, their violation or contradiction is experienced as deliberate human interference with the natural and moral order of things. The ability to project one's expectations onto and realize one's goals in the world is the essence of the autonomous, effective self.

Powerlessness, the experience of events that are beyond one's control, events such as the unwanted and unexpected death of a spouse, child, or sibling (always seen to be caused by the actions of another), violate those fundamental assumptions about how the world *is* and how it *should be,* and unleash murderous rage.

In a similar way, the experience of envy violates the egalitarian assumption. Both perceived powerlessness and perceived inequality are experienced as assaults on the self, situations where the appropriate emotional response is rage and the culturally and psychologically appropriate behavioral response, one that restores the sense of power and effectiveness, is homicide.

Both of these can be seen in the attribution of homicidal motives to others in accusations of sorcery. Sorcerers' motives for murder by sorcery are seen to be expressions of *their* anger and envy, rooted in the same assumptions. Rage and homicide are the assumed natural consequences of a refusal to grant a request or accede to a marriage, envy of someone's beautiful child or a woman's gold teeth.

EXPLAINING WAORANI WAR

It should be apparent by now that we are not going to uncover a "cause" for Waorani violence and war, at least not the kind of unitary cause that sociobiology or ecological functionalism envisions, or that medical researchers announce when they report their discovery that HIV "causes" AIDS or that X-rays "cause" cancer.

In reality, of course, this is not an adequate model of disease causation, either;[4] nonetheless, this image of one entity acting on another—like one billiard ball striking another and determining a specific result—has become the model of "scientific" explanation for most laymen as well as for a good many social scientists, especially those who see people as reacting more or less mechanically to forces that act on them.

We have found nothing remotely like that in our exploration of the dynamics of Waorani violence and war. Rather, what we found, and what we have tried to describe here, are the multiple contexts—environmental, ecological, biological, historical, social, cultural, and psychological—that constitute the behavioral environment within which purposive action takes place. Together, they push behavior toward violence, defining a reality in which homicidal violence is seen to be a legitimate and appropriate option.

As with human behavior everywhere, Waorani behavior—including violence— is motivated by what individuals want to achieve in their world as they perceive and understand it. Within their experienced reality, people make choices based on the information that they have available to them: information about themselves, the world around them, and potential goals and objectives in that world. Violence, like

---

[4]See Dubos, 1959.

other behaviors, occurs when it is perceived and selected, from a field of possible alternatives, as a viable means of achieving those goals and objectives.

This was, for generations, an essentially closed system insulated by war and language from new inputs of information. All social relations, whether with other Waorani or with *kowudï,* were premised on this closed knowledge structure. Those relations, under the direction of the cultural and individual schemata that we have been defining and describing, all have a strong and barely latent potential to erupt into violence. Under such circumstances, the conflicts that are an inevitable concomitant of human social life are essentially unconstrained. Any dispute or perceived conflict—made even more volatile by the homicidal rage that these engender here—can, and still occasionally does, precipitate a mass killing. It was only with the input of new information that altered these cultural and individual constructions of reality that it was possible for substantive change to occur.

PART 3

CONTEXTS REVISED

9 / The Renunciation of Violence

INFORMATION AND THE DECLINE OF WAR

The idea that the sum of the knowledge of a society's members constitutes the cultural information that the society has at its disposal in defining and adapting to its reality has some important implications:

1. Not all people have access to the same information, and no single individual has access to the totality. Rather, different people have access to different, overlapping bodies of knowledge, some of which may be inconsistent or contradictory. Different people's behavior, therefore, may be rooted in somewhat different information, in different sets of assumptions and values.
2. The new information that constitutes culture change and generates changes in social behavior, derives ultimately from the experiences of individuals. Thus, cultural and social change have their roots in individual experience and the information that it makes available.

The crucial role of information in the dynamic of Waorani violence and warfare can be seen most clearly in the dramatic decline of violence that followed immediately upon the input of new information. Almost overnight, killings declined by more than 90%, and the pattern of intense internal and external raiding and warfare that had persisted for generations virtually ceased.

THE FIRST PEACEFUL CONTACTS

The most recent attempts to "pacify" the Waorani began in the late 1950s with attempts by evangelical Protestant missionaries to make contact with a band living along the tributaries of the upper Curaray. The primary players in the pacification process have been Protestant and Catholic missionaries and national and international oil companies.

Waorani isolation was, according to accounts of elders, not always absolute. From time to time, peaceful contacts between individual bands and other Indians were established and maintained, sometimes for a number of years. We have accounts of a period, around the turn of the century, when Waorani from the Upriver band reportedly traded and intermarried with Quichua from the Arajuno River at the western edge of Waorani territory.

There is another account from around the turn of the century of a hacienda owner who, for ten years, carried on a "dumb barter" exchange with a band of Waorani. They would collect rubber and leave it at the edge of his property, and he would replace it with axes, machetes, and cloth (Elliot, 1957, p. 97). Inevitably, however, these relations broke down and were replaced by renewed hostility.

The result was that most bands had no regular (or irregular) trade or traffic with the outside world. Even more important from the perspective developed here, they also had no access to new information. Their cultural knowledge schema was, with a few exceptions such as these, essentially a closed system, insulated by warfare and language from new information from outside.

Protestant missionaries from North America had been working in the Oriente among the Quichua and Shuar since before World War II, but their activity increased in the years after the war. In the mid-1950s, some of these missionaries began to see themselves as God's instruments for civilizing the "Aucas." One of those, Peter Fleming, wrote in his diary, "It is a grave and solemn problem; an unreachable people who murder and kill with extreme hatred. It comes to me strongly that God is leading me to do something about it . . ." (Elliot, 1957, p. 104). The result was the formulation, by Fleming and four others, of "Operation Auca," their plan to establish peaceful relations with the "savages" by ferrying themselves into Waorani territory by plane.

After locating a Waorani hamlet from the air, the missionaries spent several months dropping gifts—pots, machetes, clothes, salt— to the people on the ground. From Wïba, who had fled some years before and who was working as a laborer on a hacienda, they collected a list of phrases they hoped would put the Indians at ease when they finally met them face to face (Elliot, 1957, p. 133).

Unfortunately, there is no indication that, when they finally met the Waorani, the Indians even knew that they were trying to speak their language, much less understood them. This is not surprising, since for "I like you; I want to be your friend" they had written *"bitu miti punimupa,"* which approximates "I am coming to you." For "welcome" and "let's get together" they had phrases that roughly translate "you all come" and "I am coming to your place." None of this, even in the unlikely event that it had been understood, would have been terribly reassuring to people who suspected that all outsiders were cannibals.

In early January, 1956 the missionaries began the final phase of "Operation Auca"; they first flew over the Waorani hamlet, then landed their plane on a sandbar in the nearby Curaray River and set up a camp that they dubbed "Palm Beach."

The Waorani settlement was in turmoil and people were furiously angry, not because of the arrival of the missionaries, but because of a dispute over a violation of the incest taboo. Nëngkiwi was sleeping with Gïmari, his brother's daughter, and the two said that they wanted to be married. Not only was Nëngkiwi already married, but this liaison violated the prescriptive cross-cousin marriage rule and the incest taboo: he called Gïmari "daughter." Moreover, Gïmari's mother, Akawo, had already agreed that she would marry Nëngkiwi's nephew, Omëni (who was later our neighbor), and she refused to agree to a marriage to Nëngkiwi.

Nëngkiwi threatened to spear Akawo and her son Nämpa if they did not allow Gïmari to go with him. Gïmari's brother Nämpa was also enraged; he was so angry that he smashed his blowpipe, quiver, and poison pot. Others, too, were furious, "killing mad," *(piïntï)* they told us.

In the midst of all this, Nëngkiwi and Gïmari announced that they were going to the river to see the *kowudï,* to see what they wanted. They met the missionaries, who took their pictures and gave them food. When they returned to their own settlement, they said, "They are cannibals and are looking for us so they can eat us." Nämpa, still raging, went to get his uncle Paä to help them spear the *kowudï.* When they returned, the entire group headed for the Curaray. Omënï described what followed:

> Carrying our spears, quickly we went. Akawo held Nïmö's [Rachael Saint's] brother and Nämpa came; Nyämë and Nïmüngkä speared him. A pistol was fired and Nämpa was hit in the forehead. Another one was in the plane, Nïmüngkä speared him. Nyämë and Paä came and speared another one and he fell into the water. The river was low then; one ran to the other side of the river; Paä and Nïmüngkä speared him on the sand and he died. [Elisabeth Elliot's husband] was in the water hanging onto a tree trunk, and there they speared him. We tore the airplane apart.
>
> That evening we went uphill. Nämpa was wounded; Mïnyïmö and Këmë were with him. We stayed until dark and then we slept. Nämpa wasn't walking right, and he fell and broke his collarbone. We saw a different plane coming and we came back to Tïwënö and left Nämpa in a hammock in the house with his mother, Akawo.
>
> Paä went home to his wife, Wïwa, on the Damöïntarö River and told her that Nämpa had been shot by the *kowudï:* "he will just die; the bullet is still in his head." That morning, Nëngkiwi carried Nämpa to Paä's house in a hammock slung from poles. Everyone came along.
>
> We heard airplanes coming and going. They didn't see us there at Paä's house because he built it under the branches of the trees. We only made fires in the early morning when the mists rise up out of the valleys. After the mists rose up completely, we put out our fires so they wouldn't see us. [Nämpa recovered somewhat and lived, some say for several months, with a .22 caliber bullet in his head.]

The killing of the missionaries made headlines in Europe and North America and precipitated yet another bizarre episode in this litany of misconceived adventures. As we pieced the story together from both missionary and Waorani sources, a Canadian who may have been a psychologist apparently was inspired by the newspaper accounts of the encounter between the missionaries and the Aucas, and took it upon himself to use psychology to pacify the savages.

After making his way to the Oriente, he hired some Quichua to take him by canoe deep into the territory of the Upriver band. They went up the Tïwënö River until they encountered a Waorani hamlet. The Canadian disembarked on a sandbar and, with supplies, ammunition, several guns and, apparently, a considerable quantity of money, started off in the direction of the houses. His Quichua crew wisely wasted no time heading back downriver.

Omënï recounted the events that followed:

> One day we all went fishing together and came to a place where we had put a stick at a cross trail and the stick was gone. We knew that the Oruna had come to our fishing and hunting place. Kipa said that he knew they were *kowudï.* "I smell their stinking clothes!" he said. We thought they had come upstream, so we went downstream and found the remains of manioc mash in the leaf in which it had been carried. It was fermented to alcohol. "They are Oruna" [Quichua], we said, "and they are headed to our

dwelling place!" We were afraid that they were coming to kill us and take our women and children, so we threw down our fish, put our blowguns and dart quivers aside and, carrying only our spears, we ran as fast as we could to get home.

When we got there, Kabë [the young girl Kipa had taken for a wife after he speared everyone else in her family] was feeding her pet woolly monkey. We thought that the *kowudï* were on another trail not too far away. *"Kowudï* are coming close!" we cried. We all ran and scattered ourselves to hide. One little girl and boy (Gamï and Iniwa) hid under Paä's canoe. The *kowudï* came, but did not find them.

When night fell, we all gathered together and Kipa suggested that we go to Gïngata's house. So we all left with the women and children. Then we decided to go to Nyämë's and Nïmüngkä's house near Damöïntarö. We fled to them in the dark. It was still dark when we got there and we called out to them. There is a big cave near that place and we put all the women and children there to hide.

We men took a canoe, and feeling our way in the dark headed for Paä's house to tell him. After we got him, we headed for Boikä and Müngkä's place. When we got there, Müngkä said, "You are coming to spear me!" and Paä replied that we were running from the *kowudï*.

At dawn some of us decided to go see what the *kowudï* were doing. Kabë, Kipa, Adyïbë, Gïmari, Mïipo, Paä and I went back. When we got there, Kabë's pet woolly monkey was pacing back and forth. Paä was hiding along the trail to spear the Oruna, but they had all gone back except for one man. He was in Kipa's house, which was very high. Kipa always built his houses like that, almost up in the trees with hard chonta palm floors and walls, so that it was very hard for raiders to come in and spear. We couldn't see into the house at all. We stayed back at the edge of the forest where he couldn't see us, and we watched the house. Every morning he would look around and then climb down and look inside the other house to see if anybody was there. He always carried his gun with him everywhere. We decided to wait for him inside that house and spear him when he came to the door. When he opened the door, we tried to spear him, but the spear didn't penetrate; his clothes were too hard. [According to a missionary who had met him as he was trying to arrange transport into Waorani territory, he may have been wearing a bulletproof vest]. He ran back to Kipa's house and started shooting out of the door, shooting wildly into the forest. He shot at us out of the house, so we went away.

We kept going back and he was still there and still shooting. About a month went by; we tried to see how we could kill him, but he was too high and even though we tried, we couldn't get to him. Mïipo tried to climb a tree to see him, but the *kowudï* shot him in the shoulder and we all ran away. We kept coming back to see him. We called him *"kogïngkuu"* because he was hairy like a monkey.

Finally, late one evening, we heard a very loud shot. "Wonder what that was," we said. The next morning, Nïmüngkä, Paä and I went closer, but stayed out of firing range. The door was open and we could see his feet with red socks on them and the feet were not moving. Two women, Adyïbë and Kabë were coming downhill on a trail about that time and could see in the doorway. They could see that he was lying very still and watched for some time. They went closer. Then, "He has died," they called out to us and we all came to look. We all saw for ourselves. Müngkä, Mïipo and Künï all speared him as they entered. "He is buzzard food now," they said.

Another of our neighbors explained that the intruder, trapped and unable to flee, had remained barricaded in the house that he had commandeered until he apparently ran short of ammunition. Then he put his shotgun under his chin and pulled the trigger, nearly decapitating himself.

His lower jaw was blown off and his teeth were scattered about. We gave them to the children to play with. Inside his clothes, he had a lot of money, but we didn't know what it was then. We thought it was leaves, and we just threw it down and it blew away in the forest.

We have heard this story many times; Waorani think it is hilarious and they howl with laughter at it.

Around the same time, and in this same band, a child about three years old died suddenly, probably from a snakebite. She was entering her house when she suddenly screamed and fell down. In a very short time, she was dead. Her mother (Wɨwa) accused her sister-in-law Dyiko of witchcraft, and she and two other women announced that they were going to the *kowudɨ* and headed into the jungle. (This may or may not have been a way of committing suicide; it is impossible to reconstruct motives after so many years.)

They walked to a Quichua settlement on the upper Curaray. In Arajuno, a half-day's walk away from that settlement, Elisabeth Elliot, widow of another of the missionaries killed at "Palm Beach," was visiting with her small daughter. She, too, had become convinced that it was God's will that she bring Christianity to the "Aucas."

When she heard about the arrival of the women, she immediately set off for the Curaray, accompanied by a group of armed Quichuas. By the time they arrived, one of the Waorani women had fled back into the jungle. Since the other two seemed to be intending to stay, Elliot decided to move there and begin learning their language. By the time she arrived with her belongings, however, Waorani raiders had struck nearby. Led by Paä, the husband of the woman who had fled after her child had died, they had ambushed a young Quichua man and his wife.

As Omënɨ recalled it,

We [Gïngata, Paä, Nyämë, Kipa, Nɨmüngkä, and Omënɨ] went out to raid Oruna. An Oruna and his wife were spear-fishing and we speared the man, who broke his fish spear trying to fend us off. Paä took the woman for his wife and we ran all night.

Fearful of additional raids, Elliot decided to move with the two Waorani women to the larger Quichua village of Arajuno (Elliot, 1961, p. 38).

A few miles away, Rachael Saint, a sister of another of the slain missionaries, had, for several years, been painfully working to learn the Waorani language from Wɨba the woman who had provided the phrases of greetings for the ill-fated attempt at contact on Palm Beach. She, too, had become convinced that it was God's will that she bring the message of Christianity to the "Aucas." Over the course of the next year, the two missionaries evolved a plan to accompany the Waorani women back into the forest, to make contact with their kinsmen and to bring to them the Christian message.

The missionaries' objective was to bring God's word to the "savages" and, thereby, to bring an end to the killing. The motives of the Waorani women are less clear. In hindsight, they recall having had similar purposes, but it is also apparent from some of their comments recorded at the time by Elliot that they were very impressed by *kowudɨ* medicines and technology and that they wanted these made available to their kinsmen (Elliot, 1961).

It was decided that the three Waorani women would first go back into the forest alone to locate their relatives and prepare them for the arrival of the missionaries. In September of 1958 they reemerged from the forest, accompanied by four more women and two boys, to report that their kinsmen had agreed to allow the missionaries to come and live with them. Two weeks later the party, accompanied by six armed Quichua men, set off to meet the "Aucas"—peacefully for the first time—in their own domain.

After seeing the women settled in a hamlet on the banks of the Tïwënö River, a small tributary of the Curaray, the Quichuas departed. The missionaries and the Waorani women immediately set about preaching their message that there was a God and that he abhorred killing. Although they had as their highest priority bringing an end to the violence, they had no means of enforcing that objective. The region was, and to a great extent still remains, beyond the reach of routine police or military authority. If they were to be successful, the Waorani would have to be persuaded to abandon warfare and raiding and to forego both their generations-old blood feuds and their fear and hatred of all outsiders.

At first they made little progress; "had they not been women" (and thus not perceived as threatening), "we would have killed them right away," one of our neighbors told us; "We didn't listen to them." It was the returning Waorani women who proved to be the key. Wïba had lived with the Quichua for a decade, the others for nearly a year. They described for their kinsmen their lives on the outside: how the *kowudï* were not cannibals, how there was no raiding, how people did not constantly live in fear of attacks, how there was access to all sorts of tools, medicines, and wonderful goods. As they began to realize that the feuding could stop, some members of the Upriver band began urging their kin to heed the words of the missionaries.

What the missionaries did not know was that groups of Waorani themselves had, on numerous occasions, tried to reduce the killing by making peace with at least some of their enemies. One group would invite another to a drinking feast where both would pledge to end their vendettas and, perhaps, to marry their sons and daughters to each other. Sometimes it was simply a ruse and, when one group relaxed its vigilance, the other seized its hidden spears and commenced a slaughter.

But even when the feast concluded peacefully with a majority on both sides really intending to end their vendettas, the results were often disastrous. Since there was no way to enforce conformity with the wishes of the majority, as likely as not the visitors would be ambushed on their way home by hotheads who could not pass up the opportunity to even an old score.

There was, in short, no safe way to establish initial peaceful contacts between enemies or to promote the growth of trust. Instead there was a value system that demanded blood vengeance for the deaths of kinsmen and a cultural construction of reality and of self and emotion that equated powerlessness and grief with rage, and rage with homicide. It was a self-contained and self-perpetuating cycle of violence that very effectively insulated itself from any new information. Like the proverbial fish that couldn't discover water because it couldn't envision an alternative, Waorani could not envision an alternative to the cultural construction of reality in which they were immersed.

The returnees, however, having experienced a different world, were able to imagine alternatives, to envision new options, and to communicate these to their relatives in terms that they could understand. What they provided was new cultural knowledge—new information and new perceptions of reality—that allowed a reorganization of both cultural and individual schemata.

They enabled their kin to see new possibilities, formulate new goals, and plot courses of action based on them. They were able to imagine and to seek a new world, one without the constant fear of violent death. In a matter of months, the Upriver band abandoned the pattern of internal and external raiding that had persisted for generations, and soon the missionaries and their converts were beginning to reach out to other kindreds.

Once word that the vendettas were ending had been passed to outlying kindreds of the Upriver band, attempts began to contact their bitter enemies living on the headwater tributaries of the Tiputini. The missionaries, with the technology at their disposal, provided a way to initiate contacts safely with groups that were still at war. After a new group had been located from the air, they would be visited by overflights for several months, and goods—axes, machetes, pots, clothing, food— would be dropped from the small planes.

After some time, Waorani from "pacified" groups would speak to their hostile kin through a loudspeaker lowered to the ground as the plane flew in a tight circle above, urging them to give up their vendettas. Finally, contact would be made on the ground by volunteers who had kin among the hostile band. Each new group was persuaded to relocate to the settlement on the Tɨwënö River, where large manioc gardens had been planted to support them until they could plant their own gardens.

The technique was not always successful. As we noted in chapter 3, the young man who made the first attempt to contact the Ridge people walked into a hostile settlement and was killed by his own kin. Within a year, however, the band had been convinced to make peace and relocate. In a remarkably short time, most groups had been contacted and persuaded to abandon their old hostilities. After generations of intense warfare and violence, individual bands abandoned their vendettas within months of contact and, within only a few years, the killings virtually ceased. Years passed without a single homicide on the Protectorate.

As each new group relocated to the large settlement that was developing on the Tɨwënö River, their commitment to peace was reinforced by their dependence on the other bands for food until their own gardens matured. Their resolve was also buttressed by the Christian beliefs and values being promulgated by the missionaries and, increasingly, by other Waorani.

Not surprisingly, as remote bands came into contact with the outside world through missionaries and other Indians, they were swept by colds and other respiratory infections; "They were too sick to fight, even if they had wanted to," Rosie Jung told us. Be that as it may, when they recovered, the peace still held.

It is important to recognize that, for each new group contacted, the change in behavior from warfare to peace was the primary and crucial change. The decision to stop killing kowudɨ and enemy Waorani had to happen before any other changes could begin to occur.

It is also crucially important, in terms of the theoretical arguments that we outlined in chapter 8, that this transformation occurred, at least in its initial phases, in the absence of any other substantive changes, either within or outside of Waorani society: They were not conquered, the ecological situation had not been altered, the subsistence system had not changed, nor were there other significant changes in the material context and content of their lives. All that had changed was the information available to them.

Other factors quickly came into play, of course. The intensity of the raiding had left some bands with no potential spouses of the proper kin type except in bands with whom they were at war. The establishment of peaceful relations and the subsequent relocation made marriage partners available in bands of former enemies. Also, as peaceful contacts with *kowudï* commenced, Waorani were able to begin acquiring the knives, axes, shotguns, flashlights, snakebite antivenins, other medicines and medical care, and the other goods and services that their long isolation had denied them. The desire for continuing access to all these benefits quickly reinforced their commitment to peace, once the process had begun, but the *decision* to abandon warfare was primary, the *sine qua non* for everything that followed.

INFORMATION AND CULTURE CHANGE

Whatever the historical origins of the violence that for so long had characterized Waorani society might have been, its perpetuation clearly did not depend on biological propensities or ecological relationships (or on the interactions between them), because none of those had changed. What had maintained it was the psychocultural dynamic involving information, beliefs, attitudes, values, goals and intentions. It was a change in *that* dynamic that led to the abandonment of warfare.

In the absence of any substantive changes in the material or ecological realms or in the context of biological reproduction, but in light of new information derived from the experiences of a small group of individuals, Waorani simply decided to stop killing. With that decision, their society transformed itself, almost overnight, from the most violent on earth into one that is, at least relative to its own history, peaceful.

Moreover, the speed of this transformation—within a matter of months for each individual band—can only be explained as a consequence of the missionaries providing a means for the Waorani to accomplish something that *they* also wanted: to escape the vendettas. When new information permitted the formulation of a new image of reality and the recognition of new possibilities, the Waorani were presented with an opportunity to escape from the cycle of violence, and they seized and implemented it.

Their actions, far from being the mindless result of ecological or biological forces operating outside of human consciousness, were the result of people consciously and deliberately striving to realize their newly found objectives within the context of a cultural reality that they, themselves, were actively reconstructing.

This is clear from the fact that other groups of Waorani that did not gain access to the new information, did not make the transition. In the 1970s, the activities of the SIL were severely curtailed by the Ecuadorian government, and efforts to contact new groups came to an end. Bands far down on the Shiripuno and Yasuní rivers remained uncontacted in their traditional territories. They also remained at war.

By the mid-1970s, oil exploration was under way along the headwaters of the Tiputini and Yasuní rivers, and The Company's camps were regularly attacked and harassed by Waorani. Father Labaca, the Capuchin priest later killed by the Tagëiri, had been trying unsuccessfully to make contact with them since the mid-1960s.

In 1976, in response to a request from The Company, he began visiting the oil camps, and was finally able to initiate peaceful relations. Later, he made several trips by canoe and helicopter to settlements of the Yasuní band. When the new information that the raiding was ending became available to them, they too made a conscious decision to forego their vendettas against those groups that had abandoned theirs.

This band was never "missionized"; it was never involved with the Protestants, had only sporadic contact with the Capuchin mission, and was never relocated. Even so, they have given up their vendettas against all but the still-hostile Tagëiri. In their case, this was clearly a pragmatic decision and not a moral one, since the Tagëiri are still fair game.

As this new information became available to the various bands, it was differently accepted and incorporated; some individuals truly assimilated many of the Christian ideals and values, others adopted them more superficially, and still others rejected them and the Christian identity entirely.

Regardless of these differences, however, the new information allowed all Waorani who had access to it to transform their cultural and individual maps of reality and formulate new objectives and goals. Only the Tagëiri and perhaps one or two other groups are still immersed in their traditional world and insulated by warfare from the newly emerging construction of reality. They remain hidden in the dense forests, ridges, and swamps, still at war with each other and with the world outside. For the rest of Waorani society, however, the large-scale killing has, at least for the moment, come to an end.

CONSTRUCTING A CULTURE OF PEACE

Compared to the pre-contact period, life among the Waorani is now very peaceful. Where previously every man had been involved in multiple killings, now very few of the first generation to reach adulthood since contact have killed. This should not, however, be taken to mean that this has become an *inherently* peaceful society.

Despite the dramatic change in behavior, occasional spearings continue to occur, both on and off the reserve. In cross-cultural perspective, Waorani society remains fairly violent, with a homicide rate over the past 30 years that we have conservatively calculated (excluding, for example, any consideration of infanticide) to be at least 57/100,000 per year. (The standard way of calculating and reporting homicide rates is in numbers per 100,000 per year, but it should be obvious that numbers like that have very little reality when we are describing a society of fewer than 1,500 people.)

Such figures do, however, allow some very tentative comparisons with other societies. The figure cited is, for example, more than six times the rate for the United States as a whole. That should not, however, obscure the fact that a very real and dramatic change in behavior has occurred: a decrease in homicide rates from perhaps as high as 1,000 per 100,000 to around 60 per 100,000 per year, a decline of more than 90%.

While these behavioral changes are dramatic, they are, like the Napo River it-self, in places, a mile wide but only an inch deep. The social, cultural, and psycho-logical changes that have accompanied the new peacefulness have been remarkably superficial.

The economy and the pattern of daily life remains rooted, literally and figura-tively, in the gardens. Very little food is imported, despite the efforts of at least one missionary to discourage the consumption of the traditional manioc drink and to en-courage the consumption of rice.[1]

Many men work, at least occasionally, as laborers for The Company, but this increasing involvement with the outside money economy has, for most people, been largely confined to essentially peripheral "luxury" goods: clothes, flashlights, shot-guns, aluminum pots, and so on. Commodity production and sale have been con-fined almost entirely to a few handicrafts such as hammocks and net bags, and to parrots and monkeys captured while hunting. For most people, daily activities and daily life remain tied to the traditional subsistence system of gardening, hunting, and fishing.

Social organization and social relations are also little changed from the pre-contact period. Kinship, domestic group composition, marriage patterns, political organization, patterns of work, and cooperation remain largely unchanged from the pre-contact period.[2]

The basic social, economic, and political unit continues to be the household or, more commonly today, the house cluster of siblings and their married and unmar-ried children. Within these kindreds, patterns of cooperation and sharing are little changed from pre-contact patterns described in the earliest missionary accounts and by the Waorani themselves. Outside the kindred, of course, the range of social rela-tions has broadened dramatically to include Waorani from formerly hostile groups as well as Quichua, Shuar, and other *kowudï*.

Social organization still provides little basis for group solidarity, and there is still little sense of or concern with group cohesiveness beyond the extended family. There are still no institutionalized mechanisms for settling disputes or for restrain-ing conflict when it occurs.

Ideological continuity also is apparent. In some settlements, to be sure, many people now consider themselves to be Christians. Even among these, however, there appears to be little fundamental difference in most world view assumptions and values between those who have lived most or all of their lives in association with missionaries and those who have had little or no direct contact with them. Indi-vidual autonomy continues to be highly valued, and parents still have little control over the actions of their adult or adolescent children. Just prior to our first field study, a group of adolescents and young men speared and stomped to death an old

---

[1]We presume his opposition to manioc is because the Quichua and Shuar let their manioc drink be-come alcoholic, although the reason he gives is that it is not healthful, which is, of course, preposterous. In fact, just the opposite is the case. Studies have shown that the traditional diets of indigenous people in this region are vastly superior to the diets that follow acculturation (e.g., Benefice & Barral, 1991).

[2]Very recently, a Waorani "tribal" government has been organized; this development is discussed in chapter 10.

woman in our settlement while the elders of their kindred continued to decry vio-lence. Today, as in the past, each kindred and, ultimately, each individual remains autonomous.

In short, the present relative peacefulness has few psychological, social, or cultural underpinnings. There are still few constraints—social, cultural, or psychological—on the actions of individuals. There are neither institutional nor (except for those committed to the ideology of nonviolence transmitted by the missionaries) inter-nalized controls on violence. Lacking psychological, social, or cultural underpin-nings, the new peacefulness is currently being sustained largely by the force of conscious social will.

In this new culture of peace, lacking as it does either internalized or institution-alized controls on conflict and violence, being Christian is an important component of a new identity for many. As we have seen, however, even for many of those who consider themselves Christians, Christian theology has made little impact beyond a few Bible stories and a belief in a God who abhors killing. Still, for them and for many others, the end of the vendettas is directly attributed to the women who brought the Christian message, if not to the message itself. As an accomplished killer and survivor of many retaliatory raids explained it to us, "We were almost down to two people; if it had not been for Nïmö [Rachael Saint] and Wïba, we would all be dead by now." While other of the values, beliefs, and behaviors pro-moted by the missionaries may have been little assimilated, for many Waorani, being Christian and being peaceful are inseparably linked.

In communities that hold Christian services, the central focus of the entire rit-ual is the concern with violence (cf. Yost, 1981). Rumors or reports of a dispute that threatens to turn violent generate a great deal of public concern. The participants are urged to let go of their anger and not to allow the conflict to escalate to a spearing. Prayers are offered that the killing not begin again, and these prayers are a public reaffirmation of the commitment, by individuals and by the community as a whole, to a new way of life. Being Christian and/or participating in the weekly church ser-vices are powerful public symbols of the commitment to the new "civilized" self-image, symbols that, along with the wearing of clothes and the abandonment of the balsa wood earplugs, both reflect and support that commitment.

The personal, individual commitment to peacefulness and the "letting go" of anger over past spearings is well illustrated by the agreement between Omëni and Buka to have their children marry and, thereby, to enter into the special kinship re-lation of *yaa,* co-parents-in-law. Omëni and other members of the Upriver group killed Buka's father in a spearing raid shortly before the arrival of the missionaries, even though they were related (Buka's father was married to Omëni's grand-mother's sister). Nonetheless, their children are now intermarried, and the two old enemies share grandchildren (see the kinship diagram in chapter 3).

Nowadays, when a spearing does occur, there is pressure on the victim's kin to avoid retaliation. When, just prior to our first study, the old woman from our settle-ment was killed, her daughter, Wïba, refused even to acknowledge that her mother had been murdered. Several years later, the victim's brother, the patriarch of the Upriver band, said, "In the old days, I would have killed them all by now, but we don't spear any more."

WORLD VIEW, EMOTION, AND CULTURE CHANGE

That comment—"In the old days, I would have killed them all . . ."—highlights what was, to us, one of the most puzzling aspects of this entire process of culture change: the apparent ease with which vendettas that had persisted for generations were ended. They simply stopped. How, we wondered, could blood feuds that had cost the lives of parents, siblings, and children, and motivated people to commit wholesale slaughter, be abandoned so easily? An answer may lie in the relationship between the changes that have occurred in individual and cultural schemata.

Stability and change are the two most fundamental characteristics of the kinds of cultural and individual information structures that we have been describing (cf. Laszlo, 1969). It is the relative stability of these maps/plans that provides a coherent and consistent guide to action in the world, but it is their capacity for change, for incorporating new information, that allows for their modification, for the recognition and pursuit of new goals and opportunities in response to new conditions.

We have already described both the stability of fundamental cultural assumptions and values, and the changes in individual motives and goals that occurred in recent years. In chapter 8, we argued that the homicidal rage engendered by the deaths of relatives was, in large part, a reaction to the violation of some of these fundamental asumptions, to a perceived assault on autonomy and effectiveness through active interference with individual expectations and goals.

If that is the case, then the formulation of an alternative set of goals and objectives—escaping the constant threat of violent death, gaining access to new goods and to potential spouses, and so on—came to take precedence and provided another definition of autonomy and effectiveness. Revenge for dead relatives was abandoned in service of these new, more important, and immediate goals. Precisely this can, in fact, be seen in the differing reactions generated by recent deaths on the reserve.

When young men speared and stomped Akawo, Wïba's mother, to death a few years ago, Wïba refused to even confront the fact that her mother had been murdered. Akawo's brother similarly refrained from taking revenge. This has been the pattern of response to every killing that we are aware of that has occurred on the reserve in the last 30 years. Taking revenge against other Waorani carries the very real threat of reigniting the vendettas and impeding the achievement of all those new goals. Thus, when Waorani have killed other Waorani, the victims' kin have, in every case, forgone retaliation.

Something very different has happened, however, when Waorani deaths have been attributed to *kowudï*. In two recent cases (described in chapter 10), sudden deaths were attributed to sorcery by *kowudï*. In both cases, the "victims'" kin launched retaliatory raids that slaughtered entire families. The difference here is that killing *kowudï* does not impede the attainment of other objectives: it does not threaten to reignite the vendettas among Waorani (and *kowudï* are unlikely to retaliate), nor does it interfere with the attainment of other goals.

Waorani themselves recognize that their new relative peacefulness is a tenuous and unstable achievement. The desire on the part of most people who lived through the vendettas not to be drawn back into that abyss is very real, and they are well aware that individual decisions and actions can still bring a return to the violence of the past. This awareness is reflected in the public prayers and frequent exhortations to avoid conflict and violence and, in the case of the recent killings, in the decisions to forego retaliation.

But the old pattern remains latent, as can be seen in the continuing relatively high rate of homicides and in the continuing obsession with the raids and killings of the recent past. These are almost constant topics of conversation and almost any incident can elicit a graphic account of how some kinsman met his or her untimely end.

The endless spearing stories reflect, as does our own obsession with media portrayals of violence, an ambivalence toward violence, both in the current culture and in individual personalities. The stories express both a horror of and a fascination with the bloodshed of the recent past while, at the same time, keeping it constantly on view as a reminder of a world to which most people who remember it do not want to return.

10 / Action in a New World: Ethnogenesis and the Return of Violence

In early 1993, we were traveling up the Shiripuno River in the company of a boat-load of Waorani after spending a few days in an outlying settlement. As we passed a homestead where colonists had cleared a large area and begun to plant coffee, the Waorani pulled their boat to the riverbank and called out to several people working in a field near the river. When the settlers came over, the Waorani men began making demands for produce of various kinds, saying that they would pick up the goods when they returned downstream. The settlers made no attempt to protest, and their faces remained carefully impassive. The threat of violence that lay just below the surface of the entire incident made clear to us just how tenuous the current peace actually is.

In a paper we presented soon after we returned from our first field study, we argued that, although the decline in homicide rates has held constant for most of a generation, the current peace is unstable at best and the potential for renewed violence is great, even among those who have never experienced it directly (Robarchek & Robarchek, 1996b). Unhappily, recent events seem to bear out that prediction. In the past several years, violence has been on the rise. After a lapse of more than two decades, there have recently been at least two raids in which, in the pre-contact pattern, entire families—men, women, and children—have been killed.

Unlike the abandonment of large-scale violence, which began without major environmental, economic, political, or social changes, its resurgence is occurring in a context of dramatic transformations, both within Waorani society and in its relations with the outside world.

OIL

A key variable in this equation is oil, but we cannot even begin to discuss the politics and economics of oil here.[1] For our present purposes, it is sufficient to note that, after several decades of relatively nondisruptive exploration established the presence of extensive reserves of petroleum in Waorani territory, the extraction phase is now well under way.

The exploration phase involved cutting lines through the forest for seismic exploration, clearing areas for campsites, and helicopter landing pads, and so on. While there was certainly pollution and some damage to the forest, and game was

---

[1]For good discussions of some of these issues and the environmental costs of oil extraction in the Oriente, see Kane, 1996, and Kimerling, 1991.

often frightened away, the region is vast and the ecological consequences of oil exploration were, for the most part, more or less temporary.

Waorani were, by and large, in favor of the activities of The Company. By providing jobs, cutting trails, and clearing sites, oil exploration gave Waorani access to the cash they needed to acquire the tools, shotguns, clothes, and other goods they wanted as they strove to shed their "Auca" identity.

If the impact of the exploration phase was, at least from the Waorani perspective, largely positive, extracting the oil from beneath the Waorani homeland and transporting it to foreign markets is another matter entirely. That process is vastly more destructive, both environmentally and culturally, and it is bringing to fruition those seeds of a resurgence of violence that we saw nearly a decade ago.

In 1993, during the rainy season, we made a trip by dugout canoe down the Shiripuno River to visit a group living far off the Protectorate. We had been travelling in a driving rain for hours, and runoff water was flowing into the river from every gully and rivulet, some of it ultimately coming from drilling sites and pipeline corridors many miles away. There, the runoff water had picked up the highly toxic crude oil from spills and ruptured pipes or from flooded ponds filled with drilling sludge and waste oil. As we traveled downstream under a leaden sky, floating mile after mile, hour after hour, through the heart of the Waorani homeland, the surface of that flood-swollen river shimmered, bank to bank, under a thin, rainbow-colored sheen of oil.

COLONISTS

Even more destructive than the oil itself, from the Waorani point of view, are the roads that accompany oil extraction. Getting the oil out of the jungle requires pipelines, and pipeline construction and maintenance require roads. When the first, and in 1993 still the only road into Waorani territory, was opened, the problems it brought were acute and immediate. Foremost among these was the problem of colonists.

From the moment word first reached surrounding groups that the Waorani were abandoning warfare, outsiders began encroaching on their land and resources. Some Quichua married in, then brought their relatives to hunt and fish. Soon they were poisoning long stretches of the Curaray and other rivers, drying the fish, and hauling them by the thousands of pounds to Puyo and Tena for sale. Homesteads and gardens began to appear along the once-forbidden south bank of the Napo River. In late 1987, as we were preparing to leave for home, there was talk among some young Waorani men of burning the settlers out.

With the opening of the first pipeline road (named, with typical sensitivity, the "Via Auca," or "Highway of the Savages"), running 60 miles into the Waorani heartland from the oil boom town of Coca to the Rio Tiguino, a vast and nearly uninhabited region became instantly accessible to landless Indians and other colonists. Since produce could be exported via the pipeline road, the region immediately became commercially exploitable for cattle, coffee, and other cash commodities. Colonization increased rapidly and dramatically, as did Waorani resentment. Settlers flooded in, and military units from the base at Coca began patrolling the road to deter those Waorani who wanted to drive the settlers out. Nonetheless, clashes did occur.

The situation was partially defused when the government, responding to the Waorani's destruction of some homesteads, restricted colonization to a narrow corridor along both sides of the road. Waorani resentment persists nonetheless; this has been the homeland of some bands for generations, and it infuriates them to see *kowudï* occupying it. It was in this context that the incident described at the beginning of this chapter took place.

The conflicts along the Via Auca present, in microcosm, the multilateral conflicts of interest that exist, not only between the Waorani and the government and oil companies, but between the Waorani and other Indians as well.

ETHNO-POLITICS, ECO-POLITICS, AND THE "NOBLE SAVAGE"

In recent years, a number of organizations have been formed to represent the interests of the Oriente's indigenous people. Nominally inclusive and claiming to represent all indigenes, they have, in reality, been dominated by the vastly more numerous Quichua and Shuar.

Still, despite their numerical insignificance, the Waorani have been assiduously courted by these organizations. There are several reasons for this, not the least of which is their symbolic value in Ecuadorian and international politics. To the sophisticated urbanites of the highlands (where all the important political decisions are made), these are still the *Aucas,* the ultimate savages, both terrifying and romantic.

In the world of national and international ecology-politics, they embody the politically correct mystique of the oppressed and exploited "Noble Savages," fighting valiantly to preserve their culture and protect the ecological integrity of their lands. While, as we have seen, there is a good deal of reality in that image, it is the mystique more than the reality that has public relations value. The reality of a houseful of women and children who have been speared to death is not an image that is likely to generate much sympathy for the perpetrators, their cause, or the causes of those associated with them.

Still, the myth-image of the Noble Savage has power in the modern world of manufactured media events so, whenever one of these indigenous organizations plans a demonstration, whether in a provincial town or in Quito, they come to recruit Waorani to join, with spears in hand, in manning the barricades. Usually the novelty of a trip to a city and free food is enough to entice at least a few people from one of the more easily accessible settlements to participate, even though they often know little and care less about either the manifest purpose of the demonstration or the politics of the organizers. And if, for some reason, Waorani can't be enticed to participate or don't show up on the appointed day, Indians from other groups have been known to shed their clothes and, brandishing fake spears purchased in the tourist shops, impersonate them for the cameras.

On one occasion when we were visiting in Tönyëmpadï, a military plane landed on the airstrip and the pilot opened the door and announced a free ride to Quito. Eight or ten Waorani and at least one Quichua schoolteacher immediately jumped on board and the plane took off. Some governmental agency was obviously planning some sort of media event.

Indigenous people constitute about 40% of Ecuador's population. The government, therefore, is eager to portray itself, both internally and internationally, as committed to protecting and advancing the welfare of the Oriente's indigenous people. It also wants to avoid any confrontation with them that could generate the sort of negative national or international publicity that might precipitate a strike or a boycott or otherwise somehow interfere with the flow of oil. A group of smiling "Aucas," photographed, spears in hand, with the minister of education as he opens a new one-room clapboard school built by Maxus, is political currency on the evening news in Quito.

In addition to this symbolic value, there are solidly material reasons for the government and indigenous organizations to court the Waorani: oil and land. The bulk of the oil development now occurring is in Waorani territory and, although Ecuadorian law gives indigenous people no legal claim to the resources beneath their lands, as a practical political matter, they have sometimes been able to negotiate some compensation. Various indigenous organizations have, in the past, purported to speak for the Waorani in negotiations with the government and the oil companies, but on more than one occasion, compensation negotiated and paid on their behalf never reached them.

Then there is the land itself. That 8,000 square miles of Waorani territory, mostly unpopulated, beckons irresistibly to the populous and land-poor Quichua and Shuar. Keeping that vast territory closed to colonization has not, to say the least, been a high priority for organizations dominated by these groups.

As a result of all this, Waorani, especially a handful of young men who have received some education and can speak, read, and write Spanish, came to the realization that Waorani interests are a primary concern of no one but themselves. They now recognize that they must rely on themselves to safeguard their own patrimony, and that this requires an organization that speaks only for the Waorani, and for *all* Waorani.

But that presents an immediate problem, since, as we have seen, Waorani "society" has not traditionally been a society at all. Rather, it has been an aggregation of independent kindreds, each concerned primarily with its own well-being. It was in this context that ONHAE came into being. In ONHAE and elsewhere, one can see the beginnings of ethnogenesis—the development of an inclusive Waorani ethnic identity—and of social-structural developments that transcend kinship and kindreds.

ETHNOGENESIS

We have noted repeatedly the psychological and cultural centrality of autonomy and independence and their social expression in the behavior of both individuals and kindreds. We have seen these values expressed in the atomistic character of Waorani social organization and in the absence of social ties that cross-cut kinship or limit the autonomy of individuals and kindreds. It should not be surprising, therefore, to discover that the beginnings of social institutions and social relations reaching beyond the kindred are rooted in influences external to Waorani society and culture.

The first of those outside influences was Christian missionization. While the Protestant missionaries never succeeded in their dream of converting all the "Savage Aucas" into a community of devout believers, they did create communities of self-identified Christians in some settlements. Their weekly church meetings are the only activities that bring different kindreds together in a ritual that centers on the renunciation of violence. The Christian identity, moreover, transcends, at least to a limited extent, both kindreds and settlements. It unites its followers into a larger Christian community that comprises a significant moral and political force, especially on the Protectorate.

A second such externally derived institution is the school. The larger settlements where schools are located inevitably contain kindreds that are unrelated or only distantly related to one another. The decision to request a teacher and start a school creates a common interest among these kindreds in promoting the success of the school. A school also generates responsibilities *as a community:* the construction and maintenance of a schoolhouse and a house for the teacher; the preparation of the children's noon meal (done in rotation by the women of the community); and the provisioning of the teacher and, sometimes, his wife and children. Intragroup cooperation is also required to deal with any problems or conflicts that arise from this community-wide endeavor.

A third externally derived element is sports, especially soccer. We saw how the evening games bring the different kindreds in a settlement together, if only for a few hours a week, helping to generate a sense of community identity. Slowly, settlements are moving from being mere aggregations of autonomous kindreds to becoming social and political entities in their own right.

This nascent community identity is also reinforced by and expressed in the very recent development of the *carnavales,* the inter-village soccer tournaments. Although they are organized on the model of the traditional *ëëmë,* the units, both the hosts and the guests, are communities rather than kindreds. In the soccer games, in contrast to the vendettas, it is not *Omëníri* (Omënï's bunch) versus the *Pïgöiri* (Pïgö's bunch), but the community of Tïwënö versus the community of Kiwarö. This development truly transcends kinship: Kin who reside in different communities play on opposing teams.

Perhaps related to this weakening of kinship as the only social structural principle is the apparent weakening, decried by some of our older informants, of the distinction between cross and parallel cousins with regard to sexual relations in the context of the inter-village *carnavales.*

Of course, the strongest and most explicit manifestation of this creation of an ethnic identity is in the formation of ONHAE. This reflects a conscious and deliberate attempt to create a single "nation" from the dispersed kindreds and regional bands.

In the new political reality that accompanies this developing ethnicity, the primary structural units are again spatially and politically constituted, rather than being constituted by kinship; they are settlements, not kindreds. At the *Congreso,* unrelated people sat together, grouped by community; and when the meeting was opened, they were explicitly recognized *as communities;* for example, "there is the *Tïwënö nänikabo,*" literally, "the Tïwënö bunch of them"

Not surprisingly, the Congreso saw some of the clearest statements of this growing ethnic and political consciousness. Since Waorani territory is so vast, crossing the two Ecuadorian provinces of Pastaza and Napo, someone suggested that perhaps there should be two organizations, one representing the western part of the territory, the other the east.

A young man from the distant Yasuní band spoke up: "Our land is already divided in two provinces; we should be in one."

The vice president of ONHAE: "Who will live here? Our grandchildren! We do not want a division. No. We are one organization, not two or four."

A man from the Shiripuno: "Two provinces are not good; we are one people and one land."

While much of the impetus for ethnogenesis comes from within Waorani society, both the government and The Company are fostering the process. Both have provided food, gasoline and transport in support of these organizational efforts.

The reasons for that support are not difficult to see. It is very useful politically to have official Waorani "representatives" to deal with. Both The Company's and the government's interests are served by the emergence of Waorani "leaders" and "officials" whose signatures on official documents can be displayed as evidence of Waorani approval. This gives at least the appearance of an indigenous voice in the agreements that are being "negotiated."

But saying that there has been support from the government and from The Company in creating ONHAE is not to imply that there has been sufficient support to make it *effective*. That would require relatively little in comparison with the vast wealth being extracted: an office, a computer, a secretary, a file cabinet, some clerical supplies, two or three desks, and a dozen shortwave radios for communicating with far-flung communities. No support of that sort has been forthcoming from either the government or The Company. When we left, ONHAE's "files" consisted of letters and papers stuffed in cardboard boxes and pushed under the sleeping platforms in the ONHAE officers' bamboo houses.

Moreover, these emerging "leaders" are very young and unsophisticated; they were still schoolboys when we did our first study five years before. They are potentially vulnerable to all sorts of threats and blandishments to persuade them to legitimize The Company's and the government's activities. An American journalist reported seeing an employee of The Company try to deliver an envelope full of cash to one of these young "officials" in the middle of the night (Kane, 1996).

And, of course, this is still a society whose culture stresses that one's own best interests and those of one's kindred are primary. When funds are offered or are at hand, it is very difficult for these officers to ignore demands from their own kindreds.

THE RESURGENCE OF VIOLENCE

This developing ethnic consciousness both expresses and stimulates the growing recognition of common interests among all Waorani, and fundamental and increasing conflicts of interest with *kowudï*.

In 1992, Amö, a young Waorani man who had been elected secretary of ONHAE at the first Congreso in 1990, was killed when he fell from one of the open-sided truck/buses that ply the Via Auca providing transportation to Coca for colonists and their produce. People crowd onto these vehicles, riding inside on wooden benches and, when those are full, sitting atop the cargo piled on the roof. Somehow, as one of these bounced down the via Auca, Amö fell off the top, landed on his head, and died.

A Capuchin priest who examined the body in Coca assured us that the youth had died of a fractured skull suffered in the fall. Waorani, however, universally believe he was shot by Shuar colonists. That is what we were told when we were shown his grave, which has almost become a shrine, and whenever else the subject of colonists came up.

This incident and the Waorani response to it is indicative of a pervasive change that is taking place in Waorani perceptions of their relationships to surrounding groups. Perceptions of *kowudï* held for the past 20 years are undergoing a transformation in the direction of the pre-contact image. With the development of an inclusive Waorani identity, and with the growing recognition of fundamental structural oppositions between themselves, the oil companies, the government, missionaries, and other Indians, the old image of *kowudï,* barely submerged during the years of voluntary acculturation, is reemerging.

What seems to be occurring is a reversion of Waorani perceptions of at least some *kowudï* back into murderous enemies who should be killed. The story of Amö's death provides a powerful and immediate validation of and justification for these revitalized conceptions.

Another powerful indication of the rise of this new/old image of *kowudï* is in the resurgence of raiding. In the past several years, there have been at least two raids against *kowudï* in which, in the pre-contact pattern, entire families were wiped out.

One of these was precipitated by the sudden death of a Quichua woman who had married into a Waorani community. When she died, possibly from anaphylactic shock as a result of a scorpion sting, the accepted story—and, like the story of Amö's death, the reality for Waorani—is that she was killed by a sorcerer from her home (Quichua) village. The attributed motive was that her relatives were envious of the four gold teeth her husband bought for her with money he earned working for The Company. The story, as it was recounted to us by Ompudë and Mïngkayï, clearly reflects these current Waorani perceptions of *kowudï:*

> There was an oil well downriver on the Tzapino. The Company gave a lot of money to Itekä at Wamönö, and others got motors for their canoes, pots, axes, machetes, and so on. With this money, Itekä bought his wife, Maria, some gold teeth.
>
> Now, Itekä's wife was an *Oruna* from the Curaray, and she took many of these gifts from The Company home to her mother. There, all her relatives saw her gold teeth and became very envious and angry that she [and the Waorani] should have gotten so many good things from The Company while they had nothing.
>
> Her mother's people went to the sorcerer— Manwedo [Manuel] was his name— and gave him money and he sent a scorpion to sting her. Maria went into the house after being stung and it hurt all night and bled. Before she died, she said, "For my gold teeth, my pots, and my axes, I am about to die!" By morning, she was dead.
>
> Itekä was raging and threatening to spear. He even carried spears as he got the boards to make her coffin, saying, "We are going to bury her well." Many came to her burial, some came by motor-canoe from working for The Company. They made her grave like the Oruna, her own people, do.

Maria left behind two children: a baby boy and a girl about six years old. They were crying for their mother. Itekä was very angry over his wife's death. Omari, the children's grandmother, said, "They are not *kowudï;* I will take them and raise them." And she did.

Itekä sent for his relatives because he wanted to spear. One came from Dayünö and one came from somewhere on the Napo River. When they got there, they made really long spears. In only one day they made them. All of these men, like Itekä's siblings, were angry too and asked where the sorcerer lived. Over by the Villano River was the answer. Itekä told all of them "Tomorrow you will all go with me and spear!" All but two of them agreed.

They set out with their spears, going down the Akarö River in Tönyë's canoe with the motor. A huge storm came up with lots of wind and lightning. They finally arrived at the place where the feeder stream that the sorcerer lived on joined the river on which they were traveling. The feeder stream was too shallow to float the canoe, so they took it out of the water and hid it and started across country. They came near where The Company had been working and went on for about an hour until they came to the settlement where the sorcerer lived.

Now some of them knew this house because they had once attended an *ëëmë* there. They admired the house because it was built of real lumber and was well-cleared all around. In addition, it had a strong wood door with a real lock. They say the sorcerer made his door so strong because he had a dream that he would be speared and die. Knowing all this, the raiding party decided to wait until all the people came home in the evening before attempting the attack.

All the people of the house arrived late in the day and the door was tightly shut and locked. As they came closer, they could hear the family as they sat, eating and talking. Thinking that they could not take the sorcerer by surprise if they went directly to the locked door, they all started to shake the house on its upright supports. They shook the house just like an earthquake.

Möi made a run at the door and broke it in. The sorcerer was by the fire; Tönyë speared him, then Itekä speared him. One of his children grabbed the shotgun from the corner and pointed it at Itekä, but Möi speared the child before a shot could be fired. The child fell down on the floor and died. The wife picked up a machete, and Möi speared her and she died.

An older unmarried daughter cried out in fear to her dead parents and begged the men to let her go, but Itekä was enraged because of his wife's death and he and Möi speared her. Only one family member managed to run out the door in the confusion, a 13-year-old girl. She ran to another house, then farther, and even though the men chased her, she got away.

The next day, the radio carried the news and the *kowudï* left the Curaray in fear. The Curaray people say, "You all have done badly; you have speared our grandfather." Tönyë and the others ran upstream. People are said to have called Wïba in Tönyëmpadï from Shell-Mera [using the missionaries' shortwave radio network]. Wïba told Waorani on the radio not to be angry.

But Tönyë was angry, and he went to Coca, where even the police were looking for him. He went to a chief of police, who signed a piece of paper and said it was all right, since he had killed the sorcerer who had killed his sister-in-law. Then even Gïntadë [the elder of a band from the nearby Tiguïnö River] came down to see what had happened, and he said that it was all right as far as he was concerned; it was no kin of his who were killed, and he went back to Tiguïnö.

The Oruna sorcerers are everywhere. Now even the sorcerers way upstream are afraid because of that spearing. There are many *kowudï* sorcerers. The *kowudï* say they

are not doing sorcery, but we say they do, and now they are afraid. They say they will
go to the police if we harm them, but we say that we will just go away into the forest
and come back after four months or so.

This account clearly shows Waorani perceptions of the inevitable conflict between themselves and *kowudï,* conflict stemming from what is seen as the latter's
greedy envy of Waorani land and resources. It also exemplifies an increasingly widely
held conception of the murderous intentions of the *kowudï* who surround them.

Interestingly, it also shows an awareness (at least by the couple whose account
this is) of the opinions of outsiders (us), shown in the "self-defense" justification for
killing the wife and children (because they tried to attack the raiders with the shotgun and machete), and in the highly unlikely account of the subsequent approval of
the killings as justified by "the police."

The other recent raid was in response to a child's sudden death. This death, too,
was attributed to sorcery, this time allegedly committed by neighboring Shuar. The
avenging raiders speared to death a family of four and an unlucky visitor who happened to be staying with them.

It is clear from all of this that outsiders are increasingly seen as murderous enemies. This pre-contact image, though latent for a generation (the participants in both
the recent raids were men who grew to adulthood after the cessation of large-scale
hostilities), has reemerged to provide an orienting frame within which the sharpen-
ing conflicts are made sensible, and through which the anger and hostility that these
generate are channeled and given direction.

CONCLUSION

In truth, there is no "conclusion" to this case study of the Waorani. What we have
tried to do here is to provide a glimpse of a society in transition, indeed a society
undergoing multiple transformations simultaneously. The ultimate outcome, as
Waorani themselves recognize, is still very much in doubt.

After more than two decades of relative peace, violence is once again on the
upswing. Significantly, *kowudï,* and not other Waorani, have thus far been the targets of this renewed violence. This may be a reflection of the escalating process of
ethnogenesis, of the growing awareness of themselves as a group, deriving, at least
in part, from the recognition of their shared interests and of the fundamental oppositions between themselves and the oil companies, the government, and other indigenous groups.

One thing is abundantly clear, however: the current resurgence of homicidal violence is, like its earlier cessation, the product of complex interactions among the
historical, environmental, sociocultural, and psychological contexts of action. These
constitute a changing behavioral environment that informs Waorani perceptions of
the legitimacy and advisability of violence in human relations.

While, for most people, avoiding a return to the state of unconstrained warfare is
an immediate and pragmatic objective, there has been little time to develop a commitment to peaceful values in the abstract or to produce the psychological orientations and the social and cultural institutions that could make peace self-sustaining.
But regardless of what happens in the future, the fact remains that most Waorani

deliberately and decisively abandoned large-scale violence and the succeeding generation has largely followed their lead. After generations of warfare, and in the absence of major changes in subsistence practices or in the availability of material resources, Waorani society transformed itself from the most violent on earth to one that is, by and large, peaceful.

Even though occasional spearings continue, the old pattern of raiding and vendettas was abandoned remarkably quickly and easily. Most people agreed to forgive old grievances and abandon revenge raiding once they were convinced that their enemies would do the same. The culture of war, insulated from new information, had a momentum that had carried it across many generations. When new information became available, however, it generated new constructions of reality, and that allowed the formulation of new individual and social goals. People pursued those new goals by choosing courses of action directed toward gaining what they wanted from the new reality.

The arrival of Protestant missionaries and their introduction of Christian ideas and values played key strategic roles in this transformation. Their technology made it possible to initiate new contacts with some degree of safety, and the alternative value system that they provided was, for some people, a key factor in their abandonment of the vendettas.

Absolutely crucial, however, was the new information, the new vision of reality provided by the returning women who accompanied them. It was the desire of the Waorani themselves to end the killing—once that was revealed as a practical possibility—that ultimately made the rapid transformation possible.

When the new alternatives and possibilities became visible, most people radically altered their motives and their behavior in pursuit of new and previously unobtainable goals: personal security, access to potential spouses, medical care, new technology, and so on. The pragmatic result was that a cultural pattern of extreme violence that had persisted for at least a century, and possibly much longer, was abandoned virtually overnight. When an opportunity to escape the cycle of killing that had entrapped them presented itself, Waorani seized and implemented it. This is a powerful testimony both to the central role of information in sociocultural dynamics and to the capacity of human beings to take their destinies into their own hands.

Epilogue (Clay)

Those who cannot remember the past
are condemned to repeat it.

George Santayana

The incident on the Shiripuno that opened this chapter called to mind an incident from my childhood. In the early 1950s, my younger brother and I were standing in our back yard in a small town in Nebraska where my father, using some ancient hand tools inherited from his father, was crafting a bow from a piece of hardwood that he had been carefully seasoning.

A neighbor, a very old man (probably in his eighties), was watching from the backyard across the alley. Finally, he came over, and said something like "Boy, seeing that damn thing really brings back memories." He then proceeded to describe to us how, when he was a child living on a homestead on the Nebraska prairie, probably in the late 1870s or early 1880s, Sioux Indians would ride their horses up to the family's sod house, nock their arrows, and draw back their bows. "We would just step aside," he said, "and let them go in and take whatever they wanted."

Seeing that scene from the North American plains reenacted 120 years later in the South American rainforest generated a strange sense of something like *déjà vu*, as we witnessed another warlike but vastly outnumbered group of Indians trying to cope, in the only ways they knew how, with a new world that would inevitably overwhelm them. Since we know that the driving force behind much of what is happening in the Oriente is oil, and most of that oil is destined for the United States, Santayana's observation seems poignantly appropriate here.

Afterword

Our 1993 study was our fourth field project in twenty years of studying peacefulness and violence in remote jungle-dwelling societies. People often ask us if this kind of research has anything useful to tell us about violence in our own society. We believe that it does, and that analyzing the dynamics of peacefulness and violence in structurally less complex societies such as these can reveal processes that are also at work in our own.

While we feel that an approach that focuses on the contexts of violence will be useful in the analysis of any social conflict, we also recognize that a psychocultural analysis of world views, values, emotions, and so on, will probably not tell us a great deal about high-tech, mechanized, anonymous, nation-state warfare where the combatants may feel little animosity toward each other, may be separated by tens or hundreds of miles, and may never even see one another.

The increasingly frequent and severe ethnic conflicts that seem to be characteristic of the late twentieth century, however, are another matter entirely. In violent conflicts such as those in Bosnia-Herzegovina, Azerbaijan, Afganistan, Rwanda, and Chechnia, group identity, values, self-image, and the emotions of rage, hatred, envy, and fear loom as large motivationally as they did among the Waorani, as is evidenced by the savagery of the atrocities inflicted, even on noncombatant civilians.

We also see some remarkable parallels between our Amazonian case study and the urban jungles to which we returned. Urban gang warfare, like Waorani warfare, is premised on loyalty to a very small group, territoriality, bravado, blood vengeance, and the use of violence, both instrumentally to achieve specific goals and for self-validation.

Human identity, here as in Amazonia, is extended only to those in a small face-to-face group, and the human emotions of empathy, sympathy, and compassion are simply not relevant in relations with those outside it. Killing a nongang member for a pair of sneakers or a leather jacket is as easy and inconsequential for a gang member as it was for a Waorani to kill a *kowudï* for an axe or a machete. The blood vendettas between the Upriver and Downriver Waorani are mirrored in our city by those between the Insane Crips and the Junior Boys.

Here, as among the Waorani, there is a self-perpetuating culture of violence. Regardless of whether or not it has its ultimate origins in the socioeconomic "roots of violence" that obsess social reformers, it is clear that, here as in Amazonia, it is maintained and perpetuated by a psychocultural dynamic. For those caught up in it, gang violence is a way of life that gives identity, meaning, and purpose.

The Waorani case offers us a particularly valuable perspective because, in many ways, they are an extreme version of ourselves. They, too, see humankind as dominant over nature and in charge of its own destiny; their fundamental orientations to themselves, to each other, and to the world around them, manifested in their world view and value system, are strikingly similar to our own. It was impossible for us, as American observers, not to admire them because they manifest so many of the same values that we espouse, including egalitarianism, autonomy, individualism, and courage.

Moreover, their culture, like our own, is suffused with violence. Although the mass killing has largely ceased, violence lurks just below the consciousness of even those young people who did not experience it directly. Their obsession with the spearings of the recent past mirrors our own fascination with and ambivalence toward violence, as is reflected in our mass media.

If there is even a possibility that these resemblances reflect the operation of fundamentally similar psychological and sociocultural processes, then they deserve much closer examination, particularly in view of the fact that the Waorani were able, very rapidly, to transform their culture of violence and reduce their rate of homicide by more than 90%.

As we compare our own society with that of the Waorani (and as we contrast both with the Semai), one common feature stands out starkly, both in urban neighborhoods and in the Amazon: the lack of any encompassing, psychologically significant *community* acting as a moral force to constrain individual action. In neither place is there a larger moral community effectively instilling social values, monitoring behavior for compliance, or uniting individuals and kindreds in networks of obligations and responsibilities that transcend their own narrow wishes and interests.

For Waorani, as we have seen, there was, until very recently, no sense of or interest in any community beyond the immediate bilateral kindred of parents, siblings, and parallel cousins. Sole allegiance was to this group, and all those outside it were real or potential enemies. Obligations and responsibilities were confined to the immediate kindred, and even this group imposed few real constraints on the actions of individuals. The values of individualism and autonomy had been carried to their logical conclusion, to a point where a sense of obligation to and responsibility for a larger community was nonexistent. Even today that remains largely true for most Waorani; identity with the emerging Waorani "nation" is tenuous, and that community still has little moral salience for most people.

In our own society, similarly, a great many people (and not only among the poor and disadvantaged) have no primary reference group that provides a sense of identity, that teaches socially positive values, or that acts to promote and reinforce behavior consistent with those values. Like the Waorani, they lack any positive group, either kin or community, that acts as a moral force to constrain individual action or to unite individuals into social networks that transcend their own interests.

The existence of a community whose interests take precedence over the whims of individuals is the primary reason why small rural communities are much less troubled by violence than are large urban neighborhoods. The former are still *communities* where people are enmeshed in networks of long-term relationships that communicate a consistent set of expectations, and where their behavior is carefully monitored for compliance.

Individuals, regardless of their own inclinations, are expected to conform to the community's norms, and the hand of day-to-day social control, manifested in gossip, shaming, and ridicule, can be heavy if they do not. But such sanctions are effective only because the community has some psychological salience: it *matters* to individuals because they locate their identities within it and, willingly or not, they put its demands and expectations ahead of their own impulses.

By contrast, most urban neighborhoods, regardless of socioeconomic level, are not communities in this sense at all; they are merely amorphous and amoral aggregations. They have no psychological salience and they present no consistent model with which to identify and on which to build a sense of self, nor do disorganized families or public schools, preoccupied with value-neutrality and promoting "self-esteem."

But gangs do. Young people, lacking any other psychologically meaningful communities, create their own, and these most certainly *do* provide a reference group and a sense of identity. They also often present a realm of new opportunities and goals—excitement, money, drugs, sex—and they provide the means for achieving them. Some of the behaviors they promote reflect values, such as loyalty, courage, individualism, and materialism, that are shared with the wider society. Many other behaviors—intimidation, vengeance, and murder—do not.

As the epidemic of violence has spread, two kinds of prescriptions have predominated: (1) more severe and certain punishment for violent offenders, and (2) elimination of the socioeconomic conditions that purportedly "breed violence." While it can reasonably be argued that neither approach has been consistently applied, it is clear that, to the extent that they have, both have failed miserably. As expenditures for both new prisons and new social programs have soared, our streets and homes have become increasingly less secure.

This is not to imply that we should stop prosecuting violent criminals or that we should cease striving to ameliorate poverty and eliminate inequality; but it should be clear by now that, with homicide now the leading cause of death in some segments of our population, we cannot afford to wait for the millennium before seeking some other solutions.

Our analysis of the dynamics of violence and peacefulness in Waorani society also calls these current "solutions" into question. Recall that, in a relatively short time, the Waorani reduced homicides by more than 90%. The killers are still there; many were our friends and neighbors. They were not defeated or incarcerated, nor were they incorporated as equals into the Ecuadorian socioeconomic system. Yet, with relatively rare exceptions, they stopped killing.

What happened, as we saw, was that new information, new cultural knowledge, allowed people to envision new possibilities and to formulate new goals. New leaders emerged offering new alternatives and new means of achieving them. The Waorani responded by abandoning their vendettas and their generations-old culture of war to pursue what they wanted from this new reality.

Their decision was reinforced by the formation of new reference groups that transcended the narrow interests of individuals and kindreds. First came the community of Christian believers. Later, community interests and individual identities premised on the criteria of locality and ethnicity began to develop. Although this process is just beginning, none of these communities and identities even existed as social or psychological realities before. They all demand some submission of individual impulses in service of the objectives of the group.

This kind of individual and cultural reorientation is not unique to the Waorani. Their case has many features in common with other instances of rapid sociocultural change that have been documented by anthropologists. These include leaders who were "marginal," in the sense that they had been exposed to ideological and behavioral alternatives; thus, they could both see the implications of those alternatives and communicate them to their neighbors and kin in terms that the latter could comprehend.

And, as in similar cases elsewhere, major sociocultural change was not dependent on profound psychological reorganization in most members of the society (cf. Wallace, 1956, 1970). While such a reorganization of attitudes and values did occur in some individuals—our friend Omëni, a prime example—the changes were much more superficial for most people. This is evidenced by the world view and value system that we found to be largely unaltered, and by the occasional violent lapses that still occur.

What is required in our urban jungles is precisely that same kind of reorientation, and there are already models for such change available within our own society. The successes achieved in rehabilitating criminals and drug users by groups such as the Black Muslims, Synanon (in its early years), the Native American Church, the Pan-Indian religious movement, and charismatic Christianity are well-known. All these can be seen as models for generating meaningful reference groups, a sense of identity, wider senses of social responsibility, and sets of values consistent with (but not necessarily identical with) those of the wider society.

Unfortunately, the religious or quasi-religious character of most of these groups often disqualifies them from receiving financial support from government agencies. Moreover, the typically charismatic leaders of the most successful of these, and the devotion they inspire in their followers, often threaten and frighten mainstream society. Ironically, it is probably precisely those characteristics that make it possible for such leaders to present authoritatively new attitudes, values, and goals and, ultimately, to generate new identities.

Given the demonstrated success of such groups in reordering disordered and dysfunctional lives, we should be searching our cities for charismatic leaders in the mold of Martin Luther King, Jr., and Malcolm X, leaders who can articulate a new frame of reference for self-identity and a new vision of the future. Rather than demonizing these leaders and the groups they lead, we need to devise ways to make society's resources available to assist them in generating viable communities of followers.

Rehabilitation and reincorporation of the perpetrators of violence, however, is not the ultimate solution to the problem. Rather, we must find ways of enculturating socially positive values and attitudes in each new generation. Here again, generating meaningful communities is probably the key. Adult-directed peer communities have long been recognized as an effective means of inculcating society's values and goals in the next generation. From puberty rites and bush schools to the Nazi and Communist youth corps, their effectiveness has been well demonstrated.

These last two examples are, perhaps, reason enough to be wary of centralized, government-directed organizations, but there are other alternatives already available to us. Although the content of their programs may have little relevance for modern urban youth, groups such as the Cub Scouts, Girl Scouts, and Boy Scouts can provide us with structural models. If sufficient commitment existed, and resources were made available to develop new orientations and new programs and make membership desirable through activities, uniforms, field trips, weekend and summer camps, and so on, such traditional organizations could be revitalized. New ones directed to the interests and needs of our increasingly diverse society might also emerge, perhaps under the sponsorship and direction of churches, corporations, and civic organizations.

Our goal should be to replace gangs with permanent, ongoing reference groups with which young people could be affiliated from childhood through adolescence. Unlike sports teams, these would not be focused on a single activity (although they might well include sports among their activities). Rather they would encompass as many aspects of children's experience—intellectual, aesthetic, social—as possible. They should include a challenging course of skill-building activities with structured goals and activities that progress and develop as the child does. This would provide opportunities for achievement and accomplishment as a basis for genuine self-respect.

Under adult direction, these peer communities would provide a consistent model for and reflection of a positive sense of self. Making continuing participation contingent on appropriate behavior and putting the responsibility for discipline in the hands of the members would mobilize peer pressure in support of society's values.

Finally, successful participation in well designed activities that relate directly to adult career options would communicate realistic possibilities and goals to young people while helping them to develop the attitudes and skills necessary to achieve those goals, replacing hopelessness, aimlessness, and anomie with realistic aspirations and achievable objectives.

Certainly, some caution must be exercised in any such endeavor. The transformative power of groups always carries the potential for fanaticism, as Jonestown, Synanon's latter phase, the Branch Davidians, and Heaven's Gate all demonstrated. And, as we have seen all too often, there is always the danger that group identity, particularly when it is rooted in ethnicity, can turn toward demagoguery. Nevertheless, given the current state of affairs and what is at stake, the potential payoff is surely worth the gamble.

Glossary

acculturation: culture change resulting from one society's adoption of cultural elements from another (often more powerful) society

agouti: a jackrabbit-size rodent

Auca: "savage" (from Quichua); used in Ecuador, usually pejoratively, to refer to Waorani

bilateral descent: descent reckoned through both the father and mother

chonta: a species of palm tree; source of wood for spears and blowguns and of highly prized starchy fruit

cross cousin: mother's brother's or father's sister's child

ethnogenesis: the development of a sense of ethnic identity

increased inclusive fitness: an increase, relative to others, of one's own genes in the next generation

kindred: a group of individuals who can trace relationships to one another through either mother or father

kowudï: outsider; foreigner

manioc: a starchy tuber

nuclear family: father, mother, and children

Oriente: term used in Ecuador to designate the rainforested region east of the Andes

paradigm: originally a structure of information that defined a set of something, such as pronouns or kin terms; now used to describe an explanatory framework that accounts for how some aspect of the world works

parallel cousin: mother's sister's or father's brother's child

peccary: either of two species of wild pig-like mammals native to the new world

phonemes: the basic meaningful sounds of a language

phonetic: (adj.) refers to the distinguishable features of spoken sounds

phonology: referring to the sounds that are meaningful in a given language

plantains: several kinds of bananas that are usually eaten cooked

schema: (pl., schemata) a system of information that constitutes both a map of some reality and a plan for action in it

swidden: method of gardening based on clearing an area of rainforest, burning the cut vegetation or allowing it to rot, planting gardens for a year or two, and then allowing the area to reforest itself

tipë: a drink made of manioc that is mashed, pre-chewed, and left to ferment slightly

tutelary spirit: a supernatural guardian or protector

vendetta: an ongoing cycle of reciprocal revenge-raiding among kin groups

References Cited

Bennett Ross, J. (1980). Ecology and the problem of the tribe: A critique of the Hobbesian model of preindustrial warfare. In E. B. Ross (Ed.), *Beyond myths of culture*. (p. 33–60). New York: Academic Press.

Benefice, E., & Barral, H. (1991). Differences in life style and nutritional status between settlers and Siona–Secoya Indians living in the same Amazonian milieu. *Ecology of Food and Nutrition, 25,* 307–322.

Blomberg, R. (1957). *The naked Aucas: An account of the Indians of Ecuador.* London: George Allen & Unwin, Ltd.

Chagnon, N. (1988). Life histories, blood revenge, and warfare in a tribal population. *Science, 239,* 985–992.

Davis, W. E., & Yost, J. A. (1983). The ethnobotany of the Waorani of eastern Ecuador. *Botanical Museum Leaflets: Harvard University, 29*(3), 159–217.

Dentan, R. K. (1968). *The Semai: A nonviolent people of Malaysia.* New York: Holt, Rinehart and Winston.

Dubos, R. (1959). *Mirage of health.* New York: Harper and Row.

Elliot, E. (1957). *Through gates of splendor.* New York: Harper & Brothers.

Elliot, E. (1961). *The savage my kinsman.* New York: Harper & Brothers.

Farabee, W. C. (1922). *Indian tribes of Eastern Peru.* Cambridge, MA, The Museum, New York: Kraus Reprint Co.

Ferguson, R. B. (1992). A savage encounter: Western contact and the Yanomamo war complex. In R. B. Ferguson and N. L. Whitehead (Eds.), *War in the tribal zone.* (pp. 199–228). Santa Fe, NM: School of American Research Press.

Greenberg, J. H. (1987). *Language in the Americas.* Stanford, CA: Stanford University Press.

Gross, D. R. (Ed.). (1975). Protein capture and cultural development in the Amazon Basin. *American Anthropologist, 77*(3), 526–549.

Harner, M. J. (1972). *The Jivaro: People of the sacred waterfalls.* Garden City, NY: Doubleday Natural History Press.

Harris, M. (1971). *Culture, man, and nature.* New York: Crowell.

Harris, M. (1974). *Cows, pigs, wars, and witches: The riddles of culture.* New York: Random House.

Harris, M. (1977). *Cannibals and kings.* New York: Random House.

Harris, M. (1979). The Yanomamö and the causes of war in band and village societies. In M. L. Margolis & W. E. Carter (Eds.), *Brazil: Anthropological Perspectives.* (pp. 121–133). New York: Columbia University Press.

Holloway, H. L. (1932). East of the Ecuadorian Andes. *The Geographical Journal, 80*(5), 410–419.

Kane, J. (1996). *Savages.* New York: Alfred A. Knopf.

Kimerling, J. (1991). *Amazon crude.* Natural Resources Defense Council.

Larrick, J. W., Yost, J. A., & Kaplan, J. (1978). Snake bite among the Waorani Indians of eastern Ecuador. *Transactions of the Royal Society of tropical medicine and hygiene, 72*(5), 542–543.

Laszlo, E. (1969). *System, structure, and experience.* New York: Gordon and Breach.

Meyers, F. R. (1988). The logic and meaning of anger among Pintupi aborigines. *Man 25,* 589–610.

Milton, K. (1984). Protein and carbohydrate resources of the Maku Indians of northwestern Amazonia. *American Anthropologist, 86*(1), 7–27.

Muratorio, B. (1991). *The life and times of Grandfather Alonso: Culture and history in the Upper Amazon.* New Brunswick, NJ: Rutgers University Press.

Orton, J. (1876). *The Andes and the Amazon: Or, across the continent of South America.* (3rd ed.). New York: Harper & Brothers.

Peeke, C. (1973). *Preliminary grammar of Auca.* Norman, OK: Summer Institute of Linguistics.

Rival, L. (1992). *Social transformations and the impact of formal schooling on the Huaorani of Amazonian Ecuador.* Doctoral dissertation, London School of Economics, University of London.

Rival, L. (1993). The growth of family trees: Understanding Huaorani perceptions of the forest. *Man* (n.s.), *28,* 635–652.

Robarchek, C. A. (1977). Frustration, aggression, and the nonviolent Semai. *American Ethnologist, 4*(4), 762–779.

Robarchek, C. A. (1979). Learning to fear: A case study of emotional conditioning. *American Ethnologist, 6*(3), 555–567.

Robarchek, C. A. (1980). The image of nonviolence: World view of the Semai Senoi. *The Journal of the Federated States Museums, 25,* 103–117.

Robarchek, C. A. (1989). Primitive warfare and the ratomorphic image of mankind. *American Anthropologist, 91*(4), 903–920.

Robarchek, C. A. (1990). Motivations and material causes: On the explanation of conflict and war. In J. Haas (Ed.), *The anthropology of war.* (pp. 56–76). New York, Cambridge University Press.

Robarchek, C. A., & Robarchek, C. J. (1989). The Waorani: From warfare to peacefulness. *The World and I, 4*(1), 624–635.

Robarchek, C. A., & Robarchek, C. J. (1992). Culture of war, culture of peace: A comparative study of Semai and Waorani. In J. Silverberg & J. P. Gray (Eds.), *Aggression and peacefulness in humans and other primates.* (pp. 189-213). Oxford: Oxford University Press.

Robarchek, C. A., & Robarchek, C. J. (1996a). *Waging peace: The psychological and sociocultural dynamics of positive peace.* In A. Wolfe & H. Yang (Eds.), Anthropological Contributions to Conflict Resolution. (pp. 64–80). Athens, Georgia: University of Georgia Press.

Robarchek, C. A., & Robarchek, C. J. (1996b). The Aucas, the cannibals, and the missionaries: From warfare to peacefulness among the Waorani. In T. Gregor (Ed.), *A Natural History of Peace.* (pp. 189–212). Nashville: Vanderbilt University Press.

Ross, E. B. (1978). Food taboos, diet, and hunting strategy: The adaptation to animals in Amazonian cultural ecology. *Current Anthropology, 19*(1), 1–36.

Saint, R. (1964). *Aucas and cannibals: How the Aucas came to Ecuador as told by Uncle Gikita and translated by Rachel Saint.* Summer Institute of Linguistics. University of Oklahoma.

Schoeck, H. (1966). *Envy. A theory of social behavior.* New York: Harcourt, Brace and World.

Sinclair, J. H., & Wasson, T. (1923). Exploration in Eastern Ecuador. *The Geographical Review, 13*(2), 190–213.

Smith, R. (1993). *Crisis under the canopy: Tourism and other problems facing the present day Huaorani.* ABYA-YALA: Quito, Ecuador.

Spiller, M. M. (1974). *Historia de la Mision Josefina del Napo. 1922–1974.* (Vol. 1). Quito, Ecuador: Artes Graficas.

Spiro, M. E. (1967). *Burmese supernaturalism.* Englewood Cliffs, New Jersey: Prentice-Hall, Inc.

Steward, J. H. (Ed.). (1948). *Handbook of South American Indians.* (Vol. 3), *The tropical forest tribes.* (Bulletin 143. 986 p.) Smithsonian Institution, Bureau of American Ethnology, Washington, DC: U.S. Government Printing Office.

Sweet, D. G. (1969). *The population of the Upper Amazon Valley, 17th and 18th Centuries.* Master's thesis, University of Wisconsin, Madison.

Taussig, M. (1987). *Shamanism, colonialism, and the wild man: A study in terror and healing.* Chicago: University of Chicago Press.

Wallace, A. F. C. (1956). Revitalization movements. *American Anthropologist, 58,* 264–281.

Wallace, A. F. C. (1970). *Culture and personality.* New York: Random House.

Wallis, E. E. (1960). *The Dayuma story.* New York: Harper & Brothers.

Wallis, E. E. (1973). *Aucas downriver.* New York: Harper & Row.

Watson, G. (1991). Rewriting culture. In R. Fox (Ed.), *Recapturing anthropology: Working in the present.* (pp. 73–92). Santa Fe: School of American Research.

Whitten, N. E. (1981). Amazonia today at the base of the Andes: An ethnic interface in ecological, social, and ideological perspectives. In N. E. Whitten (Ed.), *Cultural transformations and ethnicity in modern Ecuador.* Urbana: University of Illinois Press.

Wilson, M., & Daly, M. (1985). Competitiveness, risk taking and violence: The young male syndrome. *Ethology and Sociobiology, 6*(2), 59–73.

Yost, J. A. (1981). Twenty years of contact: The mechanisms of change in Wao (Auca) culture. In N. E. Whitten (Ed.), *Cultural transformations and ethnicity in modern Ecuador.* Urbana: University of Illinois Press.

Yost, J. A., & Kelley, P. M. (1983). Shotguns, blowguns, and spears: The analysis of technological efficiency. In R. B. Hames and W. Vickers (Eds.), *Adaptive Responses of Native Amazonians.* New York: Academic Press.

Index

Page numbers followed by "n" refer to notes.

A

Accidents, 25–26
Acculturation, 96
Achuar, 91
Agoutis, 38, 58, 104
Ahuano, 62
Airstrips, 13, 15–16, 17, 46, 76, 95, 101
Akawo, 109, 124–125, 152, 153, 162
Alas de Socorro ("Wings of Mercy"), 11
Alcohol use, 45, 49–50, 160n
Amazon River, 85, 89
Amö, 69, 143, 170–171
Anacondas, 9, 74, 109
Ancestors (*duuräni*), 53
Andes, 13–15, 73
Anger and rage, 35, 36, 58, 63, 65–66, 69, 104, 120–125, 144, 146, 152–153. *See also* Violence
Antesana, 14
Arajuno River, 62, 95–96, 151
Arango, Sister Inés, 59–60
Archidona, 13, 86
Auca language. *See* Waorani language
Aucas, 9, 21, 98, 113, 120, 152, 155, 168. *See also* Waorani
Aushiris, 21, 90
Authority and social control, 102–104
Autonomy, 102–104, 118–123, 168, 177, 178
Avishiiri, 90
Awä, 46–47
Ayahuasca, 106, 112–113

B

Babëiri, 98, 99
Baeza, 13
Baï, 38, 39, 46, 47, 50
Baiwäiri, 98
Balsa wood plugs in earlobes, 16, 98
Banisteriopsis muricata, 106
Baños, 13
Barral, H., 160n
Benefice, E., 160n
Bennet Ross, J., 128n
Bibängkä, 52, 53–55, 57
Bible stories, 34–36, 56, 113
Bible translation, 10, 13, 31, 34, 36
Bilateral descent, 99, 102
Biological explanations of warfare, 128, 131–136
Birds
    hunting of, 46, 48
    as omens, 110
    as pets, 37, 38
    in rainforest, 73–74
Birth
    during woman's flight from raiding party, 47
    multiple births, 48
    self-reliance of women during, 119

Blancos (whites), 45, 87, 92–93. *See also* Missionaries; Outsiders (*kowudɨ*)
Blomberg, R., 21, 23, 24, 89, 93
Blowpipes, 46, 53, 81
Boundary demarcation, 64, 65–66
Buka, 161

C
Cannibalism, 9, 90, 97, 109, 152
Capuchins, 95, 159, 171. *See also* Missionaries
Carnaval, 61–62, 169
Catholic missionaries. *See* Missionaries
Caucheros (rubber collectors), 89–91
Cecco, Monsignor, 21, 22–23
Chagnon, Napoleon, 131–132
Children
    capture of, in raids, 88–89
    at church, 34, 35
    deaths of, 89, 122, 125, 134–135, 155, 173
    illnesses of, 69
    infanticide, 48, 113, 134
    kidnapping of, 59, 143
    of killers, 133–135
    life of, in family, 57–58, 59
    violence by, 58
Chonta palm fruit, 79
Christianity, 34–36, 42–43, 56, 113–114, 144, 145, 159–161, 169, 174. *See also* Missionaries
Church, 34–36, 42–43, 56, 113–114, 169. *See also* Christianity
Clothing, 16–17, 35, 38
Coca, 58, 60, 73, 85, 95, 166, 170–171, 172
Cofan, 91
Colonists in Oriente, 60, 65–66, 69, 96, 165, 166–167
Community identity, 169–170, 178–181
Company, The (*La Compania*), 45, 52, 56, 67, 158–159, 160, 166, 170, 171
Cononaco River, 65, 98, 99, 101
Cooking. *See* Food
Cross cousin marriage, 41, 47, 99–100, 138, 144
Cross cousin sexuality, 56, 57, 105–106, 133, 138
Cuchiyacu River, 98
Culture
    and construction of self, 118–119, 145–146
    definition of, 3–4, 114–115
    information and culture change, 158–159
    of peace, 159–161
    rage and, 120–125, 146
    and self and emotion, 117–118
    of Waorani, 115–116, 117–123
    world view, emotion, and culture change, 162–163
Curaray River, 9, 11, 23, 86, 89, 95, 96, 105, 113, 152, 166
Curare-tipped darts, 81–83

D
Dagëngapë, 79
Daily routine of authors, 38–41
Daly, M., 131, 134
Damöïntarö, 55, 56
Dancing, 54, 63, 64
Darts tipped with curare, 81–83
Data collection
    economic and social relations survey, 45
    genealogies, 41–45
    participant observation for, 46–56

Davis, W. E., 10
Deaths. *See also* Homicides; Warfare
    of children, 89, 122, 125, 134–135, 155, 173
    of missionaries, 9–10, 27, 54, 58–60, 87, 105, 113, 142–143, 152–153
    from snakebites, 24, 25–26, 140
    stories of, during genealogies, 44–45
Deer, 48, 74, 108
Dentan, R. K., 1
Development, 12
Diet. *See* Food
Disabilities. *See* Handicaps
Diseases. *See* Illnesses
Dïtë
    agouti killed by, 104
    on Awä, 46–47
    family of, 36, 38, 41–43, 59, 111
    and food exchange with authors, 48, 49, 59
    house of, 36, 39
    hunting magic and, 107
    and kidnapping of children, 59, 143
    on omens, 110
    on taboos, 108
Dogs, 37, 108
Domestic relations. *See* Family relationships
Domestic violence, 57
Downriver group, 24–25, 41, 42, 111–112, 177
Drinking feasts (*ëëmë*), 52–55, 57, 61, 100, 106, 156
Dubos, R., 146n
Duuräni (ancestors), 53, 109
Dyiko
    in church, 34
    drinking feasts (ëëmë) and, 53
    family of, 38, 41–44
    home of, 39
    and joking about spearing, 55
    naming of authors by, 32–33, 49
    omens and, 109
    in red dress for authors' first meetings with, 16, 32
    sorcery and, 111–112, 124, 125, 155
    spearing raids and, 32, 105

E
Earlobe holes, 16, 28
Earlobes with balsa wood plugs, 16, 98
Ecological adaptation, 74–84
Ecological functionalism and warfare, 128–130
Economic and social relations survey, 45
Economic relations, 103–104, 160
Ecuador. *See also* Waorani
    authors' field research in, 1–5, 10–18, 31–33, 41–47, 60–61, 165
    authors in Quito, 11–13
    authors' travel to Waorani Protectorate, 13–18
    boundary demarcation of Waorani territory, 64, 65–66
    colonists in Oriente, 60, 65–66, 69, 96, 165, 166–167
    location of Waorani Protectorate, 11
    maps of, 2, 25
    Oriente in, 9, 10, 73–74
    Peru's annexation of Amazonian Ecuador, 95
    physical environment of, 73–74, 129
    population of indigenous people in, 168
Education, 36, 168, 169

Ëëmë (drinking feasts), 52–55, 57, 61, 100, 106, 156
Egalitarianism, 102–104, 118, 119, 123, 177
Elliot, Elisabeth, 26, 61, 103, 120, 152, 155
Emotions. *See* Anger and rage
Employment, by The Company, 45, 52, 56, 67, 102, 160, 166
Encomiendas (land grants), 87
Envy, 123, 123n, 124–125
Eru, 47
Ethnocentrism of natives, 96, 97
Ethnogenesis, 168–170

F
Family relationships. *See also* Marriage
   children, 34, 35, 57–58, 59, 69, 88–89
   cross cousin marriage, 41, 47, 99–100
   genealogies, 41–45
   generalized reciprocity and, 49
   households in Tɨwënö, 17, 36–39
   husband–wife relationship, 57–58
   and naming of anthropologists by Dyiko, 32–33, 49
   residence patterns and, 74–76, 101–102
   sexual division of labor not found, 57, 104–105, 144
   warfare and, 25
Farabee, W. C., 97
Feasts, 52–55, 57, 61, 100, 106, 156
Ferguson, R. B., 128n
Fish and fishing, 55, 57, 74, 79–81, 103–104, 108, 129, 166
Fleming, Peter, 152
Flirting, 52
Food, 26, 36, 37, 40, 47–50, 58, 64, 78–79, 103–104, 108, 129–130, 160, 160n. *See also* Gardening
Franciscans, 86. *See also* Missionaries
Frustration–Aggression Theory of violence, 120, 121
Furniture, 32

G
Gämɨ, 34, 36, 38, 39, 41, 43, 52–55, 121, 124–125
Gang warfare in United States, 177–181
Gardening, 45–47, 57, 76–79, 101, 110–111, 129, 160. *See also* Food
Gender dichotomy, 57, 103, 104–105, 144
Genealogies, 41–45
Generalized reciprocity, 47–49
Gɨkitairi group, 98
Gïmari, 144, 152–153
Gïngata, 38, 41–43, 47, 111, 154, 155
Girïnäni, 99, 100
Gold, 92, 93
Government. *See* "Tribal" government
Government officials, 62–63, 65–66, 94
Greenberg, J. H., 33n
Gross, D. R., 128n
Guahibo, 127
Guggenheim Foundation. *See* Harry Frank Guggenheim Foundation
Guns. *See* Shotguns; Weapons

H
Haciendas, 22–23, 87–89, 93–94, 95, 141, 152
Hallucinogenic drugs, 106
Handbook of South American Indians, 90
Handicaps, 47
Harner, M. J., 85, 92
Harris, M., 128n, 129

Harry Frank Guggenheim Foundation, 10
Health care, 67–68
Health of Waorani, 26, 130, 139. *See also* Illnesses
Historical perspectives, 21–24, 26, 85–96, 140–143, 151–158
Holloway, H. L., 21
Homicidal rage, 120–125, 146, 152–153. *See also* Anger and rage
Homicides. *See also* Deaths; Warfare
    data on Waorani killers, 132–136
    infanticide, 48, 113, 134
    joking about, 55
    of kidnapped women, 98
    of killers, 134–135
    of killers' wives, 134–136
    men and women as killers, 105
    of missionaries, 9–10, 27, 54, 58–60, 87, 105, 113, 152–153
    of oil camp workers, 60, 95–96
    omens of, 109–110
    purported homicide of Waorani by *kowudï* colonists, 69
    of Quichua, 60
    rage and, 120–125, 146, 152–153
    recent resurgence of, 160–162, 165, 170–174
    revenge as motive for, 25, 26, 27
    of sorcerers, 24, 26, 124–125, 172
    statistics on, 1, 3, 19, 27, 159
    vendettas, 24–26, 99, 100, 101–102, 134–136, 159, 174, 177
    and Waorani attitude on outsiders, 66
Homosexuality, 56–57, 106, 138
Hookworms, 74
Hooting, 53, 54
Households, 17, 36–38, 39, 41–45, 74–76
Houses, 17, 18, 32, 36–38, 39, 41–42, 74–76
Hunting, 46, 48, 57, 76, 81–84, 104, 105, 107–110, 112, 129, 130

I
Illnesses. *See also* Snakebites
    of anthropologists, 50
    contact with outside world as cause of, 69, 157
    epidemic diseases introduced by Spanish, 86–87, 91, 92
    polio epidemic, 101, 118, 133
    of Semai, 139
    sorcery as cause of, 25–26, 110–112, 124
    of Waorani, 25–26, 69, 74, 86–87, 89, 91, 92, 101
Imäa, 31, 33, 38, 40, 47, 52, 112
Inca Empire, 73, 85, 139, 140
Incest taboo, 152–153
Individual/psychological context, 3–4, 105, 117–125, 145–146
Individualism. *See* Autonomy
Industrial megaculture, 12
Infanticide, 48, 113, 134
Information and culture change, 151, 158–159
Institute of Agrarian Reform and Colonization, 65
Instituto De Patrimonio Cultural (Institute of Cultural Heritage), 11
Internal war, 24–26, 99, 100, 101–102, 134–136
Iquitos, Peru, 89
Irö. See Sorcery
Itekä, 171–172

J
Jaguar shamans, 112–113
Jaguars, 9, 74, 108, 109, 112
Jesuits, 86, 87. *See also* Missionaries

Jivaro. *See* Shuar (Jivaro)
Jobs. *See* Employment
Josephina Mission, 87, 94–95
Jung, R. ("Rosie"), 13, 15–18, 31, 34, 35, 38, 39, 157

K
Kane, J., 165n, 170
Kaplan, J., 26, 130
Kelley, P. M., 129
Kï, 99, 100, 105–106
Kidnapping
    of children, 59, 143
    of *kowudï* women, 98
Kimerling, J., 129, 165n
Kinship, 25, 32–33, 36–38, 39, 41–45, 49, 99–100, 144, 178. *See also* Family relationships
Kipa, 154, 155
Kitchens, 36, 37
Kiwarö, 34, 65
Kogi, 57
Kowudï. See Outsiders (*kowudï*)
Kupë, 122

L
Labaca, Father Alejandro, 59–60, 106, 159
Lago Agrio, 96
Language
    English numbers, 56
    Quichua language, 36, 86, 92
    Spanish language, 33, 36, 45, 56, 65, 168
    Waorani language, 5–6, 10, 17, 33–34, 40, 141
Larrick, J. W., 26, 130
Laszlo, E., 162
Laziness, 46, 47
Leaders among Waorani, 61, 63, 65, 170
Limoncocha, 90
Lying, 46

M
Mäapo, 99, 100
MAF. *See* Mission Aviation Fellowship (MAF)
Magic, 107, 108, 109, 139, 145
Malaria, 74
Malay Peninsula, 1, 74. *See also* Semai
Malinowski, Bronislaw, 107
Manaus, Brazil, 89
Manioc, 37, 46–50, 78, 79, 103, 108, 111, 160n
Marañon River, 91
Marmosets, 34, 35, 38
Marriage. *See also* Family relationships
    complaints against wife, 52
    conflicts over, 100, 144
    cross cousin marriage, 41, 47, 99–100, 138, 144
    formalized at drinking feasts (*ëëmë*), 100
    of mentally retarded woman, 47
    parental arrangement of, 100
    relations between husbands and wives, 57–58
    between Waorani and Quichua and other outsiders, 62, 65–66, 67, 102, 151
Marxist ideology, 11, 12
Maxus Ecuador, 62, 63, 64, 66–67, 69, 168
Maxus Energy, 62

Maynas Province, 85, 86
Measles, 86
Medical care. *See* Health care
Mëmpo, 99, 100
Mera, 95
Meyers, F. R., 123n
Mïï, 106, 112, 125
Milton, K., 129
Mïmä, 38, 39, 41–44, 47, 110–112, 124
Mïngkaiyï, 38, 39, 53, 55, 107, 111–112, 171–173
Mïnta, 38, 39, 47
Mïnyï mëmpo (jaguar shaman), 112–113
Mishahuallí, 73
Mission Aviation Fellowship (MAF), 11, 12, 13, 15, 52, 55, 76, 95, 104
Missionaries. *See also* Religion; and specific missionaries
    authors' contacts with, 11–12, 31
    bias of, in writing about Waorani, 19
    and creation of Waorani Protectorate, 12
    goal of, 12, 27, 151, 152, 155–156, 169, 174
    health care and, 67–68
    historical perspectives on, 86–87, 91, 92, 93, 94–95, 96, 151, 152
    killing of, 9–10, 27, 54, 58–60, 87, 105, 113, 142–143, 152–153
Marxist criticism of, 11, 12
Summer Institute of Linguistics, 10–12
    in Tïwënö, 15, 16–18
    as tourists, 68–69
    on Waorani and warfare, 21, 22–23
Waorani women and, 26–27, 155–156
Möipa, 26
Monkeys
    cooking of, 49
    hunting of, 48, 108
    as pets, 38, 59
    in rainforest, 73
Montaña, 15, 141
Muratorio, B., 21, 93, 94

N
Names
    Dyiko's naming of anthropologists, 32–33, 49
    of Waorani, 41
Nämpa, 152–153
Nängkä, 34, 35, 36, 39, 56
Näntowë, 38, 39, 55
Napo (town), 93
Napo River, 22–23, 85, 86, 89, 90, 91, 92, 93, 95, 97, 160, 166
Nashiño River, 98, 99
Native ethnocentrism, 96, 97
Nëngkiwi, 144, 152–153
New Guinea, 127
"Noble Savage" myth–image, 167
Nonviolence. *See* Peace and nonviolence
Nuevo Rocafuerte, 60, 95
Nutrition. *See* Food
Nyäwadë, 38, 39, 47, 155

O
Oa, 90
Ocelots, 74, 109
Oil exploration, 23, 45, 60, 62, 64, 66–67, 73, 95–96, 102, 106, 151, 158–159, 165–166, 168

Omakä, 124
Omëni̇̈
  abandonment by mother, 118
  Akawo and, 152
  approval for authors' fieldwork by, 18
  on attitude toward outsiders, 22, 69
  and change in attitudes and values, 113, 180
  Christianity and, 34, 35, 41, 113, 161
  on death of Canadian outsider, 153–155
  family of, 36, 38, 41, 43, 53, 111, 161
  fishing and, 104
  house of, 36, 39
  house repairs by, 31
  household of, 36
  on killing of missionaries, 153
  killings by, 16, 69, 113, 144, 153, 155, 161
  at ONHAE Congress, 69
  at soccer tournament, 63
Omens, 109–110
Ompudë, 38, 39, 109, 112, 119, 121, 171–173
Ongkayi̇̈, 38, 39, 55
ONHAE, 60, 63, 64–69, 168, 169–170
Orejones, 90
Orellana, Francisco, 85
Organización de las Nación Huaorani de la Amazonia Ecuatoriana (ONHAE), 60, 63, 64–69, 168, 169–170
Organization of the Waorani Nation of Ecuatorial Amazonia (ONHAE), 60, 63, 64–69, 168, 169–170
Oriente region, 9, 10, 73–74. See also Waorani
Orthography, 5–6
Orton, J., 86
Oruna, 97–98, 118, 153–154, 171–173. See also Quichua Indians
Outsiders (kowudi̇̈). See also Missionaries; Quichua Indians
  as cannibals, 97, 152
  colonists in Oriente, 60, 65–66, 69, 96, 165, 166–167
  Dyiko's naming of anthropologists, 32–33, 49
  exposure to, through paid employment, 45
  food not offered to, 50
  joking about spearing, 55
  kidnapping of kowudi̇̈ women, 98
  tourism and, 68–69
  Waorani attitude toward, 22–23, 27, 66, 91, 97–98, 171–173
  Waorani's marriage to, 61, 102

P
Paä, 23, 54, 124, 153, 154, 155
Pacification process, 27–29
Pañacocha, 60
Participant observation, 46–56
Patrons, patronas, 88, 94
Peace and nonviolence, 27–29, 34–36, 113, 144, 145, 151–163
Peccaries
  hunting of, 48, 81, 82, 104, 105, 107, 109, 112
  jaguar shamans and, 112
  as pets, 38, 40
  in rainforest, 74
Peeke, Catherine ("Cathy"), 5, 10, 13, 15–18, 31, 33–35, 38, 39, 55
Pëënëmë (banana drink), 50, 52, 79
Personality
  autonomy and, 102–104, 118–123, 168, 177, 178
  characteristics of Waorani, 105
  cultural construction of self, 118–119, 145–146
  culture, self, and emotion, 117–118

definition of, 3–4, 117
    egalitarianism and, 102–104, 118, 119, 123
    warfare and, 145–146
Peru, 89, 95
Petroecuador, 67
Petroleum industry. *See* Oil industry
Pets, 34, 35, 37, 38, 40, 59
Physical environment, 73–74, 129, 138–140, 168
Pigs. *See* Peccaries
Piyĕmöiri, 98
Pizarro, Francisco, 85
Pizarro, Gonzalo, 85
Plantains, 50, 52, 53, 78–79
Polio epidemic, 101, 118, 133
Political structure, 102–104, 144, 167–170
Postmodernism, 138n
Pronunciation guide, 5–6
"Protein scarcity" argument, 129–130, 138
Protestant missionaries. *See* Missionaries
Psychological context, 3–4, 105, 117–125, 145–146
Puerto Francisco de Orellana, 73
Pumas, 74
Pïïntï. See Homicidal rage
Putomayo River, 97
Puyo, 73, 124, 166

Q
Quichua Indians
    airstrips near missionary outposts among, 95
    alcohol and, 49, 160n
    colonists and, 96
    historical perspectives on, 86
    houses of, 36
    and jobs with The Company, 45
    killings of, 60
    language of, 36, 86, 92
    Lowland Quichua, 86, 92, 97
    marriages between Waorani and, 62, 65, 151
    and raids of/by Waorani, 22–24, 61, 62, 92, 155, 171–173
    at soccer tournaments, 63
    sorcery and, 171–173
    and "tribal" government, 167
    Waorani fear and resentment of, 63, 153–154
    Waorani women's flight to, 26, 97–98, 155
    wife beating by, 57
    Záparo cultural elements and, 91

R
Rage. *See* Anger and rage
Raids. *See* Warfare
Rainforest Information Center, 65
Reading skills, 34, 36
Reciprocity. *See* Generalized reciprocity
Reducciones (permanent settlements), 86
Reference groups for youth, 180–181
Religion. *See also* Missionaries
    Christianity, 34–36, 42–43, 56, 113–114, 144, 145, 159–161, 169, 174
    jaguar shamans, 112–113
    magic, 107, 108, 109, 139, 145
    omens, 109–110
    sorcery, 24, 25–26, 38, 101, 105, 106, 110–112, 122–125, 140, 145, 146, 155, 162, 171–173

    taboos, 107–109, 152–153
    in U.S. urban areas, 180
Repair service, 51
Residence patterns, 74–76, 101–102
Retaliation. *See* Revenge
Revenge, as motive for murder, 25, 26, 27, 161, 162
Ridge group, 24–25, 42, 49, 63, 111–112, 157
Rival, L., 5
Rivera, E., 89
Rivers, 40, 73, 74, 79, 166. *See also* specific rivers
Roads, 166–167
Robarchek, Clay and Carole
    daily routine of, 38–40
    and economic and social relations survey, 45, 46
    food for, 47–49, 108
    genealogies collected by, 41–45
    house of, 31–32, 39
    illnesses of, 50
    incident of Clay's childhood, 174–175
    and kidnapping of children, 59, 143
    naming of, by Dyiko, 32–33, 49
    participant observation and, 46–47
    research cited, 2, 19, 114, 115, 120n, 121, 128n, 131, 165
    shotgun repair by Clay, 51, 91
    snakebite of Carole, 51–52
    and snakebite of Wämönyï, 55
    uneasiness of, among Waorani, 55, 59
    Waorani language learning by, 33–34
Rocafuerte, 95
Rosaldo, 123n
Ross, E. B., 128n
Royal Dutch Shell, 23, 95–96
Rubber boom, 89–91, 93, 141

S
Saint, Rachel, 26–27, 57, 60–61, 65, 90, 113, 155, 161
Santayana, George, 174
Schema, schemata, 3–4
Schoeck, H., 123n
School, 36, 169
Schoolhouse, 18, 31–32
Secoya, 91
Self. *See* Personality
Self-reliance. *See* Autonomy
Semai, 1, 2, 10, 12, 45, 48, 97, 106–108, 115, 120n, 129, 139, 178
Settlement pattern, 74–76, 101–102
Sevilla, Mrs. Esther, 94
Sex roles, 57, 103, 104–106, 144
Sexuality
    carnaval and, 61–62
    cross cousin sexuality, 56, 57, 105–106, 133, 138
    and drinking feasts (*ëëmë*), 55, 62, 106
    and face painting with red pigment, 61–62
    homosexuality, 56–57, 106, 138
Shamans, 112–113
Sharanahua, 127
Shell–Mera, 11, 13, 55, 67, 95, 104
Shell Oil Company, 23, 93, 95–96
Shiripuno River, 65, 67, 68, 98, 101, 102, 158, 165, 166, 170
Shotguns, 48, 51, 84, 91, 108, 166
Shuar (Jivaro), 45, 65, 91–92, 95, 96, 127, 141, 160n, 167, 173

SIL. *See* Summer Institute of Linguistics (SIL)
Sinclair, J. H., 93
Singing and chanting, 54, 63, 66
Siona, 91
Sioux Indians, 175
Slave raiding, 89, 90, 91, 141
Sleeping houses, 38
Smallpox, 86
Snakebites, 25–26, 35, 51–55, 68, 74, 104, 107, 115–116, 139–140, 155
Snakes, 74, 75, 108, 115, 139
Soccer and soccer tournaments, 45, 52, 53, 55–56, 57, 60, 61–64, 169
Social control, 102–104
Social organization, 97–116, 143–145, 160, 178. *See also* Family relationships; Kinship
Sociobiology of warfare, 128, 131–136
Songs. *See* Singing and chanting
Sorcery, 24, 25–26, 38, 101, 105, 106, 110–112, 122–125, 140, 145, 146, 155, 162, 171–173
Spanish colonialism, 85–89, 91
Spanish language, 33, 36, 45, 56, 65, 168
Spears, 21, 81, 83–84
Spiller, M. M., 21, 23, 87, 88, 94, 95
Spiro, Melford, 140
Sports. *See* Soccer
Ssabela, 90, 90n
Stealing, 46
String making, 35, 40–41, 56
Suicides, 97–98, 154–155, 155
Summer Institute of Linguistics (SIL), 10–12, 13, 31, 60–61, 90, 158
Supernatural. *See* Religion
Sweet, D. G., 85, 86, 87

T
Taboos, 107–109, 152–153
Tagë, 27
Tagëiri, 27, 59–60, 98, 99, 109, 122, 124, 143, 159
Tarömïnäni, 98–99
Taussig, M., 98
Tena, 13, 15–16, 21, 73, 87, 93, 94–95, 166
Texaco, 96
Tigres mojanos, 9, 98
Tiguino River, 98, 102
Tïpë (porridge from manioc), 49–50, 78, 79
Tiputini River, 98, 158
Tivacuno River, 98
Tïwënö. *See also* Waorani
    altitude of, 38
    approval for fieldwork in, 18, 31
    authors' choice of, for fieldwork, 18
    authors' daily routine in, 38–41
    authors' house in, 31–32
    church in, 34–36, 42–43, 56
    drinking feasts (ëëmë) in, 52–55, 57, 61
    households in, 17, 36–38, 39, 41–45
    map of, 39
    missionaries in, 15, 16–18, 31
    population of, 18
    settlement of, 101, 157
    soccer tournament in, 61–62
    weather of, 38
Tïwënö River, 40, 101, 156, 157
Tönyë, 31, 61
Tönyëmpadï, 34, 35, 60–65, 69, 76, 113, 124, 167–168

Tools, 21, 22, 77, 91, 141, 157, 158, 166
Torres de Peñaherrera, Sra. Josefina, 88–89
Tourism, 68–69
Trade, 152
"Tribal" government, 60, 63, 64–69, 102, 160n, 167–168
Tuka, 53, 57
Twins, 48
Tzapino River, 22, 52, 56, 68, 69

U
Umï, 111–112, 124
UNESCO, 129
United States urban violence, 177–181
Upriver group, 24–25, 42, 98, 153, 157, 161, 177
Urban violence in United States, 177–181

V
Vendettas, 24–26, 99, 100, 101–102, 134–136, 144, 159, 174, 177
Via Auca, 166–167, 170
Violence. *See also* Anger; Warfare
    anthropology of, 19–20, 127–137
    data on Waorani killers, 132–136
    death of Canadian outsider, 153–155
    decline in and renunciation of, 3, 10, 26–29, 34–36, 113, 144, 151–163, 179
    domestic violence, 57
    Frustration–Aggression Theory of, 120, 121
    historical context of, 85–96
    homicide statistics, 1, 3, 19, 27, 159
    information and decline of, 151, 158–159
    killing of kidnapped women, 98
    killing of missionaries, 9–10, 27, 54, 58–60, 87, 105, 113, 142–143, 152–153
    against oil camps, 60, 95–96, 106, 158–159
    omens of, 109–110
    rage and, 120–125, 146, 152–153
    recent resurgence of, 160–162, 165, 170–174
    stories of deaths during genealogies, 44–45
    U.S. urban violence, 177–181
    vendettas, 24–26, 99, 100, 101–102, 134–136, 144, 159, 174, 177
    Waorani as most violent society, 1, 3, 9–10, 19–20, 159
    and Waorani attitude on outsiders, 66
    women's involvement in, 105
Volleyball, 45

W
Wäapo, 99, 100
Wakabo, 100
Wallace, A. F. C., 180
Wallis, E. E., 10
Wämönyï, 38, 41, 43, 52–55
Wänï, 52, 57
Waorani. *See also* Warfare
    attitude toward outsiders, 22–23, 27, 66, 91, 97–98, 171–173
    authority and social control, 102–104
    authors' field research with, 1–5, 10–18, 31–33, 41–47, 60–61, 165
    bilateral descent and, 99, 102
    boundary demarcation of territory of, 64, 65–66
    changes affecting in 1993, 60–69, 102
    clothing of, 16–17, 35, 38
    culture of, 114–116, 117–123
    ecological adaptation of, 74–84
    economic relations of, 103–104, 160

ethnocentrism of, 97
ethnogenesis and, 168–170
in fifteenth through nineteenth centuries, 85–91
generalized reciprocity and, 47–49
health of, 26, 130
historical perspectives on, 21–24, 26, 85–96, 140–143, 151–158
houses and households of, 17, 18, 32, 36–38, 39, 41–45, 74–76
individual/psychological context of, 117–125, 145–146
kinship and marriage, 25, 32–33, 36–38, 39, 41–45, 49, 99–100, 144, 178
leadership among, 61, 63, 65, 170
meaning of name, 97
as most violent society, 1, 9–10, 19–20, 159
names of, 41
officials and, 62–63
oldest living Waorani, 54
outside influences on, 169
personality of, 105
physical environment of, 73–74, 129, 138–140, 168
politics and, 102–104, 167–170
population density of, 129, 138
religion of, 106–114
settlement pattern of, 74–76, 101–102
sexuality of, 55, 56–57, 61–62, 105–106
social/cultural context of, 97–116, 143–145, 160
story on early life of, 90
subgroups of, 24–25, 42, 49, 98–99
in Tɨwënö, 16–17
"tribal" government of, 102, 160n
world view of, 115–116, 143, 162–163
Waorani language, 5–6, 10, 17, 33–34, 40, 141
Waorani men. *See also* names of specific men
clothing of, 17
earlobe holes and, 16, 28
homosexuality and, 56–57, 106, 138
hunting by, 81–84, 104, 105
as killers, 105, 132–136
soccer and, 55–56
Waorani Protectorate, 11–18, 25
Waorani women. *See also* names of specific women
childbirth experiences of, 47, 119
clothing of, 16–17, 35
fishing by, 80, 104
flight from raiders, 47, 97–98, 118, 134–135
food preparation by, 49, 50
gardening by, 77–79, 81
homicides of killers' wives, 134–136
as killers, 105
missionaries and, 26–27, 155–156
prominent women, 61, 63
soccer and, 56
as sorcerers, 110–112, 124, 155
string making and, 40–41
weaving and, 42
Waräni, 100
Warfare. *See also* Homicides; Violence
anthropology of, 127–137
data on Waorani killers, 132–136
decline in and renunciation of, 3, 10, 26–29, 34–36, 113, 144, 151–163, 173–174, 179
ecological functionalism and, 128–130
explanation of Waorani war, 146–147
external war, 20–24

frequency of raids, 20
gang warfare in U.S., 177–181
historical context of, 21–24, 26, 85–96, 140–143
individual/psychological context of, 145–146
information and decline of, 151, 158–159
internal war, 24–26, 99, 100, 101–102, 134–136
joking about, 55
material context of, 138–140
rage and, 120–125, 146
social/cultural context of, 143–145
sociobiology of, 128, 131–136
vendettas, 24–26, 99, 100, 101–102, 134–136, 144, 159, 174, 177
Wasson, T., 93
Watson, G., 138n
Weapons, 21, 36–37, 48, 51, 81–84, 91, 108, 141, 166
Weather of Tiwёnö, 38
Weaving, 42
Wёmpo, 99, 100
Whites. *See* Blancos (whites)
Whitten, N. E., 86, 91, 92
Wɨba, 61, 63, 65, 69, 101–102, 161, 162
Wild pigs. *See* Peccaries
Wilson, M., 131, 134
Wɨnёiri (spirit familiars), 112–113
Wɨpɨiri, 98
Witoto, 97
Work. *See* Employment
World view of Waorani, 115–116, 118, 143, 162–163

Y
Yanomamö, 127, 131–132
Yasuní National Park, 129
Yasuní River, 95, 98, 101, 158
Yasuní River band, 58–60, 66, 69, 106, 170
Yost, James A., 1, 10, 19, 24, 26, 108, 113, 114, 129, 130, 161

Z
Záparos, 51, 91